Literature and Revolution

Literature and Revolution
Leon Trotsky

Edited by William Keach
Translated by Rose Strunsky

Chicago, Illinois

Haymarket Books
PO Box 180165, Chicago, IL 60618
www.haymarketbooks.org

First published in 1925 by International Publishers, New York
Compilation © 2005 William Keach
For additional copyright information, see page 332.

ISBN-10: 1-931859-16-7
ISBN-13: 978-1931859-16-5

Cover design by Josh On
Cover painting, "Dynamic Composition" by Alexandra Exter, 1916
Interior design by Alan Maass

Library of Congress Cataloging-in-Publication data

Trotsky, Leon, 1879–1940.
    [Literatura i revolëiiuëtìsièïia. English]
    Literature and revolution / Leon Trotsky ; [translated by Rose
Strunsky ; introduction to the new edition by William Keach].
        p. cm.
    Originally published: New York : International Publishers, 1925.
With new introd.
    Includes bibliographical references and index.
    ISBN 1-931859-16-7 (pbk. : alk. paper)
    1. Russian literature—20th century—History and criticism.
2. Russian literature—20th century—Political aspects. 3. Socialism
in literature. I. Title.

PG3026.P64T7613 2005
891.709'358—dc22   2004021408

10 9 8 7 6 5 4 3

Contents

Acknowledgements

Special thanks are due to Elizabeth Terzakis, both for her detailed help with the glossary and for her wide-ranging advice about this edition as a whole. Julie Fain and Anthony Arnove contributed indispensably—in many different ways, at every stage of the project. Sheila Emerson read a draft of the introduction with great care and suggested some helpful improvements. I am grateful to Josh On, who designed the cover, to Alan Maass, who is responsible for the inside layout, and to Dao Tran and Deborah Roberts, for their essential help in proofreading. And I wish to thank Victor Erlich for a very illuminating and suggestive conversation about Trotsky's views on contemporary Russian poets and on Russian Formalism.

Introduction

The man the world came to know as Leon Trotsky (his parents named him Lev Davidovich Bronstein) is by any measure one of the major political figures of the twentieth century. Because he was a revolutionary socialist and a leading force in the Russian Revolution of 1917, Trotsky has had enemies as well as admirers. He was and still is denounced as a dangerous radical by those for whom the revolutionary overthrow of tsarism and the relatively brief creation of a workers' state in Russia were destructive, threatening developments. At the same time, because he relentlessly opposed Joseph Stalin's rise to power in the new Soviet Union and saw in it the ruin of everything Russian workers and peasants had fought for, Trotsky has also been vilified by self-proclaimed leftists who identify revolutionary socialism with Stalinism, or with some other version of state control and dictatorship.

Despite such animosity from both sides of the conventional political spectrum, the integrity of what Trotsky stood for has been recognized, and not just by activists who have attempted to build on Trotsky's example. In *A History of the Modern World,* the eminent American historian R.R. Palmer wrote that, as Stalin began to consolidate his power in 1925, Trotsky "inveighed against the lassitude that had descended upon socialism....He denounced the tendency to bureaucratic ossification...and urged a new movement of the masses to give it life."[1]

What anyone thinks about Trotsky's ideas and achievements will depend importantly on his or her broader understanding of the Russian Revolution. It is still fashionable these days to see the

Revolution as a misguided or malevolently motivated mistake—a bloody, conspiratorial revolt against the barbarity of tsarism and of capitalist imperialism (the Revolution grew directly out of World War I) that led inevitably to the brutality of Stalin's police state, show trials, and gulags. Although the collapse of the Soviet Union and its East Bloc satellites at the end of the 1980s created fresh opportunities for historical and political analysis outside the confines of a Cold War mindset, a confidently progressive and open-minded rethinking of the Revolution has been slow to emerge and take hold. Trotsky himself saw the Revolution as the first great movement in the self-emancipation of humanity, a movement led by workers organized through an awareness of their power to transform society. Yet his remarkable *History of the Russian Revolution,* published in 1931, is more often recognized as a "brilliant and essentially literary work" merely "representing Trotsky's version of the revolution"[2] than as a critically relevant contribution to the ongoing effort to understand one of the foundational moments in modern history.

As for *Literature and Revolution,* the book has been more widely known among radical leftists and academic specialists in Russian literature than among ordinary students and general readers. It deserves a wider audience. This edition is being published in the belief that Trotsky makes a unique contribution to our understanding of cultural conflict and change in the period of the Russian Revolution—and also to our ways of thinking about the relationship between cultural and political change at any historical moment, including our own.

One of the remarkable things about *Literature and Revolution* is that Trotsky wrote it in the first place. He drafted the essays that make up the book as we know it during the summers of 1922 and 1923.[3] Although the civil war of 1918–1921 ended with the Bolshevik-led workers' state victorious over the forces that wanted to return Russia to tsarism, the country was economically and socially devastated. Many of the most effective working-class revolutionaries died fighting the counterrevolutionary White Army. Industrial production had fallen to catastrophic levels, forcing the government to adopt a series of measures known as the New Economic Policy (NEP), which permitted a return to small-scale capitalist trade. The Revolution was increasingly isolated: the international revolutionary movement, without which a socialist society in Russia was impossible, had suffered severe defeats—particularly in Germany in 1918 and again in 1923.[4] In addition, Vladimir Lenin, leader of the Bolshevik Party and chairman of the Council of People's Commissars, had suffered debilitating strokes in May 1922 and March 1923, making it easier for Stalin to consolidate his power base within the bureaucracy and to form his alliance (or *troika*) with Grigory Zinoviev and Lev Kamenev for the primary purpose of weakening Trotsky's influence.

Under such circumstances, it does at first seem surprising that Trotsky would have turned his attention to questions of culture, art, and literature. But in fact, the genesis and argument of *Literature and Revolution* demonstrate some of the deepest impulses in Trotsky's political thinking. As head of the Red Army, he understood as well as anyone that revolutionary moments in history are most decisively defined and driven by the material necessities of life. "The nightingale of poetry," he says near the beginning of Chapter 1, "...is heard only after the sun is set. The day is a time for action...all through history, mind limps after reality" (34).[5] At the same time, Trotsky argues in his Introduction, human cultural needs are in their own way as real as any other needs:

> ...even a successful solution of the elementary problems of food, clothing, shelter, and even of literacy, would in no way signify a complete victory of the new historic principle, that is, of socialism. Only a movement of scientific thought on a national scale and the development of a new art would signify that the historic seed has not only grown into a plant, but has even flowered. In this sense, the development of art is the highest test of the vitality and significance of each epoch. (29)

Art, as a distinctive form of culture understood most broadly as the "sum of knowledge and capacity that characterizes the entire society" (165), at once follows and completes a society's response to the "elementary problems" of human need, production, and distribution.

It is through this dynamic understanding of the social relationship between economic life and culture that Trotsky also grasps the immediate political debate about the status of art in the Soviet Union in 1923–1924.[6] Isaac Deutscher is right in one sense to claim that "the refutation of the idea of 'proletarian culture' forms the central and most controversial part of *Literature and Revolution.*"[7] Proponents of "proletarian culture," most notably the theoretician A.A. Bogdanov, had founded a journal called *Proletkult* and were organizing conferences, workshops, and public celebrations of new writing by working-class poets, novelists, and playwrights. Trotsky believed this initiative to be founded on misunderstanding and illusion, and though he defended its right to exist, he criticized it in an acute and sustained way. Trotsky's polemic against the advocates of *Proletkult* is ultimately inseparable from his opposition to the Stalinist bureaucratization of the Communist Party, and to all that follows from Stalin's turning the Soviet Union's struggle for survival as a workers' state into the cult of "socialism in one country."

At issue is Trotsky's understanding of what a socialist revolution and a socialist society are in themselves, as historical possibilities and as actualities. His most important contribution to Marxist analysis, the theory of "permanent revolution," rests on his account of "combined and uneven development." Under the conditions of twentieth-century international capitalism and imperialism, Trotsky argued, it was not necessary for backward countries to go through a prolonged stage of bourgeois economic and social dominance before socialism was possible. Russia, for obvious reasons, was the prime example. At the time of the 1917 Revolution, Russia was both a very backward, predominantly peasant society with a relatively weak bourgeoisie that still depended on and cowered under tsarism, and a society with sectors of concentrated and advanced industrial capitalism (in cities such as Petrograd and Moscow) and, consequently, centers of working-class power.

Culturally and artistically, Russia was also strikingly uneven in its development.[8] Vast numbers of workers and peasants were illiterate and lived their lives desperately absorbed in the struggle for survival. At the same time, early twentieth-century Russian literature was continuing a rich array of past traditions and achievements, even as it participated in the major currents of European modernism: Symbolism, Futurism, Imagism, Surrealism, Constructivism. This marked cultural unevenness, together with the realities of sustaining an isolated workers' state in the aftermath of a brutal civil war, form the historical foundation of Trotsky's analysis of what the writing and reading of literature could be in post-Revolutionary Soviet society and could become in the socialist society of the future.

Fundamental to Trotsky's argument is the distinction between the transitional workers' state established and maintained through a "proletarian dictatorship"—through rule by the class on whose labor all modern societies depend—and a subsequent socialist society that will emerge when the working class no longer has to defend itself against and rule over adversarial classes. The social and cultural possibilities of the post-Revolutionary workers' state are different in principle both from what came before and from what may be expected in the future:

> In contrast to the regime of the slave owners and of the feudal lords and of the bourgeoisie, the proletariat regards its dictatorship as a brief period of transition....the proletariat will be more and more dissolved into a socialist community and will free itself from its class characteristics and thus cease to be a proletariat....The proletariat acquires power for the purpose of doing away forever with class culture and to make way for human culture. We frequently seem to forget this.[9] (155–56)

Utopian? Unrealistic about the time needed to abolish class society ("the period of the social revolution, on a world scale, will last not months and not years, but decades—decades, but not centuries, and certainly not thousands of years")? Readers of *Literature and Revolution* may well want to ask themselves such questions about Trotsky's perspective. What needs emphasis here is that, for Trotsky, a concept of "proletarian culture" analogous to "feudal culture" or "bourgeois culture"—or to a real "socialist culture," for that matter—is inherently contradictory. And in the Russia of 1923–1924, the entire process of creating the conditions for a new culture was in its infancy: "If a line were extended from present art to the socialist art of the future, one would say that we have hardly now passed through the stage of even preparing for its preparation" (32).

It is from this basic position on "revolutionary and socialist art" (the title of his last chapter) that Trotsky mounts his argument for maximum possible freedom in both literary production and reception. When it comes to production—to who should write what in the new workers' state—Trotsky is exuberant about the opening up of all kinds of literature to workers and peasants, some of whom had only recently learned to read and write while serving in the Red Army. "It is not to be questioned," he writes, "but that the proletariat, during the time of its dictatorship, will put its stamp upon culture" (160). Fostering such activity means continuing to expand all modes of literacy,[10] and also encouraging the broadest possible range of representation and expression.

> [It] does not at all mean a desire to dominate art by means of decrees and orders. It is not true that we regard only that art as new and revolutionary that speaks of the workers, and it is nonsense to say that we demand that the poets should describe inevitably a factory chimney, or the uprising against capital!" (144)

"Personal lyrics of the very smallest scope have an absolute right to exist within the new art," Trotsky continues. "No one is going to prescribe themes to a poet or intends to prescribe them. Please write about anything you can think of!"

Even as he makes the case for this kind of freedom for the writer, Trotsky insists that such freedom should not be mistaken for artistic accomplishment. The *Proletkultists* reduce all aesthetic value to its most rudimentary social and political content, he argues, and this both patronizes new working-class writers and deprives them of the cultural knowledge and practice they need to develop a new art. Acutely aware of the cultural backwardness forced on Russian workers and peasants by centuries of tsarist deprivation, and of the gap between these newly liberated classes and the existing literary intelligentsia,[11] Trotsky sees that those who "speak with great eloquence and even pompously of proletarian art" do working-class writers no favor by pretending that any and every thing they write is a literary work of art. These writers, like all writers, need to be enabled to study "literary technique" and to cultivate their own standards of literary judgment. The working class is producing "significant cultural and historical documents. But this does not at all mean that they are artistic documents....illiterate poems do not make up proletarian poetry, because they do not make up poetry at all" (164). "The proletarian poets are going through an apprenticeship" (172) that will lead to serious literary achievement only if these poets are given the freedom, time, and encouragement to absorb and make use of the cultural history previously withheld from them.

This means, obviously, that not only writers but also all people in the new society must be able to know as much as they want and need to about Russian literature—about world literature. "Though the proletariat is spiritually, and therefore, artistically, very sensitive," Trotsky writes, "it is uneducated aesthetically" (185). As a "non-possessing class," workers were restricted in the past "from acquiring those elements of bourgeois culture which have entered into the inventory of mankind forever" (159). Telling workers that they need not, much less that they should not or cannot, bother with the literature of the bourgeois, feudal, or ancient classical past is ridiculous.

> It is childish to think that bourgeois belles-lettres can make a breach in class solidarity. What the workers will take from Shakespeare, Goethe, Pushkin, or Dostoyevsky will be a more complex idea of human personality, of its passions and feelings. ...In the final analysis, the worker will become richer. (184)

Trotsky's confidence in working-class self-education and creativity underlies his repudiation of any attempt to keep workers from being "contaminated" by the literary productions of capitalist culture. Furthermore, the working class "cannot begin the construction of a new culture without absorbing and assimilating the elements of the old cultures" (185). As for the Communist Party telling workers what they can read, the "domain of art is not one in which the Party is called upon to command. It can and must protect and help it, but it can only lead it indirectly" by defending "the historic interests of the working class in its entirety" (179). For Trotsky, these interests include maximum literacy, maximum education, maximum freedom of self-expression and self-education.

Trotsky's case for artistic freedom depends conceptually on ideas about art itself that are articulated most fully in his chapter on "The Formalist School of Poetry and Marxism." For readers of *Literature and Revolution* working on literary criticism and theory, this is likely to be the most provocative section of the book. The Russian Formalists were professional academics attempting to develop a more scientific approach to the understanding and analysis of literature.[12] Figures such as Victor Shklovsky, a founder in 1916 of the Society for the Study of Poetic Language (Opoyaz), and Roman Jakobson, founder in 1915 of the Moscow Linguistic Circle, brought contemporary work in linguistics, psychology, and the philosophy of language to bear on literary analysis by studying the formal features of a poem or fictional narrative apart from the social and historical reality represented in such literary texts. Although Trotsky fundamentally disagrees with the Formalist way of prioritizing artistic form over sociohistorical content, he recognizes the value as well as the limitations of the exercise. "This analysis, which the Formalists regard as the essence of...poetics, is undoubtedly necessary and useful, but one must understand its partial, scrappy, subsidiary, and preparatory character. It can become an essential element of poetic technique and of the rules of the craft" (139).

What enables Trotsky to critically value Russian Formalism is a principle that, as we have seen, is important to his criticism of the *Proletkultists*—and to his entire perspective on Marxism and artistic culture:

> ...one cannot always go by the principles of Marxism in deciding whether to reject or to accept a work of art. A work of art should, in the first place, be judged by its own law, that is, by the law of art. But Marxism alone can explain why and how a given tendency in art has originated in a given period of history; in other words, who it was who made a demand for such an artistic form and not for another, and why. (150)

That Trotsky insists on judging art "by its own law, that is, by the law of art," is striking and important. But what precisely is "the law of art"? Trotsky does not elaborate this concept systematically, leading some commentators to conclude that while Trotsky clearly familiarized himself at a serious level with the writings of Shklovsky, Jakobson, and their Formalist colleagues, he had not really worked through the linguistic and philosophical technicalities on which they based their research.[13] There is some justice in this: given everything else he was doing, it is not surprising that Trotsky had not yet found time to read, say, Ferdinand de Saussure's *Course in General Linguistics* or other works of specialized academic theory and analysis. The critic Terry Eagleton concludes that "if Trotsky is acutely conscious of the asymmetries of the aesthetic and historical, he lacks the theoretical instruments to define them precisely."[14]

Maybe. But Trotsky can be both precise and suggestive in arguing that neither the writer nor the reader of literature can escape the defining significance of form in any work of art. Paying attention to "the artistic and psychological peculiarities of form," he says, "may open a path—one of the paths—to the artist's feeling for the world, and may facilitate the discovery of the relations of an individual artist, or a whole artistic school, to the social environment" (139). Form, Trotsky is arguing, may be a way toward, rather than a barrier to, our understanding of the social contexts, motivations, and values of literature. Since a "new artistic form, taken in a large historic way, is born in reply to new needs" (141), the reader may come to grasp those "new needs" through an open curiosity about new forms. Literary expression and representation may even be determined by formal experimentation and unpredictability: "In its striving toward artistic materialization, [the] subjective idea will be stimulated and jolted by form and may be sometimes pushed on to a path which was entirely unforeseen. This simply means that verbal form is not a passive reflection of a preconceived artistic idea, but an active element which influences the idea itself" (146). This distinctive sense of the constitutive force of formal exploration and elaboration is one of Trotsky's underappreciated contributions to literary theory. His engagement with the Formalists is productive in itself and in many respects foundational to the rest of what he says about artistic freedom and the creation of a new artistic culture.

It is sometimes assumed that Trotsky's ideas about the freedom and potential development of art were unique in Russian revolutionary culture and at odds not only with the *Proletkultists* and the emerging Stalinists but also with Bolshevism itself. As it happens, Lenin forcefully agreed with Trotsky on virtually all the key points at issue in the debates about "proletarian art." In 1919, Lenin expressed his "hostility" to "all 'proletarian cultures'" as the "inventions of intellectuals":

> Proletarian culture is not something that suddenly springs from nobody knows where, and is not invented by people who set up as specialists in proletarian culture. Proletarian culture is the regular development of those stores of knowledge which mankind has worked out for itself under the yoke of capitalist society, of feudal society, of bureaucratic society.[15]

In a speech to the Central Committee of the Communist Party in May 1924, Trotsky reminded members upset with his criticisms of the *Proletkult* movement that his position was consistent with Lenin's own. Specifically addressing "Comrade Pletnov," who with the help of two other *Proletkult* enthusiasts had attempted to use quotations from Lenin in an attack on *Literature and Revolution,* Trotsky recalls that "Lenin mercilessly condemned 'chatter about proletarian culture.'"[16] Lenin was so much against narrow and misleading efforts to define and promote "proletarian culture" that he threatened "to close down *Proletkult* altogether," a move which Trotsky successfully opposed.

There is one inescapable limit to the artistic freedom Trotsky argues for in *Literature and Revolution,* a limit first set out near the end of the Introduction. "Our policy in art, during a transitional period, can and must be...to allow [the various groups and schools of art] complete freedom of self-determination in the field of art, after putting before them the categorical standard of being for or against the Revolution" (33). Many of Trotsky's readers these days are likely to dismiss this limit and the "categorical standard" on which it is based without thinking about it very carefully. The editors of the *Norton Anthology of Theory and Criticism,* for example, after recognizing Trotsky's "laudable respect for artistic autonomy," go on to lament what they see as his "tendency towards dogmatism" when it comes to defending the revolution.[17] Those inclined to follow the *Norton* editors in this line of thinking should at least consider what Trotsky is actually saying. His position is not that all literary discourse must explicitly praise the Revolution or the cause of working-class emancipation, or that it must refrain from dissent, debate, or satire; as we have seen, Trotsky argues just the opposite. What he says is that writers must not use literature as part of a serious attempt to destroy a society still struggling—against great odds—to survive.[18] Those inclined to reject Trotsky's position might consider the positions taken by governing regimes during the revolutionary moments from which our own modern capitalist democracies arose: the English Revolution of the mid-seventeenth century; the French Revolution; the American Revolution of the 1770s and its second phase, the American Civil War. Did the political leaders in those conflicts fail to put before all citizens a "categorical standard of being for or against the Revolution"? In his introduction to *Art and Revolution,* Paul Siegel quotes a telling passage from John Milton's *Areopagitica* (1644), perhaps the most celebrated case for intellectual and literary freedom in British literature.[19] Writing as a future member of Oliver Cromwell's Council of State and for an audience who understood political and class conflict mainly in religious terms, Milton, the Protestant revolutionary (and later the author of *Paradise Lost*), is decisive on the question of toleration for his unredeemable Roman Catholic and Anglican enemies: "Yet if all cannot be of one mind,—as who looks they should be?—this doubtless is more wholesome, more prudent, and more Christian, that many be tolerated, rather than all compelled. I mean not tolerated popery and open superstition, which, as it extirpates all religions and civil supremacies, so itself should be extirpate."[20]

I am not arguing that we should equate the first successful bourgeois revolution with the first successful socialist revolution in respect to literary freedom and its limits. But I am suggesting that in historical moments when one socioeconomic order is replaced by another, literature and art have never existed outside the constraints inherent in revolutionary conflict.

In addition to his general analysis of the conditions and possibilities of literary culture in the Soviet Union of the 1920s, Trotsky comments extensively in *Literature and Revolution* on specific writers, movements, and institutional developments. His detailed knowledge of the literary scene is remarkable, impressive—and sometimes daunting. Readers unfamiliar with Russian literature will find some assistance in the glossary at the end of this edition, and in the section "Trotsky, the Poets and the Russain Revolution," which contains biographies of the poets that Trotsky discusses as well as a selection of their poems. His assessment of individual writers reflects above all else the confidence he still felt in 1923–1924 that the tremendous potential released by the 1917 Revolution would eventually triumph over the devastations of civil war and the shift of political power away from workers and their organizations toward the State and Party bureaucracy. In hindsight, of course, Trotsky can seem too confident, too hopeful. Little more than a year after the publication of *Literature and Revolution,* he was forced by Stalin and his followers to resign his position as head of the Red Army. Within three years he was expelled from the Communist Party. And in January 1928, he was sent into exile.

The final chapter of *Literature and Revolution* begins by re-emphasizing the exacting critical honesty of its opening pages. "There is no revolutionary art as yet," only "the elements of this art...hints and attempts at it, and...the revolutionary man, who is forming the new generation in his own image and who is more and more in need of this art" (187–88). As for "socialist art," which is something quite different, "no basis has as yet been made," even though eventually socialist art "will grow out of the art of this transition period." As Trotsky's attention shifts in this chapter from the present and past to the future, the promise contained in that last-quoted sentence opens out into an extraordinary vision of artistic and cultural potential.

But the shift is gradual: Trotsky still has plenty to say about the literary past and present. He returns, for instance, to the question of form and to the conventional distinction between form and content as he surveys "the large periods in the development of Russian literature" (190). "Each...tendency," he says, "contained a definite social and group attitude toward the world that laid its impress upon the themes of the works, upon their content." "Content" for Trotsky "does not refer to subject matter, in the ordinary sense of the term, but to social purpose. A lyric without a theme can express an epoch or a class or its point of view as well as a social novel" (190). This shift from "subject matter" to "social purpose" generates a corresponding shift around "the question of form." The "relation of form and content" involves more than just the verbal representation of "subject matter": it "is determined by the fact that a new form is discovered, proclaimed, and developed under the pressure of an inner need, of a collective psychological demand, which, like all human psychology, has its roots in society" (191). Alan Wald is mistaken when he claims that Trotsky's method in *Literature and Revolution* is "problematic on a theoretical plane due to its separation of content from technique," that "Trotsky seems to conceive of art as 'technique'—devoid of a particular content."[21] It is a dynamic, reciprocally-defining interaction of "form" and "content" that Trotsky asserts, and that leads him to redefine both concepts in terms of their rootedness in historically changing "social purpose."

Trotsky's rethinking of "form" and "content" in the chapter on "Revolutionary and Socialist Art" is fundamental to his analysis of literary tendencies such as Symbolism and Futurism, and to his commentary on the great works of bourgeois culture such as Shakespeare's tragedies and Goethe's *Faust*. It is also fundamental to his imagining of future transformations:

> The powerful force of competition, which, in bourgeois society, has the character of market competition, will not disappear in a socialist society, but, to use the language of psychoanalysis, will be sublimated, that is, will assume a higher and more fertile *form*. (188, my emphasis)

The "art" of the socialist future, he envisions, will not depend for its value on being separated from the practicalities of social existence. "All *forms* of life" [my emphasis] will be permeated by artistic impulses and techniques: "the cultivation of land, the planning of human habitations, the building of theatres, the methods of socially educating children, the solution of scientific problems, the creation of new styles" (189). The "direct cooperation between art and all branches of technique will become of paramount importance" (203).[22]

This concluding vision of a time when the "wall will fall... between art and industry" (203) and such rudimentary social processes as the "care for food and education...will become the subject of social initiative and of an endless collective creativeness" (205–206) has led some readers of *Literature and Revolution*—even sympathetic ones—to draw back critically from Trotsky's "utopianism." Some find it easy to smile at the sentence near the very end prophesying that "Man will become immeasurably stronger, wiser, and subtler; his body will become more harmonized, his movements more rhythmic, his voice more musical" (207). Deutscher was, quite appropriately, reminded of Percy Shelley's *Prometheus Unbound* (1819) by such radical optimism —and of Thomas Jefferson's anticipation of human "progress... physical or intellectual—until every man is potentially an athlete in body and an Aristotle in mind."[23] But Trotsky was never out of touch with the difficult struggles that had to come between the revolutionary beginnings of his own moment and a fully realized socialist culture. Near the end of the speech on "Class and Art" which he gave in the year following the publication of *Literature and Revolution*, Trotsky again argues against assuming an unbroken evolution toward a "genuine proletarian literature,... which later will change into socialist literature." "After the present breathing space, when a literature strongly colored by the 'fellow travelers' is being created—not by the party, not by the State—there will come a period of new, terrible spasms of civil war."[24] "[I]f we are victorious," he goes on—not "When," but "If"—the economic and social basis of a real socialist culture will be laid.

Trotsky's optimism about the future of art and culture never grows out of an idealized abstraction about where human history is headed. It grows out of that tenacious honesty about cultural accomplishment and political struggle that often seems to contradict his exuberant belief in the possibilities of socialist art, but is actually its precondition.

William Keach
Boston, December 2004

---

1. R.R. Palmer, *A History of the Modern World*, 2nd Edition, revised (New York: Knopf, 1963), 737. Palmer's book, first published in 1950, is still in print and widely used in schools and universities.
2. *The Norton Anthology of Theory and Criticism*, ed. Vincent B. Leitch (New York and London: W.W. Norton, 2001), 1004.
3. "My book on literature, which caused so much alarm among certain comrades, appeared originally…in the form of articles for *Pravda*. I wrote this book over a period of two years, during two summer breaks": Leon Trotsky, "Class and Art," *Art and Revolution: Writings on Literature, Politics, and Culture*, ed. Paul N. Siegel (New York: Pathfinder Press, 1970; first published under this title, 1992), 76. For the circumstances and context of Trotsky's writing *Literature and Revolution*, see Isaac Deutscher, *The Prophet Unarmed: Trotsky: 1921–1929*, vol. 2 of Deutscher's three-volume biography (New York: Vintage Books, 1959), 164–201; and Tony Cliff, *Trotsky: 1923–1927*, vol. 3 of Cliff's four-volume biography (London: Bookmarks, 1991). Chapter 5 of the latter study was written by Chanie Rosenberg.
4. On the German revolutions and their relation to developments in Russia, see Chris Harman, *The Lost Revolution: Germany 1918 to 1923* (London, Chicago and Sydney: Bookmarks, 1982).
5. All parenthetical citations refer to pages in this edition.
6. See Cliff/Rosenberg, *Trotsky: 1923–1927*, 98–100.
7. Deutscher, *Prophet Unarmed*, 188.
8. See Cliff/Rosenberg, *Trotsky: 1923–1927*, 99, 116–17.
9. See Deutscher, *Prophet Unarmed*, 188–90.
10. See Trotsky, "Class and Art," *Art and Revolution*, 84: "Well, and

what about the party?...its fundamental task in relation to literature and culture is raising the level of literacy—simple literacy, political literacy, scientific literacy—of the working masses, and thereby laying the foundation for a new art."

11. Cliff/Rosenberg, *Trotsky: 1923–1927*, 99: "How to bridge the vast chasm between the immensely idealistic aims of the revolution and the barbarous backwardness of the masses that hampered their ability to shape society in their own interests, inevitably became a key problem for the Bolshevik leaders."

12. The classic study is by Victor Erlich, *Russian Formalism: History-Doctrine* (The Hague, Paris, New York: Mouton, 1955, 4th edition 1980).

13. See Erlich, *Russian Formalism*, 99–108.

14. Terry Eagleton, *Criticism and Ideology: A Study in Marxist Literary Theory* (London: Verso, 1978), 171. See also Tony Bennett, *Formalism and Marxism* (London and New York: Methuen, 1979), 28–9, 101.

15. From Lenin, *Sochineniia*, vol. 24, quoted in Cliff/Rosenberg, *Trotsky: 1923–1927*, 115. See also Deutscher, *Prophet Unarmed*, 169.

16. Trotsky, "Class and Art," *Art and Revolution*, 75–6.

17. *The Norton Anthology of Theory and Criticism*, 1005.

18. Trotsky, "Class and Art," *Art and Revolution*, 179, note: "...we need a resolute and severe, but, of course, not petty, censorship. This means that...we need a severe political struggle against all attempts made by restorationists to bring the new Soviet art under bourgeois influence." The distinction here is between censoring bourgeois art, which Trotsky consistently opposes, and censoring the use of bourgeois art by those actively engaged in undermining the Soviet state and restoring tsarism.

19. See Trotsky, *Art and Revolution*, 22.

20. John Milton, *Complete Poems and Major Prose*, ed. Merritt Y. Hughes (New York: Odyssey Press, 1957), 747. "Extirpate" (the current form would be "extirpated") means uprooted, cut out, entirely destroyed.

21. Alan Wald, "Literature and Revolution: Leon Trotsky's Contribution to Marxist Cultural Theory and Literary Criticism," *The Ideas of Leon Trotsky*, ed. Hillel Ticktin and Michael Cox (London: Porcupine Press, 1995), 221, 224.

22. Trotsky's ideas about practical cultural are articulated in a series of essays collected and published in the volume entitled *Problems of Everyday Life* in 1923. See Deutscher, *Prophet Unarmed*, 164–65 and Cliff/Rosenberg, *Trotsky: 1923–1927*, 100–07.

23. Quoted in Deutscher, *Prophet Unarmed*, 197.

24. Trotsky, "Class and Art," *Art and Revolution*, 86.

Note on the Text and the Translation

Literature and Revolution was first published in Moscow in 1923, in an edition organized in two sections. The first consists of Trotsky's introduction and the eight chapters that make up what we have come to think of as *Literature and Revolution.* The second section, a collection of essays on literature published between 1908 and 1914, has never been entirely translated into English and published in its entirety.

The first and only complete English translation of the first part of *Literature and Revolution,* by Rose Strunsky, was published in New York by International Publishers in 1925. Rose Strunsky's father, Elias Strunsky, brought the Russian Jewish family to the United States in 1886, settling first in New York and then moving to San Francisco in 1893. There Rose and her older sister Anna joined the Socialist Labor Party when they were still in their teens. Through socialist politics they came to know the writer Jack London, who was intimately involved with Anna for several years. Rose attended Stanford for a time but left in 1905 to go to Russia with Anna and her husband, the socialist William English Walling. They lived in Petrograd and were arrested in 1907 for political activities deemed dangerous to the tsar. In 1908, they returned to the United States and lived in New York. Rose and Anna remained active in socialist politics for the rest of their lives.

Jack London's daughter, Joan, was an active Trotskyist. In 1937, she sent Trotsky a copy of London's *The Iron Heel,* first published in 1907. Trotsky's comments on the novel—from a letter written to Joan London in 1937—were printed in *New In-*

ternational (April 1945); see Leon Trotsky, *Art and Revolution: Writings on Literature, Politics, and Culture*, edited by Paul N. Siegel (New York: Pathfinder Press, 1970), pages 230–32.

The present edition reproduces the text of the Strunsky translation with a few modifications in the grammar and punctuation to bring it into line with current usage.

Literature and Revolution

To
Christian Georgievich Rakovsky
Warrior, man, and friend,
I dedicate this book.

Introduction

The place of art can be determined by the following general argument.

If the victorious Russian proletariat had not created its own army, the workers' state would have been dead long ago, and we would not be thinking now about economic problems, and much less about intellectual and cultural ones.

If the dictatorship of the proletariat should prove incapable, in the next few years, of organizing its economic life and of securing at least a living minimum of material comforts for its population, then the proletarian regime will inevitably turn to dust. The economic problem at present is the problem above all problems.

But even a successful solution of the elementary problems of food, clothing, shelter, and even of literacy, would in no way signify a complete victory of the new historic principle, that is, of socialism. Only a movement of scientific thought on a national scale and the development of a new art would signify that the historic seed has not only grown into a plant, but has even flowered. In this sense, the development of art is the highest test of the vitality and significance of each epoch.

Culture feeds on the sap of economics, and a material surplus is necessary, so that culture may grow, develop, and become subtle. Our bourgeoisie laid its hand on literature, and did this very quickly at the time when it was growing rich. The proletariat will be able to prepare the formation of a new, that is, a socialist culture and literature, not by the laboratory method on the basis of our present-day poverty, want, and illiteracy, but by large social, economic, and cultural means. Art needs comfort, even abundance. Furnaces have to be hotter, wheels have to move faster, looms have to turn more quickly, schools have to work better.

Our old literature and "culture" were the expressions of the nobleman and the bureaucrat, and were based on the peasant. The nobleman who did not doubt himself as well as the "repentant nobleman" laid their imprints upon the most significant period of Russian literature. Later the intellectual-commoner arose, based on the peasant and bourgeois, and he, too, wrote his chapter into the history of Russian literature. After going through a period of fullest "simplification" [of leading the simple life of the people] the intellectual-commoner became modernized, differentiated, and individualized, in the bourgeois sense of the term. Here lies the role of the Decadent and Symbolic schools. Already at the beginning of the century, but especially after 1907–1908, the rebirth of the bourgeois intelligentsia and its literature proceeds at full speed. The War made this process end patriotically.

The Revolution overthrew the bourgeoisie and this decisive fact burst into literature. The literature, which was formed around a bourgeois center, is no more. Everything more or less vital, which remained in the field of culture, and this is especially true of literature, tried, and still tries, to find a new orientation. In view of the fact that the bourgeoisie no longer exists, its center can be only the people, without the bourgeoisie. But who are the people? First of all, they are the peasantry, and to some extent the small burghers of the city, and after that those workers who cannot be separated from the protoplasm of peasant and folk. This is the basic approach of all the "fellow travelers" of the Revolution. So thought the late Blok. Thus Pilnyak, the "Serapion Fraternity," the Imagists, who are still alive and doing well. Thus some of the Futurists (Khlebnikov, Kruchenikh, and V. Kamensky). The peasant basis of our culture—or rather, of our lack of culture—reveals indirectly all its strength.

Our revolution is the expression of the peasant turned proletarian, who yet leans upon the peasant and lays out the path to be followed. Our art is the expression of the intellectual, who hesitates between the peasant and the proletarian and who is incapable organically of merging either with one or the other, but who gravitates more toward the peasant, because of his intermediary position, and because of his connections. He cannot become a peasant, but he can sing the peasant. At the same time, however, there can be no revolution without the leadership of the worker. That is the source of the fundamental contradiction at the very approach to the subject. One can say that the poets and writers of these sharply critical years differ from one another in the way they escape from this contradiction, and in the manner in which they fill in the gaps; one with mysticism, another with romanticism, a third with cautious aloofness, and a fourth with a cry which drowns everything. Regardless of the variety of methods of overcoming the contradiction, its essence remains one and the same. It consists in the separation created by bourgeois society of intellectual work, including art, from physical work, and it appears that the Revolution is the work of men doing physical work. One of the ultimate aims of the Revolution is to overcome completely the separation of these two kinds of activity. In this sense, as in all other senses, the problem of creating a new art proceeds entirely along the lines of the fundamental problem of constructing a socialist culture.

It is silly, absurd, stupid to the highest degree, to pretend that art will remain indifferent to the convulsions of our epoch. The events are prepared by people, they are made by people, they fall upon people, and change these people. Art, directly or indirectly, affects the lives of the people who make or experience the events. This refers to all art, to the grandest, as well as to the most intimate. If nature, love, or friendship had no connection with the social spirit of an epoch, lyric poetry would long ago have ceased to exist. A profound break in history, that is, a rearrangement of classes in society, shakes up individuality, establishes the perception of the fundamental problems of lyric poetry from a new angle, and so saves art from eternal repetition.

But does not the "spirit" of an epoch work imperceptibly and independently of the subjective will? Of course in the final analysis, this spirit is reflected in everybody, in those who accept it and who embody it, as well as in those who hopelessly struggle against it, and in those who passively try to hide from it. But those who hide themselves passively are imperceptibly dying off. Those who resist are able to revive the old art with one kind of antiquated flame or another. But the new art, which will lay out new landmarks, and which will expand the channel of creative art, can be created only by those who are at one with their epoch.

If a line were extended from present art to the socialist art of the future, one would say that we have hardly now passed through the stage of even preparing for its preparation.

A short outline of the groups of present-day Russian literature is as follows:

Nonrevolutionary literature, from the *feuilleton* writers in Suvorin's newspaper to the subtlest lyricists of the aristocrat's vale of tears, is dying, together with the classes which it served. Genealogically, as far as form is concerned, it represents the completion of the elder line of our old literature, which began as a nobleman's literature, and finished as bourgeois literature from beginning to end.

The "Soviet" rustic or peasant-singing literature can trace its genealogy, in the sense of form, though less clearly, from the Slavophil and populist tendencies of the old literature. To be sure, the peasant-singing writers are not directly the product of the peasant. They would be unthinkable without the preceding literature of the nobility and the bourgeoisie, the junior line of which they represent. At present, they are all adjusting themselves to be more in tune with the new social situation.

Futurism also undoubtedly represents an offshoot of the old literature. But Russian Futurism did not reach its full development under the old literature, and did not undergo the necessary bourgeois transformation, which would have given it official recognition. When the War and the Revolution began, Futurism was still Bohemian, which is a normal condition for every new literary school in capitalistic cities. Under the impulse of events, Futurism directed its development into the new channels of the Revolution. In the very nature of the thing, this could not and did not result in a revolutionary art. But though remaining, in some respects, a Bohemian revolutionary offshoot of the old art, Futurism contributes to a greater degree and more directly and actively than all other tendencies, in forming the new art.

However significant the achievements of individual proletarian poets may be in general, their so-called "proletarian art" is only passing through an apprenticeship. It sows the elements of artistic culture widely, it helps a new class to assimilate the old achievements, even though in a very thin veneer, and in this way it is one of the currents of the socialist art of the future.

It is fundamentally incorrect to contrast bourgeois culture

and bourgeois art with proletarian culture and proletarian art. The latter will never exist, because the proletarian regime is temporary and transient. The historic significance and the moral grandeur of the proletarian revolution consist in the fact that it is laying the foundations of a culture which is above classes and which will be the first culture that is truly human.

Our policy in art, during a transitional period, can and must be to help the various groups and schools of art which have come over to the Revolution to grasp correctly the historic meaning of the Revolution, and to allow them complete freedom of self-determination in the field of art, after putting before them the categorical standard of being for or against the Revolution.

The Revolution is reflected in art, for the time being only partially so, to the extent to which the artist ceases to regard it as an external catastrophe, and to the extent to which the guild of new and old poets and artists becomes a part of the living tissue of the Revolution and learns to see it from within and not from without.

The social whirlpool will not calm down so soon. There are decades of struggle ahead of us, in Europe and in America. Not only the men and women of our generation, but of the coming one, will be its participants, its heroes and its victims. The art of this epoch will be entirely under the influence of revolution. This art needs a new self-consciousness. It is, above all, incompatible with mysticism, whether it be frank, or whether it masquerades as romanticism, because the Revolution starts from the central idea that collective man must become sole master, and that the limits of his power are determined by his knowledge of natural forces and by his capacity to use them. This new art is incompatible with pessimism, with skepticism, and with all the other forms of spiritual collapse. It is realistic, active, vitally collectivist, and filled with a limitless creative faith in the Future.

L. Trotsky
July 29, 1924

CHAPTER ONE

Pre-Revolutionary Art

The Bolshevik Revolution of October 1917,* did not overthrow the Kerensky government alone, it overthrew the whole social system that was based on private property. This system had its own culture and its own official literature and its collapse could not but be the collapse of pre-revolutionary literature.

The nightingale of poetry, like that bird of wisdom, the owl, is heard only after the sun is set. The day is a time for action, but at twilight feeling and reason come to take account of what has been accomplished. The idealists and their almost deaf and blind disciples, the Russian subjectivists, thought that mind and critical reason moved the world, or, in other words, that the intelligentsia directed progress. As a matter of fact, all through history, mind limps after reality. Nor does the reactionary stupidity of the professional intelligentsia need to be proven now after our experience of the Russian Revolution. The working of this law can also be seen clearly in the field of art. The traditional identification of poet and prophet is acceptable only in the sense that the poet is about as slow in reflecting his epoch as the prophet. If there are prophets and poets who can be said to have been "ahead of their time," it is because they have expressed certain demands of social evolution not quite as slowly as the rest of their kind.

---

*Old Style, October 25, New Style, November 7. The term "October" in this book is used synonymously for the Bolshevist Revolution. [Trans. note.]

Before even a tremor of revolutionary presentiment could pass through Russian literature at the end of the last century and the beginning of this, history had to produce the deepest changes in the basis of economics, in land tenure, in social relations, and in the feelings of the masses. There had to be the collapse of the Revolution of 1905 through its own inner contradictions, there had to be the crushing of the workers in December of that year by the Minister of the Interior, Durnovo, two Dumas had to be dispersed and a third formed by the Prime Minister, Stolypin, before the so-called individualists, mystics, and epileptics could occupy the literary arena. A whole generation of Russian intelligentsia was formed (or rather deformed) by the efforts to conciliate monarchy, nobility, and bourgeoisie, which filled the inter-revolutionary period [between the first Revolution of 1905 and that of 1917]. Social determinism does not necessarily mean conscious self-interest, but the intelligentsia and the ruling class that keeps it are like connecting vessels and the law of levels is equally applicable here. The old radicalism and iconoclasm of the intelligentsia, which during the Russo-Japanese War found expression in a defeatist state of mind, vanished quickly under the star of June 3, 1907 [when Stolypin introduced the so-called "organic reforms"]. With the metaphysical and poetic props of nearly all centuries and all peoples and with the aid of the Fathers of the Church, the intelligentsia "self-determined" itself and proclaimed that it had its own value, regardless of its relation to the "people." The crudeness with which it turned bourgeois was its revenge on the people for the anguish that they had inflicted on it in 1905 by their stubbornness and their lack of respect toward it. The fact, for instance, that Leonid Andreyev, the most popular, if not the most profound, artistic figure of the inter-revolutionary period, finished his career as a writer on a reactionary journal belonging to Protopopov and Amphiteatrov, is in its way a symbolic indication of the social sources of Andreyev's symbolism. In this case, social self-determinism obviously shades off into self-interest. Under the skin of the subtlest individualism, of the unhurried mystic searchings of a well-bred *weltschmerz*, the fat of bourgeois reconciliation to reactionary forces was being deposited. This became manifest in the common patriotic doggerel that our writers began to turn out at once, when the "organic" development of the "reform" régime of June 3rd was upset by the catastrophe of the World War.

The strain of the War, however, proved to be too great, not only for the poetry of the régime of June 3rd, but for its social foundations as well; the military collapse of that regime broke the spine of the inter-revolutionary intelligentsia. Leonid Andreyev, feeling that his plot of ground, which had been so solid and on which had been planted his tower of glory, was disappearing under his feet, tried, by shouting and heaving and foaming at the mouth and waving of hands, to save this and to defend that.

Regardless of the lesson of 1905, the intelligentsia still cherished the hope of re-establishing its spiritual and political hegemony over the masses. The War strengthened it in this illusion. Patriotic ideology was the psychological cement for this, the cement that the new religious consciousness, scrofulous from the day of its birth, could not produce and which the vague symbolism did not attempt to produce. The democratic Revolution of March 1917, which grew out of the War and which ended the War, gave the greatest impetus, though only for a short time, to a revival on the part of the intelligentsia of the idea of Messianism. But the March Revolution was its last historic flare. The smoldering wick began to smell of Kerenskyism.

Then came the October Revolution—a landmark that is more significant than the history of the intelligentsia, and which at the same time marks its unqualified defeat. Yet despite its defeat, and its being crushed to earth by the sins of its past, it raved loudly of its glory. In its mind, the world was completely turned upside down. It was the born representative of the people. In its hands lay the pharmacopoeia of history. The Bolsheviks operated with Chinese and Letts. They could not last long against the people.

The New Year's toasts of the émigré intelligentsia were on this theme: "In Moscow, within a year!" What vicious foolishness—what floundering! It soon became evident that it was really impossible to rule against the will of the people, but that it was not impossible to rule against émigré intellectuals, and even to rule successfully, quite independently of which émigré one meant, the external or the internal.

The pre-revolutionary ripple at the beginning of the century, the unsuccessful first revolution in 1905, the tense but unstable equilibrium of the counter-revolution, the eruption of the War, the prologue of March 1917, the October drama—all these struck the intelligentsia heavily and continuously, as with a battering-ram. Where was there time to assimilate facts, to recreate them into images, and to find for these images expression in words? True, there is "The Twelve" by Blok, and there are several works of Mayakovsky. They are something—a hint—a modest deposit, but not a payment on the account of history—not even the beginning of a payment. Art showed a terrifying helplessness, as always in the beginning of a great epoch. The poets, uncalled to the holy sacrifice, proved themselves, as was to be expected, the most insignificant of all insignificant children of the earth. Symbolists, Parnassians, Acméists, who had flown above social interests and passions, as if in the clouds, found themselves in Ekaterinodar with the Whites, or on the Defense Staff of Marshal Pilsudski. Inspired by a mighty Wrangell passion, they anathematized us in verse and in prose.

The more sensitive ones, and, to some extent, the more cautious ones, were silent. Marietta Shaginyan tells an interesting story how, in the first months of the Revolution, she became active on the Don, in the role of a teacher of weaving. She had not only to go away from the writing table to the loom, but to go away from herself too, in order to lose herself entirely. Others plunged into the Proletkult [the organization for proletarian culture], into the Politprosoviet [the Department of Political Education], or did museum work, and so sat through the most tragic and terrible events that the world had ever lived through. The years of revolution became the years of almost utter poetic silence. Nor was this entirely because of the lack of paper. If poetry could not have been printed then, it could be printed now. Nor was it necessary for such poetry to have been for the Revolution; it could have been against. We know the émigré literature—it is a complete zero. But even our own literature has not given us anything that could measure up to the times.

Literature after October 1917 wished to pretend that nothing special had happened and that this period in general did not concern it. But it came to pass that somehow October began to assert itself in literature, to order and manage it and not only administratively, but in a deeper sense, too. A significant portion of the old literature found itself, and not accidentally so, across the border and thus it happened that, in a literary sense, it became nonexistent. Does Bunin exist? One cannot say that Merezhkovsky has ceased to exist since he had never been. Or Kuprin, or Balmont, or even Chirikov? Or the magazine *Zhar Ptitza* or the *Spolokhi* almanacs or the other editions, whose most significant literary feature consists in retaining the old orthography. They are all, without exception, as in Chekhov's story, scribblings in the complaint-book of the Berlin Railway Station. It will take a long time before the horses will be got ready for Moscow and the passengers express their emotions in the meantime. In the provincial *Spolokhi* almanacs, *belles lettres* is represented by Nemirovich-Dantchenko, Amphiteatrov, Chirikov, Pervukhin, and other stately dead—supposing they have ever been born. Alexey Tolstoy shows some signs of life, though not very strong ones, but for this he is excluded from the magic circle of the preservers of the old orthography and from all the rest of that retired clique of drum-bangers.

Here is a little lesson in practical sociology on the theme that it is impossible to cheat history. Well then—let us take up the subject of violence. The land was taken, the factories were taken, the bank deposits were taken, safes were opened; but what about talents, ideas? Were not these imponderable values exported abroad and in quantities terrifying to Russian culture and especially to its amiable psalm-singer, Gorky? Why didn't something come of all this? Why can't the émigrés name one name or one book worth lingering on? Because one cannot cheat history or true culture (not the psalm-singer's). October entered into the destinies of the Russian people, as a decisive event and gave to everything its own meaning and its own value. The past receded at once, faded and drooped, and art can be revived only from the point of view of October. He who is outside of the October perspective is utterly and hopelessly reduced to nothing and it is therefore that the wiseacres and poets, who do not "agree with this" or whom "this does not concern," are nobodies. They simply have nothing to say. For this and for no other reason, émigré literature does not exist. And what is not, cannot be judged.

In the death-like disintegration of the émigrés there was evolved a certain polished type of mocking cynic. All currents and tendencies entered into his blood like a bad disease that immunized him against further infection from ideas. A perfect example of this type is the unembarrassed Vetlugin. Perhaps someone knows how he began. But that is unessential. His little books *The Third Russia, Heroes* are evidence that the author read, saw, and heard various and sundry things and can push a pen (*manier la plume*). He starts his little book almost with an elegy over the lost and most subtle souls of the intelligentsia and ends it with an ode to the speculating bagman [those who went to the villages with bags to trade for food and speculated illegally]. This bagman, it seems, is going to be the master of the coming "Third Russia." And that is going to be the real Russia, sincere, on the defense for private property and growing rich and merciless in its greed. Vetlugin, who was with the Whites and who rejected them when they lost out, advances his candidacy with foresight as the ideologist of this bagman's Russia. In the sense of determining his avocation, this is clever. But what about the "Third Russia"? Whichever way you take it, the knave of clubs, alas! creeps out unmistakably from his clear-cut style. His first book was written approximately at the time of the Kronstadt uprising against the Soviets (1921), and Vetlugin thought that Soviet Russia was done for. But after a short number of months, the expected did not happen, and Vetlugin, if we are not mistaken, finds himself now with the "Changing Landmarks" group [with those who have accepted the Bolshevik Revolution as a landmark in the national development of Russia and have made peace with it]. But this is all the same. He is fundamentally protected by cynicism from any conceptual waverings, even from backsliding. Let us add that Vetlugin is also writing a cheap novel with the suggestive title, *Memoirs of a Scoundrel*—and of such there are not a few, only Vetlugin is the most brilliant of them. They even lie disinterestedly, because they have lost interest in distinguishing truth from lies. Perhaps they are the real dregs of the "second" Russia, which is awaiting the "third."

On a higher plane, but weaker, stands Aldanov. He is more of a Constitutional Democrat and therefore more of a Pharisee. Aldanov belongs to those wise ones who have assumed a tone of higher skepticism (not cynicism, oh no!). Rejecting progress, these people are ready to accept Vico's childish theory of historic cycles. In general, no people are more superstitious than skeptics. The Aldanovs are not mystics in the full sense of the word. That is, they do not have their own positive mythology, but their political skepticism gives them an excuse to regard all political manifestation from the point of view of eternity. This is conducive to a special style, with a very aristocratic lisp.

The Aldanovs take almost seriously their great superiority over revolutionists in general and over communists in particular. It seems to them that we do not understand what they understand. Revolution is to them the result of the fact that not all of the intelligentsia has passed through that school of political skepticism and literary style that forms the spiritual capital of the Aldanovs.

In their émigré leisure they counted the formal and real contradictions in the speeches and statements of the Soviet leaders (and can they be imagined without contradictions?); the wrongly constructed sentences and editorials of *Pravda* (and of such sentences it must be admitted there are many enough) and as a result the word *stupidity* (ours) in contrast to *sense* (theirs) colors their written pages. It is true they were blind to history, foresaw nothing, lost their power and with it their capital, but all this is explained by other reasons and chiefly, *entre nous*, by the vulgar character of the Russian people. But above all, the Aldanovs consider themselves stylists, because they overcame the mushy sentences of Miliukov and the arrogant and legalistic phraseology of Hessen, his associate. Their style, simply coy, without accent or character, is suited most admirably for the literary use of people who have nothing to say. Their self-sufficient manner of speech, void of content, their worldliness of mind and style, which was unknown to our old intelligentsia, was already being developed in the inter-revolutionary period (1907–1917). And now, in addition, they have noticed something in Europe and they are writing booklets. They are ironical, they reminisce, they pretend to yawn somewhat; but, out of politeness, suppress the yawn. They quote in various tongues, make skeptical predictions and immediately deny them. At first this appears amusing, then boring, and in the end disgusting. What charlatanism of impudent phrases, what bookish philandering, what spiritual flunkeyism!

But all the moods of the Vetlugins, Aldanovs, and others are expressed best of all in the form of an amiable poem by a certain Don Aminado, who is living in Paris:

> And who can guarantee that the ideal is true?
> That mankind will be better off?
> Where is the measure of things? Forward, General!
> Ten years more! That is enough for me and you!

As we see, the Spaniard is not proud. Forward, General!

The generals (and even the admirals) went forward. The trouble was, they never arrived.

          ■   ■   ■

But on our side of the frontier there remained a goodly number of pre-October writers akin to those on the other side, internal émigrés of the Revolution. Pre-October will sound to the future historian of culture just as ponderous as is to us the word medieval when contrasted with modern history. October appeared very sincerely to the majority of those who adhered to pre-October culture on principle, as an invasion of the Hun from whom they had to flee to the catacombs with the so-called "torches of knowledge and faith." However, those who hid themselves and those who, having fenced themselves off, stand aloof, have not said a new word. It is true that pre-October or non-October literature in Russia is more significant than that of the émigré. But it is only a survival, struck with impotence.

So many books of poetry have appeared, many bearing well-sounding names. They have small pages and short lines, none of which are bad. They are connected into poems where there is quite a little art, and even an echo of a once-existent feeling—yet taken altogether these books are completely and entirely superfluous to a modern post-October man, like a glass bead to a soldier on the battlefield. The gem of this literature of renunciation, of this literature of discarded thoughts and feelings, is the fat, well-meaning almanac *Streletz*, where poems, articles, and letters by Sologub, Rozanov, Belenson, Kuzmin, Hollerbakh, and others, are printed and to the quantity of 300 numbered copies. A novel of Roman life, letters about the erotic cult of the bull Apis, an article about St. Sophia, the Earthly and the Heavenly; three hundred numbered copies—what hopelessness, what desolation! It were better to curse and rage! That, at least, would resemble life.

"And swiftly you will be driven to the old stable with a club, O people, disrespectful of holy things." (Hippius, *Last Poems*, 1914–1918.) This, of course, is not poetry, but nevertheless, what natural journalism! What an inimitable slice of life is this effort of the decadent mystic poetess to wield a club (in iambics!). When Hippius threatens the people with her whips "for eternity," she is, of course, exaggerating, if she wants it to be understood that her curses will shatter hearts in the course of the ages. But through this exaggeration, fully excusable under the circumstances, one can see her nature quite clearly. Only yesterday she was a Petrograd lady, languid, decorated with talents, liberal, modern. Suddenly today, this lady, so full of her own subtleties, sees the black outrageous ingratitude on the part of the mob "in nailed boots," and, offended in her holy of holies, transforms her impotent rage into a shrill womanish squeak (in iambics). And indeed, if her squeak will not shatter hearts, it will arouse interest. A hundred years hence, the historian of the Russian Revolution will perhaps point out how a nailed boot stepped on the lyrical little toe of a Petrograd lady, who immediately showed the real property-owning witch under her decadent-mystic-erotic Christian covering. Because of the real witch in Zinaida Hippius, her poems tower above the others and are more perfect, though they are more "neutral" and therefore dead.

When you find among so many "neutral" booklets and pamphlets *The House of Miracles* by Irene Odoevtzeva, then you can almost make peace with the falsity of the modernized romanticism of salamanders, of knights, of bats, of the dying moon, for the sake of the two or three stories reflecting the cruel life of the Soviet. Here is a ballad about an *isvostchik* whom the Commissar Zon drove to death, together with his horse; a story about a soldier who sold salt mixed with ground glass, and finally a ballad on how the water mains were polluted in Petrograd. Their patterns are on a small scale and ought to please Cousin George and Aunt Nan very much. But for all that, they show a tiny reflection of life and are not merely belated echoes of melodies sung long ago and recorded in encyclopedias. And for a moment we are ready to join with Cousin George. They are very, very nice poems; go on, Mademoiselle!

We are not talking only about those "old ones" who have survived October. There is a group of young litterateurs and poets who are non-October. I am not very sure how young these young ones are. But, at any rate, in the pre-revolutionary and pre-war period they were either beginners, or had not yet begun. They write stories, novels, poems, with the unindividualized art that was customary not so very long ago, in order to receive the recognition that was customary. The Revolution crushed their hopes ("the nailed boot"). They make believe, as much as they can, that nothing, in fact, has happened and voice their wounded arrogance in their unindividualized verses and prose. But from time to time they relieve their souls by secretly thumbing their noses.

The master of this whole group is Zamyatin, the author of *The Islanders*. Properly speaking, his theme is about the English. Zamyatin knows them and paints them not badly, in a series of sketches, but very externally, like an observant and gifted, but not very exacting, foreigner. But between the same covers, he has sketches about Russian "islanders," about the intelligentsia who live on an island in the strange and hostile ocean of Soviet reality. Zamyatin is more subtle in these sketches, but not deeper. After all, the author is an "islander" himself, and lives on a very small island at that, to which he migrated from the present Russia. And whether Zamyatin writes about the Russians in London, or about the English in Leningrad, he himself undoubtedly remains an internal émigré. By his somewhat strained style, in which he expresses his particular literary gentlemanliness (bordering on snobbism), Zamyatin is as if cut out to be a teacher to groups of young, enlightened, and sterile "islanders."**

The most indisputable "islanders" are the members of the Moscow Art Theater group. They do not know what to do with their high technique, nor with themselves. They consider all that is happening around them as hostile, or, at any rate, strange. Just imagine: these people are living, to this day, in the mood of the Chekhov Theater. *The Three Sisters* and *Uncle Vanya* today! In

---

**After this was written, I became acquainted with a group of poets who, for some reason, call themselves "Islanders" (Tikhonov and others). But live notes are heard among them, at least from Tikhonov, young and fresh and promising. Whence this exotic nomenclature?

order to wait for the bad weather to pass—bad weather does not last long—they played *The Daughter of Madame Angot,* which, apart from everything else, gave them a little chance to show off their opposition to the Revolutionary authorities. Now they disclose to the blasé European and to the all-paying American how beautiful was the cherry orchard of old feudal Russia and how subtle and languid were its theaters. What a noble moribund cast from a jewel theater! Does not also the very gifted Akhmatova belong here?

The "Poets' Guild" is made up of the most enlightened composers of poetry; they know geography, they can distinguish the rococo from the Gothic, they express themselves in the French tongue, and they are to the highest degree adepts of culture. They think and rightly so, that "our culture has still a weak childish lisp" (Georgi Adamovich). Superficial veneer does not buy them. "Polish cannot take the place of real culture" (George Ivanov). Their taste is sufficiently exact to feel that Oscar Wilde is, after all, a snob and not a poet, in which it is impossible not to agree with them. They have contempt for those who do not value "a school," that is, a discipline, a knowledge, a struggling forward, and to such a sin we are no strangers. They revise their poems very carefully. Several of them, for example Otsup, have talent. Otsup is a poet of reminiscences, of dreams, and of fears. At every step he falls through into the past. The only thing that opens up the "happiness of life" for him is memory. "I have even found a place for myself; a poet observer and a bourgeois saving my life from death," he says, with tender irony about himself. But his fear is in no way hysterical, it is almost a balanced fear, that of a self-possessed European, and, what is really comforting, it is an entirely cultivated fear, without any mystic twitches. But why does their poetry never flower? Because they are not the creators of life, they do not participate in the creation of its sentiments and moods, they are only tardy skimmers, leftovers of a culture created by the blood of others. They are imitators, educated and even exquisite; they are imitators of sound, well read and even gifted; but nothing more.

Under the mask of being a citizen of the civilized world, the nobleman Versilov was, in his time, the most enlightened sponger on foreign culture. He had a taste that had been cultivated by several generations of the nobility. He felt almost at home in Europe. He looked down with condescension or malicious contempt on the radical seminarist, who quoted Pisarev or who pronounced French with the accents of a pastry cook and whose manners—well, we had better not speak of manners. And nonetheless, this seminarist of the 1860s and his successor of the 1870s were the builders of Russian culture at the time when Versilov had already definitely revealed himself as a most futile culture-skimmer.

The Russian Constitutional Democrats, who are the belated bourgeois liberals of the beginning of the twentieth century, are thoroughly imbued with respect and even "awe" for culture, for its stable foundations, for its style, and for its aroma, but in themselves are nothing more than empty zeros. Look back and measure the sincere contempt with which these Constitutional Democrats regarded Bolshevism from the height of their professional-lawyer-writer's culture and compare it with the contempt that history has shown for these very same Constitutional Democrats. What is the matter? Because, as in the case of Versilov, only translated into a bourgeois professorial tongue, the culture of the Constitutional Democrats proved to be wholly a belated reflection of foreign cultures on the superficial soil of Russian social life. Liberalism meant, in the history of the West, a mighty movement against heavenly and earthly authorities and in the heat of its revolutionary struggle it heightened both material and spiritual culture. France, such as we know her, with her cultivated folk, with perfected forms, and with the politeness that has become absorbed in the blood of the masses, came out as she is, molded in the furnace of several revolutions. The "barbaric" process of dislocations, of upheavals, of catastrophes, has left its deposits in the present-day French language, with its strength and weaknesses, its exactness and its inflexibility—and in the styles of French art also. In order to again give flexibility and malleability to the French tongue, another great revolution, let us say in passing, is needed (not in the language, but in the social life of France). Such a revolution is also needed to elevate French art, so conservative in all its innovations, to another higher plane.

But our own Constitutional Democrats, those belated imitators of liberalism, tried to skim from history, free of charge, the cream of parliamentarism, of cultured courtesy, of balanced art (on the solid basis of profits and rents). To examine the individual or group styles of Europe, to think them over or even to absorb them, in order afterwards to show in all of these styles that they have really nothing to say, is what Adamovich, Iretzky, and many of the others, are good for. But this is not creating culture, it is merely skimming its cream.

When some Constitutional Democratic aesthete makes a long journey in a cattle car and then tells about it, muttering through his teeth, how he, a most educated European, with the very best false teeth and the most exact knowledge of the technique of the Egyptian ballet, was reduced by the vulgar Revolution to the necessity of traveling with lousy bagmen, a feeling of physical disgust rises in your throat against the false teeth, the aesthetics of the ballet, and against all this culture stolen from the shelves of Europe in general. A conviction begins to grow that the very least louse of the ragged bagman is more significant in the mechanism of history, that is, is more needed, than this thoroughly cultivated and utterly futile egoist.

In the period before the War, before these culture-skimmers had risen on all fours to howl patriotically, a journalistic style had begun to develop in our midst. True, Miliukov still continued long-windedly to mumble and scribble professorial-parliamentary editorials and his associate-editor Hessen served up the best samples of divorce proceedings. But, in general, we were beginning to unlearn our traditional and domestic slipshod ways through the respectable lean and Lenten fat of the *Russkiya Viedomosti*. This tiny stylistic progress in journalism in the manner of Europe (that was paid for, by the way, with the blood of the Revolution of 1905, from which came the parties and the Duma), was drowned leaving hardly a trace of itself in the waves of the Revolution of 1905. The Constitutional Democrats who are living abroad today, divorced or otherwise, point most maliciously to the literary weakness of the Soviet press. And truly, we write badly, stylelessly, imitatively, even after the manner of the *Russkiya Viedomosti*. Does that mean that we have regressed? No, it means a transition period between the skimming imitation of progress, between the hired lawyer's claptrap, and the great cultural movement forward of a whole people, which, given but a little time, will create for itself its own style, in journalism as well as in everything else.

Then there is still another category, the *Ralliés*. This is a term from French politics and means "they who have joined." The former Royalists who made peace with the Republic were thus called. They gave up the struggle for the King and even their hope in him and loyally translated their royalism into Republican language. There was hardly one among them who could have written the *Marseillaise,* even if it had never been written before. It is to be doubted whether they sang the strophes against tyrants with enthusiasm. But these *Ralliés* live and let live. There are a number of such Ralliés among the present-day poets, artists, and actors. They do not libel and they do not curse; on the contrary, they accept the state of affairs, but in general terms and "without assuming any responsibility." Where it is seemly, they are diplomatically silent, or loyally pass things by and in general they are patient and take part, as much as they are able. I am not referring to the "Changing Landmarks" group —the latter have their own ideology. I am speaking merely of the pacified Philistines of art, its ordinary civil servants, often not ungifted. Such Ralliés we find everywhere, even among portrait painters; they paint "Soviet" portraits and sometimes great artists do the painting. They have experience, technique, everything. Yet somehow the portraits are not good likenesses. Why? Because the artist has no inner interest in his subjects, no spiritual kinship, and he paints a Russian or a German Bolshevik as he used to paint a carafe or a turnip for the Academy, and even more neutrally, perhaps.

I do not name names, because they form a whole class. These Ralliés will not snatch the Polar Star from the heavens, nor invent smokeless powder; but they are useful and necessary and will be the manure for the new culture. And this is not so little.

■　　■　　■

The castrated state of non-October art is evident in the fate of the intellectualist and religious searchings and findings that have "fertilized" the main currents of pre-revolutionary literature, that is, Symbolism. A few words about this are in place here.

The intelligentsia moved at the beginning of the century from materialism and "positivism," and even to some extent from Marxism, through critical philosophy (Kantism), to mysticism. In the inter-revolutionary years, this new religious consciousness flickered and smoldered with many dull fires. At present, however, when the rock of official orthodoxy has been seriously moved from its place, these parlor-mystics, each one queer in his own way, are depressed and hang their tails, for the new scale of things is too big for them. Without the help of parlor prophets and journalistic saints, who were formerly Marxists, even against all the opposition that was in them, the waves of the revolutionary tide rolled up to the very walls of the Russian church, which knew no reformation. She defended herself against history by a hard immobility of form, by automatic ritual and by governmental support. She had bowed very low before Tsarism and she held her own almost unchanged several years longer than her autocratic ally and protector. But her turn came, too. The "Changing Landmark" tendency in the church, renovating as it is, is a belated attempt at a bourgeois reformation, under the guise of adaptation to the Soviet state. Our political revolution was completed—and this even against the wish of the bourgeoisie—only a few months before the Revolution of the working-classes. The reformation of the church began almost four years after the proletarian upheaval. If the "Living Church" sanctions a social revolution, it is only because it seeks protective coloring. A proletarian church is impossible. The church reformation is pursuing essentially bourgeois aims, such as the liberation of the church from the medieval unwieldiness of caste, the substitution of a more individualized relation to the heavenly hierarchy for the mimicry of ritual and Shamanism; in a word, the general aim of giving to religion and to the church a greater flexibility and adaptability. In the first four years the church fenced herself off from the proletarian Revolution by a somber defensive conservatism. Now she is going over to the NEP [the New Economic Policy]. If the Soviet NEP is a mating of socialist economy with capitalism, then the church NEP is a bourgeois grafting on to the feudal stem. The recognition of the workers' rule is dictated, as was said before, by the law of imitation.

But the tottering of the age-old structure of the church has begun. To the left—the "Living Church" also has its left wing—more radical voices are being raised. Still more to the left are the radical sects. A naive rationalism, which is only just awakening, is breaking up the soil for atheistic and materialistic seeds. An era of great upheavals and downfalls has arrived in this kingdom, that had announced itself not of this world. Where now is the "new religious consciousness"? Where are the prophets and reformers from the Leningrad and Moscow literary parlors and circles? Where is anthroposophy? There is no sound or breath of them. The poor mystic homeopaths feel like petted house-cats thrown at high flood on the breaking ice. The heavy-headed aftermath of the first Revolution brought forth their "new religious consciousness," and the second Revolution crushed it.

Berdayev, for instance, still accuses those who do not believe in God and who do not bother themselves about a future life, of being bourgeois. This is really amusing. This writer's brief connection with the socialists left him with the word "bourgeoisdom" with which he is now beating off the Soviet anti-Christ. The trouble is that the Russian workers are not religious at all, but the bourgeoisie have become believers in toto—after losing their estates. Here lies one of the many inconveniences of revolution that it bares to the very bottom the social sources of ideology.

In this way, the "new religious consciousness" vanished, leaving, however, quite a few traces of itself in literature. A whole generation of poets who had accepted the Revolution of 1905 as a Saint John's Night and who had singed their delicate wings in its bonfires, began to introduce the heavenly hierarchy into their rhythms. They were joined by the inter-revolutionary youth. But, just as the poets, following a bad tradition, used to turn formerly at difficult moments to nymphs, Pan, Mars, and Venus, so here Olympus was nationalized under the aegis of poetic form. After all, whether it was to be a Mars or a Saint George depended upon whether they had to fit a trochee or an iambus. Undoubtedly many, or at least some, hid their experiences, which were mostly fear, under this. Then came the War, which dissolved the intelligentsia's fear into a general feverish anxiety. Later came the Revolution, which thickened this fear into panic. What was to be expected? To whom could it turn? To what could it cling? Nothing but the Church Calendar, nothing else remained. Very few are eager now to stir the new religious liquid that had been distilled before the War in the Berdayev and other pharmacies, for they who have the mystic urge simply cross themselves with the cross of their forefathers. The Revolution scrubbed and washed off the personal tattooing, disclosing the traditional, the tribal, that thing that had been received with the mother's milk and that had not been dissolved by critical reason because of its weakness and cowardice. In poetry, Jesus is never absent. And the robe of the Virgin is the most popular poetic texture in an age of a textile machinery industry.

One reads with dismay most of the poetic collections, especially those of the women. Here, indeed, one cannot take a step without God. The lyric circle of Akhmatova, Tsvetaeva, Radlova, and other real and near-poetesses, is very small. It embraces the poetess herself, an unknown one in a derby or in spurs, and inevitably God, without any special marks. He is a very convenient and portable third person, quite domestic, a friend of the family who fulfills from time to time the duties of a doctor of female ailments. How this individual, no longer young, and burdened with the personal and too often bothersome errands of Akhmatova, Tsvetaeva, and others, can manage in his spare time to direct the destinies of the universe is simply incomprehensible. For Schkapskaya, who is so organic, so biologic, so gynecologic (Schkapskaya's talent is real), God is something in the nature of a go-between and a midwife; that is, he has the attributes of an all-powerful scandalmonger. And if a subjective note may be permitted here, we willingly concede that if this feminine wide-hipped God is not very imposing, he is far more sympathetic than the incubated chick of mystic philosophy beyond the stars.

How can one not come, finally, to the conclusion that the normal head of an educated Philistine is a dustbin in which history in passing throws the shell and the husk of its various achievements? Here is the apocalypse—Voltaire and Darwin and the psalm-book and comparative philology and two times two and the waxed candle. A shameful hash much lower than the ignorance of the cave. Man, "the king of nature" who infallibly wants to "serve," wags his tail and sees in this the voice of his "immortal soul"! But on examination, the so-called soul represents an "organ," far less perfect and harmonious than the stomach or the kidney, because the "immortal" has many rudimentary appendices and blind sacs, which are clogged up by every kind of putrid dreg, continually causing itch and spiritual ulcer. Sometimes they erupt into rhythmic lines; the latter are then handed out as individualistic and mystic poetry and printed in neat booklets.

■   ■   ■

But nothing, perhaps, has revealed so intimately and so convincingly the desolation and decay of the individualism of the intelligentsia as the present-day wholesale canonizing of Rozanov —a "genius" philosopher, a seer, a poet, and a knight of the spirit as well. Yet Rozanov was a notorious rascal, a coward, a sponger, and a lickspittle. And this was his very essence. His talent lay within the boundaries of this essence.

When the "genius" of Rozanov is spoken of, it is chiefly his revelations in the field of sex that are emphasized. But if some one of his admirers would try to bring together and to systematize what Rozanov said in his peculiar language, adapted to omissions and ambiguities, about the influence of sex on poetry, on religion, on government, he would get something very meager and very little that is new. The Austrian psychoanalytic school (Freud, Jung, Alfred Adler, and others) made an immeasurably greater contribution to the question of the role of the sex-element in the forming of individual character and of social consciousness. In fact, there can be no comparison here. Even the most paradoxical exaggerations of Freud are much more significant and fertile than the broad surmises of Rozanov who constantly falls into intentional half-wittedness, or simple babble, repeats himself and lies for two.

However, one has to admit that those external and internal émigrés who are not ashamed to praise Rozanov and to bow before him, have hit the nail on the head; in his spiritual sponging, in his flunkeyism, in his cowardice, Rozanov only carried to the logical conclusion their fundamental spiritual traits—cowardice before life and cowardice before death.

A certain Victor Khovin—the theorist of Futurism, or whatever he is—assures us that Rozanov's vulgar changeability was the result of the most complex and subtle causes; that if Rozanov ran to the Revolution (1905) without leaving, by the way, the reactionary newspaper *Novoe Vremya* and then turned to the right, it was only because he was frightened for the manifested superman stuff and nonsense in him, and if he went as far as carrying out the Minister of Justice's orders [in the Beiliss ritual case], and if he wrote at the same time in the *Novoe Vremya* in a reactionary way and in the *Russkoe Slovo* under a pseudonym in a liberal [way], and if he served as a go-between to entice young writers to Suvorin, this was all only because of the complexity and the depth of his spiritual nature. These silly and driveling apologetics would at least have been a little more convincing if Rozanov had come nearer to the Revolution at the time of its persecution, in order afterwards to withdraw from it at the time of its victory. But this is the very thing that Rozanov did not do and could not have done. He sang of the catastrophe at the Khodynka field [at the coronation of Nicholas II] as a purifying sacrifice in an era when the reactionary Pobedonostzev was triumphant. The Constituent Assembly and the Terror, all that which was most revolutionary, he accepted in the October period of 1905 when the young Revolution seemed to have thrown to the ground the powers that were. After the 3rd of June 1907, he sang of the men of June 3rd. At the time of the Beiliss trial he tried to prove the use of Christian blood by Jews for religious purposes. Not long before his death he wrote with his habitual grimace of the simpleton that the Jews were the "first people on earth," which naturally was not much better than what he had done at the Beiliss trial, though from the opposite direction. The truest and most consistent thing in Rozanov is his worm-like wriggling before power. A wormish man and a writer; a wriggling, slippery, sticky worm, contracting and stretching according to need, and like a worm, disgusting. Rozanov called the orthodox church unceremoniously—in his own circle, of course—a dung heap. But he kept to the ritual (out of cowardice and for any eventuality) and when he came to die he took communion five times—also for any eventuality. He was underhanded with heaven as with his publisher and his reader.

Rozanov sold himself publicly for pieces of silver. His philosophy was in accordance with this and was so adapted. And so was his style. He was the poet of the cozy corner, of a lodging with all comforts. Making fun of teachers and prophets, he invariably taught that the most important thing in life is the soft, the warm, the fat, the sweet. The intelligentsia in the last few decades was rapidly becoming bourgeois and was leaning very much to the soft and the sweet, but at the same time it was embarrassed by Rozanov as a young bourgeois is embarrassed by a loose cocotte who imparts her knowledge publicly. But in essence, Rozanov always belonged to it, and now when the old partitions within "educated" society have lost all meaning as well as decency, the figure of Rozanov assumes titanic proportions in their eyes. And today they are united in a cult of Rozanov; among them are the theorists of Futurism (Shklovsky, Khovin) and Remizov, and the Dreamers-Anthroposophists, and the unimaginative Joseph Hessen, the former rights and the former lefts! "Hosanna to the hanger-on! He taught us how to like sweets and we dreamed of the albatross and lost all. And here we have been left behind by history—and without sweets."

■   ■   ■

A catastrophe, whether it be personal or social, is always a great touchstone, because it infallibly reveals the true personal or social connections, not the showy ones. And so owing to October, pre-October art, which became almost entirely anti-October, showed its indissoluble connection with the governing classes of old Russia. This is so clear now that one does not even have to touch it with one's hands. The landlord, the capitalist, the military and civil general, went into the emigration together with their lawyer and their poet. And they all decided that culture had perished. Certainly the poet had considered himself independent of the bourgeois, and had even quarreled with him, But when the problem was put with revolutionary earnestness, then the poet immediately revealed himself a hanger-on to the marrow of his bones. This history lesson in the "free" art developed parallel with the lesson concerning the other "freedoms" of democracy—that same democracy which swept and mopped after Yudenich. In modern history, art, both individual and professional, in contrast to the old, collective folk art, flourished in the abundance and in the leisure of the governing classes and remained in their keeping. The element of keeping that was almost intangible when social relations were undisturbed was bared in all its crudity when the ax of the Revolution cut down the old props.

The psychology of hanging on and of being kept is not at all equivalent to that of submission, politeness, or respectfulness. On the contrary, it implies very severe scenes, outbursts, differences, threats of a full break—but only threats. Foma Fomich Opiskin, the classic type of old noble hanger-on, found himself almost always "with psychology" in a state of domestic insurrection. But if I remember rightly, he never got farther than the barn. This is very crude, of course, and in any case, it is impolite to compare Opiskin with the Academicians and the near classics: Bunin, Merezhkovsky, Zinaida Hippius, Kotlyarevsky, Zaitzev, Zamyatin, and others. But you have to sing the song of history as it is. They have revealed themselves kept ones and hangers-on. And though some of them manifest this trait in violent ways, the majority of the internal émigrés, partly because of circumstances over which they have no control, and mainly, one must think, because of their temperament, are merely sad that their state of being kept has been cut at the root, and their melancholy peters out into reminiscences and into retold experiences.

Andrey Biely

The inter-revolutionary (1905–1917) literature, which is decadent in its mood and reach and overrefined in its technique, which is a literature of individualism, of symbolism, and of mysticism, finds in Biely its most condensed expression, and through Biely was most loudly destroyed by October. Biely believes in the magic of words. It is permitted to say about him, therefore, that his very pen name testifies to his antithesis to the Revolution, for the greatest fighting period of the Revolution passed in the struggle between Red and White.***

Biely's memoirs of Blok, which are amazing in their meaningless detail and in their arbitrary mosaic of psychology, make one feel tenfold to what an extent they are people of another epoch, of another world, of a past epoch, of an unreturnable world. This is not a question of the difference in generations, for they are people of our own generation, but of the difference in social makeup, in spiritual type, in historic roots. For Biely, "Russia is a large meadow, green, like [Tolstoy's] Yasnaya-Polyana or [Blok's] Shakhmatov estate." In this image of pre-revolutionary and revolutionary Russia, as a green meadow, as a Yasnaya-Polyana and Shakhmatov meadow at that, one feels how deep is buried the

---

***Biely means white in Russian. [Trans. note.]

old Russia, the landlord and official Russia, or at best a Russia of Turgenev and of Goncharov. How astronomically remote this is from us, how good it is that it is remote, and what a jump through the ages from this to October!

Whether it be the Bezhin meadow of Turgenev, or the Shakhmatov one of Blok, or Tolstoy's Yasnaya-Polyana, or the Oblomov one of Goncharov, it is an image of peace and vegetating harmony. Biely's roots are in the past. But where is the old harmony now? On the contrary, everything seems shaken up to Biely, everything is aslant, everything is thrown out of equilibrium. To him, the peace of a Yasnaya-Polyana has not been changed into dynamics, but into excitements and a jumping up and down in one spot. Biely's apparent dynamics mean only a running around and a struggling on the mounds of a disappearing and disintegrating old regime. His verbal twists lead nowhere. He has no hint of ideal revolutionism. In his core he is a realistic and spiritual conservative who has lost the ground under his feet and is in despair. "The Memoirs of a Dreamer," a journal inspired by Blok, is a union of a despairing realist whose chimney smokes, and of an intellectual who is used to spiritual comforts, and who, without a Shakhmatov meadow, cannot even bring himself to dream of a life beyond. This "dreamer" Biely, whose feet are on the ground and whose underpinnings are those of a landlord and of a bureaucrat, is only puffing rings of smoke around himself.

Torn from the pivot of custom and individualism, Biely wishes to replace the whole world with himself, to build everything from himself and through himself, to discover everything anew in himself—but his works, with all their different artistic values, invariably represent a poetic or spiritualist sublimation of the old customs. And that is why, in the final analysis, this servile preoccupation with oneself, this apotheosis of the ordinary facts of one's personal and spiritual routine, become so unbearable in our age where mass and speed are really making a new world. If one is to write with so much ritual of the meeting with Blok, how is one to write about great events that affect the destinies of nations?

In Biely's recollections of his infancy (*Kotik Lotaev*) there are interesting moments of lucid psychology, not always artistically correct, but frequently internally convincing, yet his connecting them together with occult discussions, his make-believe profundities, his piling up of images and words, make them futile and utterly tiresome. With his knees and elbows, Biely tries to squeeze his childish soul through into the world beyond. The traces of his elbows are seen on all the pages, but the world beyond—isn't there! And, in fact, where is it to come from?

Not long ago Biely had written about himself—he is always occupied with himself, narrating about himself, walking around himself, sniffing himself, and licking himself—several very true thoughts—"Under my theoretic abstractions of the 'Maximum' perhaps was hidden the minimalist, carefully feeling his ground. I approached everything in a roundabout way. Feeling the ground from afar with a hypothesis, with a hint, with methodological proof, remaining in watchful indecision" (*Memoirs of Alexander Blok*). In calling Blok a maximalist, Biely speaks of himself straight out as a Menshevik (in the holy spirit, of course, not in politics). These words may appear unexpected from the pen of a Dreamer and a Crank (with capital letters), but after all, in talking so much about himself, one sometimes tells the truth. Biely is not a maximalist, not in the very least, but an unquestioned minimalist, a chip of the old regime and of its point of view, yearning and sighing in a new environment. And it is absolutely true that he approaches everything in a roundabout way. His whole *St. Petersburg* is built by a roundabout method. And that is why it feels like an act of labor. Even in those places where he has attained artistic results, that is, where an image arises in the consciousness of the reader, it is paid for too dearly, so that after all these roundabout ways, after the straining and the labor, the reader does not experience aesthetic satisfaction. It is just as if you were led into a house through the chimney, and on entering you saw that there was a door, and that it was much easier to enter that way.

His rhythmic prose is terrible. His sentences do not obey the inner movement of the image, but an external meter, which at first seems only superfluous and later begins to tire you with its obtrusiveness, and finally poisons your very existence. The premonition that a sentence will end rhythmically makes one extremely irritated, just as when one waits for the shutter to squeak again when one is sleepless. Side by side with Biely's march of the rhythm goes his fetish of the word. It is absolutely irrefutable that the human word expresses not only meaning, but has a sound value, and that without this attitude to the word there would be no mastery in poetry or in prose. We are not going to deny Biely the merits attributed to him in this field. However, the most weighty and high-sounding word cannot give more than is put into it. Biely seeks in the word, just as the Pythagoreans in numbers, a second special and hidden meaning. And that is why he finds himself so often in a blind alley of words. If you cross your middle finger over your index finger and touch an object, you will feel two objects and if you repeat this experiment it will make you feel queer; instead of the correct use of your sense of touch, you are abusing it to deceive yourself. Biely's artistic methods give exactly this impression. They are invariably falsely complex.

Instead of logical and psychological analysis, he characterizes his stagnant thinking, which is essentially medieval, by the play of alliteration and by the substituting of verbal twists and acoustic ties. The more convulsively Biely holds on to words, and the more mercilessly he violates them, the harder it is for his inert opinions in a world that has overcome inertia. Biely is strongest when he describes the solid old life. His manner, even there, is tiresome, but not futile. You can see clearly that Biely himself is flesh of the flesh and bone of the bone of the old state, that he is thoroughly conservative, passive, and moderate, and that his rhythm and his verbal twists are only a means of vainly struggling with his inner passivity and sobriety when torn from his life's pivot.

At the time of the World War, Biely became a follower of the German mystic, Rudolph Steiner, of course a "Doctor of Philosophy," and kept watch in Switzerland during the nights under the dome of the Anthroposophist temple. What is anthroposophy? It is a spiritual-intellectualist turning inside out of Christianity, squeezed out of philosophic and poetic quotations. I cannot give more accurate details, because I have never read Steiner and don't intend to. I consider that I have the right not to be interested in "philosophic" systems that explain the difference in the tales of the Weimar and Kiev witches (in as much as I do not believe in witches in general, not counting the above-mentioned Zinaida Hippius, in whose reality I believe absolutely, though about the length of her tail I can say nothing definite). It is different with Andrey Biely. If heavenly things are for him the most important, then he ought to expound them. Nevertheless, Biely, who is so much given to detail and who tells us about his crossing of a canal as if he had observed with his own eyes the scene in the Garden of Gethsemane, or at least the Sixth Day of Creation, that same Biely, as soon as he touches on his Anthroposophy, becomes brief and cursory and prefers the figure of silence. The only thing that he informs us is that "not I, but Christ in me, is I." And again, "We are born in God, we die in Christ, and in the Holy Ghost we resurrect." This is comforting, but really—not very clear. Biely does not express himself more popularly, apparently from a basic fear of falling into theological concreteness, which would be too dangerous, because materialism invariably tramples on every positive ontological belief that is always formed in the image of matter, however fantastically twisted the latter may become in the process. If you are a believer, then explain what kind of feathers angel wings have and of what substance are witches' tails. Out of fear for these legitimate questions, these gentlemen spiritualists have so refined their mysticism that, in the end, their astral existence becomes an ingenious pseudonym for nonexistence. Then, frightened anew (and, indeed, there was no need at all of starting all this) they fall back on the catechism. And so in this wavering between a disconsolate astral vacuity and a theological price list, the spiritual vegetation of the mystics of anthroposophy and of philosophic faith in general goes on. Biely stubbornly but vainly tries to mask his vacuity by an acoustic orchestration and by forced meters. He tries to rise mystically above the October Revolution and tries even to adopt it in passing, giving it a place among the other things of the earth, all of which, however, are to him, in his own words, "stupidities." Failing in this attempt—and how could he not but fail?—Biely becomes wrathful. The psychological mechanism of this process is as simple as the anatomy of a jumping jack: a few holes and a few strings. But from Biely's holes and strings there comes out the apocalypse, not the general one, but his own special one, Andrey Biely's—"The spirit of truth makes me state my attitude to the social problem. Yes, you know—thus and so.... Would you like some tea? What—there is no common man today? Here is one—I am the common man." Lack of taste? Yes, a forced grimacing, a sober half-wittedness. And this before a people who have lived through a Revolution! In his most arrogant introduction to his non-epic "Epic," Andrey Biely accuses our Soviet epoch of being "terrible for writers who feel the call to large monumental canvases." He, the monumentalist, is dragged, don't you see, "to the arena of everydaydom," to the painting of "bon-bon boxes"! Can one, may I ask, turn reality and logic more roughly on their heads? It is he, Biely, who is dragged by the Revolution from canvases to bon-bon boxes! With the most unusual detail, choking not so much with detail as with a foam of words, Biely narrates how, "under the dome of the Joannite Temple,"— "he was wet with a verbal rain" (literally!), how he learned of the "land of Living Thought," how the Joannite Temple became for him "an image of theoretical pilgrimage." A chaste and holy jumble! When you read it, each consecutive page seems more intolerable than the one that went before. This self-satisfied seeking for psychological nits, this mystic execution of them on the fingernail—and done not otherwise but under the dome of the Joannite Temple—this snobbish, puffed-up, cowardly, and superstitious scribbling written with a cool yawn, this is represented as "a monumental canvas," and the call to turn your face to that which the greatest Revolution is doing within the geologic strata of national psychology is regarded as an invitation to paint "bon-bon boxes"! And it is with us in Soviet Russia that the "bon-bon boxes" are! What bad taste and what verbal profligacy! And it is just the "Joannite Temple" built in Switzerland by the spiritual loungers and tourists, which is the tasteless, German doctor-of-philosophy kind of bon-bon box, stuffed with "cats' tongues" and all kinds of sugared flies.

But it is our Russia that is at present a gigantic canvas, which it would take centuries to paint in. From here, from the summits of our revolutionary ranges, begin the sources of a new art, of a new point of view, of a new union of feelings, of a new rhythm of thoughts, of a new striving for the word. In one hundred or 200 or 300 years, they will uncover and bare with great aesthetic emotion these sources of the freed human spirit and... will stumble over the "dreamer," who waved off the "bon-bon box" (bon-bon box!) of the Revolution and demanded (from it!) that he be provided with the material means to depict how he saved himself from the Great War in Switzerland and how he day in and day out caught in his immortal soul certain little insects and spread them out on his fingernail—"under the dome of the Joannite Temple."

In this same epic Biely declares that "the foundations of everyday life for me are stupidities." And this in the face of a nation that is bleeding to change the foundations of everyday life. Well, certainly, neither more nor less than stupidities! But he asks for the *payok* [the Soviet ration], and not the ordinary one, but one in proportion to great canvases. And he is indignant that they do not hasten to give it to him. Would it seem that it really paid to darken the Christian state of the soul over "stupidities"? Still, he is not he, but the Christ in him.

And he will resurrect in the Holy Ghost. Then why here, among our earthly stupidities, spread gall on a printed page over an insufficient *payok*? Anthroposophic piety frees one not only from artistic taste, but from social shame.

Biely is a corpse, and will not be resurrected in any spirit.

CHAPTER TWO

The Literary "Fellow Travelers" of the Revolution

Nonrevolutionary or non-October literature, as we characterized it in the first chapter, is now in reality a past stage. At first, the writers placed themselves in active opposition to October, denying all artistic recognition to everything connected with the Revolution, just as the teachers refused to teach the children of revolutionary Russia. The non-October character of literature, therefore, not only expressed the deep alienation that lay between the two worlds, but it became also a tool for active politics, the sabotage of the artist. This policy annihilated itself; the old literature is now not so much unwilling, as unable.

Between bourgeois art, which is wasting away either in repetitions or in silences, and the new art, which is as yet unborn, there is being created a transitional art, which is more or less organically connected with the Revolution, but that is not at the same time the art of the Revolution. Boris Pilnyak, Vsevolod Ivanov, Nicolai Tikhonov, the "Serapion Fraternity," Yessenin and his group of Imagists, and, to some extent, Kliuev—all of them were impossible without the Revolution, either as a group, or separately. They know it themselves and do not deny it, do not feel the necessity of denying it, and some even proclaim it loudly. They do not belong to the literary jobholders who are beginning little by little to "picture" the Revolution. They are not even the "Changing Landmarks" group, because in this is implied a breach with the past, a radical change of front. The majority of these writers just mentioned are very young, between twenty and thirty. They have no revolutionary past whatever and if they broke away from anything at all it was from bagatelles. In general their literary and spiritual front has been made by the Revolution, by that angle of it that caught them, and they all have accepted the Revolution, each one in his own way. But in these individual acceptances, there is one common trait that sharply divides them from communism, and always threatens to put them in opposition to it. They do not grasp the Revolution as a whole and the communist ideal is foreign to them. They are all more or less inclined to look hopefully at the peasant over the head of the worker. They are not the artists of the proletarian Revolution, but her artist "fellow travelers," in the sense in which this word was used by the old Socialists. If non-October (in essence anti-October) literature is the moribund literature of bourgeois landowning Russia, then the literary work of the "fellow travelers" is, in its way, a new Soviet populism, without the traditions of the old populism and—up to now—without political perspective. As regards a "fellow traveler," the question always comes up—how far will he go? This question cannot be answered in advance, not even approximately. The solution of it depends not so much on the personal qualities of this or that "fellow traveler," but mainly on the objective trend of things during the coming decade.

However, in the dualism of the point of view of these "fellow travelers," which makes them doubtful of themselves, there is a constant artistic and social danger. Blok felt this dualism of morals and art more deeply than the others; in general, he was deeper. In the reminiscences of him, written by Nadezhda Pavlovich, there is the following sentence: "The Bolsheviks do not hinder the writing of verses but they hinder you from feeling yourself a master; he is a master who feels the axis of his creativeness and holds the rhythm within himself." In the expression of this thought there is a certain indefiniteness so common to Blok, and besides, we are dealing here with reminiscences, which, as everyone knows, are not always accurate. But the inner resemblance to truth and the significance of this sentence make one believe it. The Bolsheviks hinder one from feeling oneself a master because a master must have within himself an organic, irrefutable axis and the Bolsheviks have displaced the main axis. None of the "fellow travelers" of the Revolution—and Blok was also a "fellow traveler," and the "fellow travelers" form at present a very important division of Russian literature—carry the axis within themselves. And therefore we have only a preparatory period for a new literature, only études, sketches, essays—but complete mastery, with a reliable axis within oneself, is still to come.

Nicolai Kliuev

Bourgeois poetry, of course, does not exist, because poetry is a free art and not a service to class. [I received from an experienced and well-read journalist a thundering letter, proving the class character of literature. My correspondent took the sarcastic sentence literally. I am afraid that this might happen with others. There are not too many attentive readers in the world. I am therefore driving this note home with this inscription: "Attention! This is irony!"] But here is Kliuev, a poet and a peasant, and he not only recognizes it, but repeats it, underlines it, and boasts of it. The difference is that a peasant poet feels no inner call to hide his face, neither from others, nor, above all, from himself. The Russian peasant, oppressed for centuries, reaching upward, spiritualized by populism in the course of the decades, never instilled in those few poets who were his own the social or artistic impulse to conceal their peasant origin. It was true in the old days as in the case of Koltzov and it is still more true these latter years in the case of Kliuev.

It is exactly in Kliuev that we see again how vital is the force of the social method of literary criticism. They tell us that a writer begins where individuality begins and that therefore the source of his creativeness is his unique soul and not his class. It is true, without individuality there can be no writer. But if the poet's individuality and only his individuality is disclosed in his work, then to what purpose is the interpretation of art? To what purpose, let us ask, is literary criticism? In any case, the artist, if he is a true artist, will tell us about his unique individuality better than his babbling critic. But the truth is that even if individuality is unique, it does not mean that it cannot be analyzed. Individuality is a welding together of tribal, national, class, temporary, and institutional elements, and, in fact, it is in the uniqueness of this welding together, in the proportions of this psychochemical mixture, that individuality is expressed. One of the most important tasks of criticism is to analyze the individuality of the artist (that is, his art) into its component elements, and to show their correlations. In this way, criticism brings the artist closer to the reader, who also has more or less of a "unique soul," "artistically" unexpressed, "unchosen," but nonetheless representing a union of the same elements as does the soul of a poet. So it can be seen that what serves as a bridge from soul to soul is not the unique, but the common. Only through the common is the unique known; the common is determined in man by the deepest and most persistent conditions that make up his "soul," by the social conditions of education, of existence, of work, and of associations. The social conditions in historic human society are, first of all, the conditions of class affiliation. That is why a class standard is so fruitful in all fields of ideology, including art, and especially in art, because the latter often expresses the deepest and most hidden social aspirations. Moreover, a social standard not only does not exclude but goes hand in hand with formal criticism, that is, with the standard of technical workmanship. This, as a matter of fact, also tests the particular by a common measure, because if one did not reduce the particular to the general there would be no contacts among people, no thoughts, and no poetry.

If you take away from Kliuev his peasanthood, his soul not only will become orphaned, but nothing at all will remain of it. For Kliuev's individuality is the artistic expression of an independent, well-fed, well-to-do peasant loving his freedom egotistically. Every peasant is a peasant, but not everyone can express himself. A peasant who can express himself and his self-sufficient world in the language of a new artistic technique, or rather, who has kept his peasant soul through bourgeois schooling, is a big individuality, and such a one is Kliuev.

The social basis of art is not always so transparent and irrefutable. But that is only because, as has already been said, the majority of poets are bound up with the exploiting classes that, because of their exploiting nature, do not speak of themselves in the way they think, nor think of themselves in the way they are. However, in spite of all the social and psychological methods by which class hypocrisy is maintained, the social essence of a poet can be found even if it is diluted in the most subtle form. And not to understand this essence leaves the criticism of art and the history of art hanging in the air.

To speak of the bourgeois character of that literature that we call non-October, does not therefore necessarily mean to slander the poets who are supposedly serving art and not the bourgeoisie. For where is it written that it is impossible to serve the bourgeoisie by means of art? Just as geologic landslides reveal the deposits of earth layers, so do social landslides reveal the class character of art. Non-October art is struck by a deathly impotence for the very reason that death has struck those classes to which it was tied by its whole past. Without the bourgeois landholding system and its customs, without the subtle suggestions of the estate and of the salon, this art sees no meaning in life, withers, becomes moribund, and is reduced to nothing.

Kliuev is not of the rustic school; he is not peasant-singing; he is not a populist; he is a real peasant (almost). His spiritual countenance is truly a peasant one, a North peasant one at that. Kliuev, like a peasant, is individualistic; he is his own master, he is his own poet. The earth is under his feet, and the sun is above his head. A well-to-do peasant proprietor has grain in his bin; milking cows in his barn; carved weathercocks on the crest of his roof—his economic self-consciousness is solid and self-reliant. He likes to boast of his household, of his prosperity, and of his clever management—as Kliuev does of his talent and of his poetic manner. It is as natural to praise oneself as to belch after a heavy feast or to make the cross over one's mouth after a yawn. Kliuev has studied. When and what we do not know, but he manages his knowledge like a well-read person and also like a miser. If a well-to-do peasant should accidentally carry a telephone receiver out of the city, he would fix it in the main corner of the room not far from the icon. In the same way, Kliuev embellishes the main corners of his verses with India, Congo, and Mont Blanc; and Kliuev loves to embellish. A simple, scraped harness yoke is only owned by a peasant out of poverty or shiftlessness. A good peasant has a carved yoke painted in several colors. Kliuev is a good poet-master endowed with abundance: he has carvings, cinnabar, vermilion, gilt, and lintels everywhere, and even brocades, satins, silver, and all kinds of precious stones. All this shines and plays in the sun and one might even think that the sun is his, a Kliuev sun, because truly in this world there exists only he, Kliuev—his talent, the earth under his feet, and the sun above his head.

Kliuev is a poet of a closed-in world, inflexible in its essence, but nonetheless of a world that has changed greatly since 1861.

Kliuev is not a Koltzov: one hundred years have not passed in vain. Koltzov is simple, submissive, and modest. Kliuev is much more complex, exacting, ingenious. He has brought his new poetic technique from the city, as a neighboring peasant might bring a phonograph; and he uses poetic technique, like the geography of India, only for the purpose of embellishing the peasant framework of his poetry. He is many-colored, often bright and expressive, often quaint, often cheap and tinsel-like—and all this is on a firm peasant basis.

Kliuev's poems, like his thought and like his life, are not dynamic. There is too much ornamentation in Kliuev's poetry for action—heavy brocades, natural colored stones, and all manner of other things. One has to move about cautiously not to break and destroy. And yet Kliuev has accepted the Revolution, which is the greatest dynamics of all. Kliuev accepted it not for himself alone, but together with all the peasantry, and accepted it in the manner of a peasant, too. The abolition of the noble estate pleases Kliuev. "Let Turgenev cry about it on a shelf." But the Revolution is, above all, a city one; without the city there could have been no abolition of the nobles' estates. Here is where Kliuev's dualism arises in relation to the Revolution—a dualism, again, which is characteristic not only of Kliuev but of the entire peasantry. Kliuev does not love the city, he does not recognize city poetry. The friendly-enemy tone of his poems is very instructive where he urges the poet Kirillov to reject the thought of factory poetry, and to come into his, the Kliuev pinewood—the one source of art. Of "industrial rhythms," of proletarian poetry, of the very principle of it, Kliuev speaks with the natural contempt that comes to the lips of every "strong" peasant when he glances at the propagandist of socialism, the houseless city worker, or, what is still worse, the vagabond. And when Kliuev condescendingly invites the blacksmith to lie down for a while on an embroidered peasant bench, it is like a rich and broad-backed peasant from Olonetz charitably offering a piece of bread to a hungry hereditary Petrograd proletarian, "in city rags, in heels worn on city stones."

Kliuev accepts the Revolution because it has freed the peasant, and he sings many of his songs to it. But his Revolution is without political dynamics and without historic perspective. To Kliuev it is like a market or a sumptuous wedding where people come together from various places, get drunk with wine and song, with embraces and dances, and then return to their own houses: their own earth under their feet and their own sun above their heads. To others it is a republic, but to Kliuev it is the old land of Russ; to others it is socialism, but to him it is the dead and gone dream-city of Kitezh. He promises paradise through the Revolution, but this paradise is only an exaggerated and embellished peasant kingdom, a wheat and honey paradise: a singing bird on the carved wing of the house and a sun shining in jasper and diamonds. Not without hesitation does Kliuev admit into his peasant paradise the radio and magnetism and electricity; and here it appears that electricity is a giant bull out of a peasant epic and that between his horns is a laden table.

Kliuev evidently was in Petrograd at the time of the Revolution. He wrote in the *Krasnaya Gazeta*, and he fraternized with the workers, but, as a shrewd peasant, Kliuev, even in those honeymoon days, weighed in his mind whether in one way or another any harm would come from all this to his, the Kliuev, household, that is, to his art. If it should seem to Kliuev that the city did not appreciate him, then he, Kliuev, would at once show his character and raise the price of his wheat-paradise as compared with the industrial hell. And if they should reproach him for something, he would not hunt long for a word, but he would lay his opponent low and praise himself strongly and convincingly. Not so long ago Kliuev started a poetic quarrel with Yessenin, who decided to put on a tailcoat and a high hat and who announced this in his poems. Kliuev saw in this treason to his peasant origin and quarrelsomely soaped the younger man's head for him in just the same way as a rich elder brother would scold a younger one who had taken into his head to marry a town hussy and join the down-and-outs.

Kliuev is jealous. Somebody advised him to refrain from holy words. Kliuev became offended:

> It seems neither saints nor villains exist
> For the industrial heavens.

It is unclear whether he himself believes or does not believe. His God suddenly spits blood and the Virgin Mother gives herself to some Hungarian for a few yellow pieces. All this sounds like blasphemy, but to exclude God from the Kliuev household, to destroy the holy corner where the light of the lamp shines on silver and gilded frames—to such destruction he does not consent. Without the lamp, everything is unfulfilled.

When Kliuev sings of Lenin in "hidden peasant verses," it is not very easy to decide whether it is for Lenin or against Lenin. What a dualism of thought, of feeling, and of words! And at the basis of all lies the dualism of the peasant, that bast-shod Janus, who turns one face to the past and the other to the future. Kliuev even rises to song in honor of the Commune. But they are just songs of praise—"in honor to." "I don't want the Commune without the peasant oven." But the Commune with a peasant oven is not a reconstruction of all the foundations of life in accordance with reason, with compass and yardstick in hand, but the same old peasant paradise.

> The golden sounds
> Hang like clusters on the tree;
> Like halcyon birds, the words
> Settle on the branches. — *The Brass Whale.*

Here are the poetics of Kliuev in their entirety. Where is there here revolution, struggle, dynamics, a striving toward the new? Here we have peace, a charmed immobility, a tinsel fairyland. "Like Halcyon birds, the words settle on the branches." This is something curious to look at, but a modern person cannot live in such an environment.

What will Kliuev's further road be—toward the Revolution or away from it? More likely away from the Revolution; he is much too saturated with the past. The spiritual isolation and the aesthetic originality of the village, despite the temporary weakening of the city, are clearly on the decline. Kliuev seems also to be on the decline.

Sergey Yessenin

Yessenin (and the entire group of Imagists—Marienhof, Shershenevich, Kusikov) stand somewhere at the crossing of the road between Kliuev and Mayakovsky. Yessenin's roots are in the village, but not so deep as those of Kliuev. Yessenin is younger. He became a poet at the time when the village was shaken up by the Revolution, when Russia was shaken up. Kliuev was formed entirely in the pre-War years, and he responded to the War and to the Revolution only within the limits of his backwoods conservatism. Yessenin is not only younger but also more flexible, more plastic, more open to influences and to possibilities. Even his peasant underpinnings are not the same as those of Kliuev; Yessenin has neither Kliuev's solidity, nor his somber and pompous sedateness. Yessenin boasts that he is arrogant and a hooligan. But if the truth must be told, his arrogance, even his purely literary arrogance ("The Confession") is not so terrible. Still, Yessenin is undoubtedly the reflection of the pre-revolutionary and revolutionary spirit of the peasant youth whom the disturbed life of the village has driven to arrogance and turbulence.

The city has told on Yessenin more sharply and clearly than on Kliuev. Here is the point where the undoubted influences of Futurism come in. Yessenin is more dynamic, to the extent that he is more nervous, more flexible, more responsive to the new. But Imagism is the reverse of dynamics. The self-sufficient meaning of the image is bought at the expense of the whole; the parts become separated and cold.

It is said incorrectly that the abundant imagery of the Imagist Yessenin flows from his individual tenderness. As a matter of fact, we find the same traits in Kliuev. His verses are weighted down with an imagery that is even more isolated and immobile. At bottom, this is not an individual but a peasant aesthetics. The poetry of the repetitive forms of life has at bottom little mobility and seeks a way out in condensed imagery.

At any rate, Imagism is overladen to such an extent with images that its poetry seems like a beast of burden and therefore slow in its movements. An abundance of imagery is not in itself an evidence of creative power; on the contrary, it may arise out of the technical immaturity of a poet who is caught unawares by events and feelings that are artistically too much for him. The poet almost chokes with images and the reader feels as nervously impatient to get on as fast as possible to the end as when one listens to a stuttering speaker. In any case, Imagism is not a literary school from which one can expect serious developments. Even the tardy arrogance of Kusikov ("the West at which we Imagists sneeze") seems curious and not even amusing. Imagism is perhaps only a stopping point for a few poets of the younger generation who are more or less talented, but who resemble one another in one thing only, that they are all still unripe.

Yessenin's effort to construct a big work by the Imagist method has proved inadequate in "Pugachev." And this is so regardless of the fact that the author has unloaded his heavy imagery quite considerably and stealthily. The dialogue nature of "Pugachev" got the better of the poet rather mercilessly. The drama in general is a most transparent and unyielding form of art; it has no room for descriptive and narrative patches, or for lyric outbursts. Through the dialogue, Yessenin came out into clear waters. Emelka Pugachev, and his enemies and his colleagues, are all without exception Imagists. And Pugachev himself is Sergey Yessenin from top to toe: he wants to be terrible, but he cannot. Yessenin's Pugachev is a sentimental romantic. When Yessenin introduces himself as a somewhat bloodthirsty hooligan, it is amusing; but when Pugachev expresses himself like a romantic, burdened with imagery, it is worse. The Imagist Pugachev becomes a bit ridiculous.

Though Imagism, having hardly existed, is gone already, Yessenin himself is still of the future. To foreign journalists he declared himself more left than the Bolsheviks. This is in the natural order of things, and frightens no one. At present Yessenin, the poet, who may be more left than we sinners, but who smells nonetheless of medievalism, has begun his "wander-years," and he will not return the same as he went. But we will not surmise. When he returns, he will tell us himself.

The "Serapion Fraternity": Vsevolod Ivanov; Nikolai Nikitin

The "Serapion Fraternity" are youngsters who still live with the brood. Some of them have not come to the Revolution through literature, but have come into literature through the Revolution. Just because they trace their brief pedigree from the Revolution, they, some of them at least, have an inner need to move away from the Revolution, and to protect the freedom of their work from its social demands. It is as if they feel for the first time that art has its own rights. The artist David (in N. Tikhonov) immortalizes at the same time both "the hand of the patriot murderer" and Marat. Why? "But so beautiful is the flash of the wrist to the elbow, splashed with the cherry-like paste." Quite often the Serapions go away from the Revolution or from modern life in general and even sometimes from man and write about Dresden students, Biblical Jews, and tigresses and dogs. All this gives merely an impression of a groping, of an attempt, of a preparing. They absorb the literary and technical achievements of the pre-revolutionary schools without which there could be no movement forward. Their general tone is realistic but as yet quite unformed. It is too early to estimate individually the "Serapion Fraternity," at least within the covers of this work. In general they indicate, among many other symptoms, the renaissance of literature on a new historic basis, after the tragic collapse. Why do we relegate them to being "fellow travelers" of ours? Because they are bound up with the Revolution, because this tie is still very unformed, because they are so very young, and because nothing definite can be said about their tomorrow.

The most dangerous trait of the Serapions is that they glory in their lack of principles. This is stupidity and thickheadedness. As if an artist ever could be "without a tendency," without a definite relation to social life, even though unformulated or unexpressed in political terms. It is true that the majority of artists form their relation to life and to its social forms during organic periods in an unnoticeable and molecular way, and almost without the participation of critical reason. The artist takes life as he finds it, coloring his relation to it with a kind of lyric tone. He considers its foundations to be immovable and approaches it as uncritically as he does the solar system. And this passive conservatism of his forms the unseen pivot of his work.

Critical periods do not allow an artist the luxury of an automatic and irresponsible elaboration of social points of view. And whoever boasts of this, whether insincerely or even without pretense, is masking a reactionary tendency or has fallen into social stupidities or is making a fool of himself. It is, of course, possible to do youthful exercises in the spirit of Sinebriuchov's stories, or in the manner of Fedin's novelette, *Anna Timofeevna*, but it is impossible to give a big or a significant picture and even in sketches one cannot hold out long without troubling one's head about social and artistic perspectives.

The novelists and poets who were born of the Revolution

and who are still very young, being almost in their swaddling clothes, try, in the search for their artistic individualities, to get away from the Revolution that has been their environment and in which milieu they have yet to find themselves. From this come the tirades of the "art for art's sake," which seem very significant and bold to the Serapions, but which in fact are a sign of growth at best and an evidence of immaturity in any case. If the Serapions would get away from the Revolution entirely, they would reveal themselves at once as a second-rate or third-rate remnant of the discarded pre-revolutionary literary schools. It is impossible to play with history. Here the punishment follows immediately upon the crime.

Vsevolod Ivanov, who is the oldest and the most notable of the Serapions, is the most significant and the most weighty. He writes about the Revolution and only about the Revolution, but exclusively about peasant and out-of-the-way revolutions. The onesidedness of his theme and the comparative narrowness of his artistic grasp put an impress of monotony on his fresh and bright colors. He is spontaneous in his moods and in his spontaneity he is not sufficiently careful and strict with himself. He is very lyrical and his lyricism flows without end. But the author makes himself felt too insistently, comes forward too often in person, expresses himself too loudly, slaps nature and people on the shoulders and back too hard. As long as one feels that his spontaneity comes from his youth, it is very attractive, but there is a great danger of its becoming a mannerism. To the degree that spontaneity decreases, a broadening of the creative grasp and a heightening of technique must come in its place. This is possible only if one is strict with oneself. The lyricism with which Ivanov warms so much, both nature and the dialogue, must become more secret, more internal, more hidden, and more miserly in its expression. A phrase must be born from a phrase by the natural force of the artistic matter without the visible aid of the artist. Ivanov learned from Gorky and learned well. Let him go through this school once again, but this time backwards.

Ivanov knows and understands the Siberian peasant, the Cossack, the Khirgiz. Against the background of revolt, of battles, of fires, and of suppressions, he shows very well the peasant's lack of political impersonality in spite of his stable social strength. While in Russia, a young Siberian peasant, a former Tsarist soldier, supports the Bolsheviks, but on his return to Siberia he serves "Tolchak" against the Reds. His father, a bored and prosperous peasant, who was looking for a new faith, imperceptibly and unexpectedly to himself becomes the leader of the Red groups. The whole family breaks up; the village is burned. But as soon as the hurricane is over, the peasant begins to mark the trees in the forest for cutting down and begins to build anew. After swinging in various directions, Roly-poly tries to settle down firmly on his leaden base. In Ivanov various individual scenes reach great power. The scenes where the "conversation" between the Far Eastern Reds and a captured American takes place, or the drunken debauch of the rebels, or the Khirgiz searching for a "big God," are splendid. But in general, whether Ivanov wants it or not, he shows that the peasant uprisings in "peasant" Russia are not yet revolution. The peasant revolt bursts forth suddenly from a small spark, unevenly, often cruel in its helplessness—and no one sees why it flared up or whither it leads. And never and in no way can the disjointed peasant revolt be victorious. In "Colored Winds" a hint is given as to the essence of a peasant uprising, in the figure of the city Bolshevik, Nikitin, but it is vague. Nikitin in Ivanov's story is an enigmatic bit of another world, and it is unclear why the peasant element turns around him. But, from all these pictures of Revolution in distant corners, there follows one undeniable conclusion, that there is being remelted in a great crucible and on a hot fire the national character of the Russian people. And Roly-poly will not come out of this crucible the same as he was.

It would be a good thing if Vsevolod Ivanov could also mature in this crucible.

■   ■   ■

Nikitin came forward clearly from among the Serapions within the past year. What he wrote in 1922 marks a big jump forward from what he did in the preceding year. But there is something just as disquieting in his rapid maturing as in the precocity of a youth. Anxiety is caused first of all by the manifest note of cynicism that is characteristic to a greater or lesser degree of almost all the youth today, but which in Nikitin assumes at times an especially evil character. The question is not of rude words, nor of naturalistic excesses—though excesses are always excesses—but in a challengingly crude and apparently realistic approach to people and events. Realism, in the broad sense of the word, that is, in the sense of an artistic affirmation of the real world with its flesh and blood and also with its will and consciousness, may be of many kinds. One can take man, not only social, but even psychophysical man and approach him from different angles—from above, from below, from the side, or walk all around him. Nikitin approaches, or more accurately steals up to him—from below. That is why all his perspectives of man become crude and sometimes even disgusting. Nikitin's talented precocity gives the fellow an especially ominous character. It is a road that leads to a blind alley.

Under these verbal improprieties and naturalistic debauches is hidden a lack of faith or a dying out of faith, and this is true not only of Nikitin. This generation was caught in the whirl of great events without any preparation, political, moral, or artistic. It had nothing that was stable, or, rather, conservative, and therefore the Revolution conquered it easily. But because the conquest was easy, it was extremely superficial. The young people were caught in the whirl and all of them, Imagists, Serapions, etc., became Dissenters, semi-consciously starting from the conviction that the fig leaf is the main emblem of the old world. It is very instructive that the generation that was caught in its adolescence by the Revolution is the worst, not only among the urban intelligentsia, but also among the peasantry and even among the working-class. It is not revolutionary, it is turbulent and has the earmarks of anarchistic individualism. The succeeding generation that rose under the new regime is much better; it is more social, more disciplined, more exacting toward itself, and its thirst for knowledge is growing seriously. It is this youth that gets along so well with the "old fellows," with those who were formed and strengthened before March and October of 1917, and even before 1914. The revolutionism of the Serapions, as of the majority of the "fellow travelers" of the Revolution, is much more related to the generation that came too late to prepare for it and too soon to be educated by it. Having approached the Revolution from the wrong side of a peasant and acquiring this half Dissenter's point of view, these "fellow travelers" become disillusioned, and the more so the more clearly it appears that a revolution is not a thing of joy, but a conception, an organization, a plan, a work. The Imagist Marienhof takes off his hat and politely and ironically bids good-bye to the Revolution, which has betrayed him (that is Marienhof). And Nikitin, in his story "Pella," in which this form of a pseudo-revolutionary Dissenter finds his most perfect expression, ends with the innerly skeptical words that are not as coy as Marienhof's but just as cynical: "You are tired and I have already thrown away the chase....And now it is futile for us to be running after. There is no sense to it. Don't look for dead places."

We had heard this once before, and remember it very well. The young novelists and versifiers who were caught by the Revolution in 1905 turned their backs to it later with almost the same words. When they took off their hats to say good-bye to this stranger in 1907, they seriously imagined that they had settled their accounts with it. But it returned a second time and much more firmly. It found the unexpected first "lovers" of 1905 prematurely aged and spiritually bald. For this reason—though to tell the truth, entirely without bothering much about it—it drew into its circle the new generation of the old society (along its very periphery and even at a tangent). But then came another 1907; chronologically, it is called 1921–1922 in the shape of the NEP. The Revolution wasn't such a splendid stranger after all. Only a trader's and nothing more!

It is true these young people are ready to maintain on many occasions that they are not thinking of breaking with the Revolution, that they were made by it, that they are unthinkable outside the Revolution and cannot think so of themselves. But all this is very indefinite and even ambiguous. Of course they cannot separate themselves from the Revolution, in so far as the Revolution, although a trader's one, is a fact and even an environment. To be outside the Revolution means to be among the émigrés. Of this there can be no discussion. But apart from the émigrés abroad, there are the internal ones. And the road to them lies along estrangement from the Revolution. He who has nothing more to run after is a candidate for spiritual emigration. And inevitably this means artistic death, because there is no use

of fooling oneself—the attractiveness, the freshness, the significance of the younger ones come entirely from the Revolution
that they touched. If this be taken away, there will be a few more
Chirikovs in the world, and nothing more.

Boris Pilnyak

Pilnyak is a realist and an excellent observer with fresh eyes
and a good ear. People and things are not old and worn out for
him and always the same, and only thrown into temporary disorder by the Revolution. He takes them in their freshness and
uniqueness, that is, alive and not dead, and he seeks support for
his artistic order in the disorder of the Revolution, which is to
him a live and fundamental fact.

In art as well as in politics—and in some respects art is like
politics and politics like art, because both are art—a "realist"
may look only at what is under his feet, notice only obstacles,
minuses, holes, torn boots, broken dishes. Then politics will be
in fear, evasive, opportunistic, and art will be petty, eaten with
skepticism, episodic. Pilnyak is a realist. The question is only as
to the standard of his realism. And a large standard is needed
for our time.

Life in Revolution is camp life. Personal life, institutions,
methods, ideas, sentiments, everything is unusual, temporary,
transitional, recognizing its temporariness and expressing this
everywhere, even in names. Hence the difficulty of an artistic approach. The transitory and the episodic have in them an element
of the accidental and the accidental bears the stamp of insignifi-
cance. The Revolution, taken episodically, appears quite insignificant. Where is the Revolution, then? Here lies the difficulty. Only
he will overcome it who fully understands and feels the inner
meaning of this episodic character and who will reveal the historic axis of crystallization that lies behind it. "Why do we need
solid houses?" the sect of Old Believers used to say. "We are
awaiting the coming of Christ." Nor is this Revolution building
solid houses, but instead, it makes removals, concentrations, and
barracks. The character of the temporary and of the barrack lies
on all its institutions. But not because it is awaiting the coming of

Christ, that is, contrasting its final aim with the present process of building life, but because, on the contrary, it is striving in endless gropings and experiments to find the best ways of building a house that is solid. Everything it does is merely sketches, études, rough drafts on a given theme. There were and there will be many of them. And there are many more unsuccessful ones than those that promised success. But all of them are filled with one thought, with one search. A single historic task inspires them. Gviu, Glavbum, are not simply correlations of sound, in which Pilnyak hears the wailing of the revolutionary elements. These are purposeful, working words, thought out and consciously put together (just as there are working hypotheses) for a conscious, purposeful, planful construction, such as has never been in the world before.

"Yes, in a hundred or one hundred and fifty years men will yearn for the present Russia, as for the days of the most beautiful manifestation of the human spirit. But my shoe is torn and I would like to sit abroad in a restaurant and drink a little whisky." (*Ivan and Mary*). Just as a train of cattle cars, because of the confusion of hands, feet, bagmen, and lights, cannot see a road two thousand versts long, so Pilnyak tells us, because of a torn shoe and because of all the other discordancies and difficulties of Soviet life, one cannot see the historic turn made in these very days. "Seas and plateaus have changed places! For in Russia there is the beautiful agony of birth! For Russia is being divided into economic zones! For in Russia there is life! For the waters are muddy with high floods from the black earth. This I know. But they see lice in the filth." The question is put with very clear precision. They (the bitter Philistines, the deposed leaders, the offended prophets, the pedants, the stupid ones, the professional dreamers) see only lice and mud, when in truth above this there is also the agony of birth. Pilnyak knows this. Can he limit himself to sighs and convulsions, to physiologic episodes? No, he wants to make one feel birth. This is a great task and a very difficult one. It is good that Pilnyak has set this task to himself. But it is not yet time to say that he has solved it.

Pilnyak has no theme because of his fear of being episodic. True, he has a hint of two, three, and even more themes that are drawn in all directions through the texture of the story; but only a hint and without the central pivotal meaning that generally belongs to a theme. Pilnyak wants to show present-day life in its relations and in its movement, and he grasps at it in this way and in that, making parallel and perpendicular crosscuts in different places, because it is nowhere the same as it was. The themes, more truly the theme possibilities, which cross his stories, are only samples of life taken at random, and life, let us note, is now much fuller of subject matter than ever before. But Pilnyak's pivot is not these episodic and sometimes anecdotal subjects. But what? Here is the stumbling block. The invisible axis (the earth's axis is also invisible) should be the Revolution itself, around which should turn the whole unsettled, chaotic, and reconstructing life. But in order that the reader should feel this axis, the author himself must have felt it and at the same time must have thought it through.

When Pilnyak, without knowing at whom he was aiming, hits Zamyatin and other "Islanders" and says that an ant does not understand the beauty of a female statue because it sees nothing but small projections and grooves as it creeps over it, he has spoken to the point and sharply. Every great epoch, whether it is the Reformation or the Renaissance or the Revolution, must be accepted as a whole, and not in sections or in little parts. The masses, with their invincible social instinct, always participate in these movements. In the individual this instinct attains the level of a generalizing reason. But the spiritually mediocre are neither with the one nor the other; they are too individualistic to share in the perceptions of the masses and too undeveloped for a synthesized understanding. Their share is the bumps and grooves on which they bruise themselves with philosophic and aesthetic curses. How is it with Pilnyak in this matter?

Pilnyak scrutinizes very aptly and sharply a section of our life and in this lies his strength, for he is a realist. Beyond this he knows and proclaims this knowledge of his aloud, that Russia is being turned into economic zones, that the beautiful agonies of birth are taking place within her, and that in the confusion of lice and curses and bagmen the greatest transition in history is being accomplished. Pilnyak must know this since he proclaims it aloud. But the trouble is that he only proclaims it, as if he were contrasting these convictions with the vital and cruel actual existence. He doesn't turn his back on revolutionary Russia; on the contrary, he accepts it and even praises it in his own fashion. But he merely says so. He cannot acquit it artistically because he cannot grasp it intellectually. Therefore Pilnyak often willfully breaks the thread of his narrative with his own hands in order to tie the knots himself quickly, end to end, to explain (somehow or other), to generalize (and very badly), and to ornament lyrically (sometimes beautifully and much more often superfluously). Pilnyak tied a great number of such purposeful authors' knots. His whole work is dualistic, sometimes it is the Revolution that is the invisible axis, sometimes, very visibly, it is the author himself who is timidly rotating around the Revolution. Such is Pilnyak today.

As to subject matter, Pilnyak is provincial. He takes the Revolution in its periphery, in its backyards, in the village, and mainly in the provincial towns. His Revolution is a small town one. Still, even such an approach can be vital. It can be even more organic. But to be that you cannot stop at the periphery. You have to find the axis of the Revolution, which is neither in the village nor in the district. You can approach the Revolution through the small town, but you cannot have a small-town line of vision on it.

A district council of the Soviets—a sled road—"Comrades, help me in"—bast shoes—sheepskins—the waiting line to the Soviet house for bread, for sausages, for tobacco—Comrades, you are the sole masters of the Revolutionary Council and township—oh, sweetheart, you give little, so little! (this in reference to sausages)—it is the last decisive battle—the International—the Entente—international capitalism....

In such bits of discussion, of life, of speeches, of sausages, and of anthems, there is something of the Revolution; a vital part of it grasped with a keen eye, but as if in a hurry, as if rushing past. But something is lacking there that would tie these bits together from within. The idea that underlies our epoch is lacking. When Pilnyak pictures a cattle car, you feel the artist in him, the future artist, the potential future artist. But you do not feel the satisfaction that comes from solving contradictions, which is the greatest sign of a work of art. It is just as perplexing as before, and even more so. Why the train? Why the cattle car, and what have they in them that is of Russia and for Russia? No one asks Pilnyak for a historical analysis of a cattle car in a cross section of life and a cross section of time, or even, what is more, for a prophetic announcement toward which he inclines so futilely himself. But if Pilnyak himself had understood the cattle car and its connection with the course of events, it would have been transmitted to the reader. But at present the foul cattle car moves along without any justification, and Pilnyak, who accepts it, only creates doubt in the reader's mind.

One of Pilnyak's latest works, *The Snowstorm*, proves the kind of great writer he is. The meaningless dreary life of the filthy provincial Philistine perishing in the midst of Revolution, the prosaic senseless routine of everyday Soviet life, and all this in the midst of the October storm, is painted by Pilnyak not as a unified picture, but as a series of bright spots, of apt silhouettes and clever sketches. The general impression is always the same—a restless dualism.

"Olga thought that a revolution was like a snowstorm—and the people in it were like flakes." Pilnyak thinks the same, not without Blok's influence, who took the Revolution exclusively as an element, and because of his temperament, as a cold element; not as a fire—as a snowstorm, "and the people in it are like snowflakes." But if a revolution is only the might of an unbridled element playing with man, then where do the days of the most beautiful manifestation of the human spirit come in? And if the agonies can be justified, because they are the agonies of birth, what is it, in fact, that is being born? If you have no answer to this you will have a torn shoe, lice, blood, snowstorm, and even leap-frog, but not revolution.

Does Pilnyak know what is being born from the agonies of Revolution? No, he does not. Certainly he has heard said (how could he not but hear!) but he does not believe it. Pilnyak is not an artist of the Revolution, but only an artistic "fellow traveler." Will he become its artist? We do not know. But at present he is not. Posterity will talk about "the most beautiful days" of the human spirit. Very well, but what was Pilnyak in those days? Unclear, hazy, dual. Is it not for this reason that Pilnyak is afraid of the events and of the people who define strictly and who give a meaning to what is happening? Often Pilnyak passes the communist by with respect, a little coldly, sometimes even with sympathy, but he passes him by. You seldom find a revolutionary workman in Pilnyak, and what is more important, the author does not see and cannot see with the latter's eyes the things that are happening. In *The Bare Year* he looks at life with the eyes of his various characters, who are also all "fellow travelers" of the Revolution, and here is disclosed another remarkable manifestation: the Red Army does not exist for this artist of 1918–1921. How does that happen? The first years of the Revolution were, above all, years of war, and the blood rushed from the heart of the country to the fronts and peripheries, and there for several years it was spilt in great quantities. During those years the workers' vanguard put all its enthusiasm, all its faith in the future, all its renunciation, its clarity of thought, and its will into the Red Army. The urban revolutionary Red Guard at the end of 1917 and the beginning of 1918, in its fight for self-preservation, spread to the front in divisions and battalions. Pilnyak pays no attention to this. The Red Army does not exist for him. That is why the year 1919 is bare for him.

But somehow Pilnyak must answer the question, what is this all for? He must have a philosophy of revolution of his own. Here is a most alarming disclosure. Pilnyak's philosophy of history is absolutely retrogressional. This artistic "fellow traveler" reasons as if the road of the Revolution leads backwards, not forwards. Pilnyak accepts the Revolution because it is national, and it is national because it pulls down Peter the Great and resurrects the seventeenth century. To him the Revolution is national, because he thinks it retrogressional.

The Bare Year, Pilnyak's principal work, is marked absolutely by this dualism. The basis, the foundation, the ground of it is made up of the snowstorm, of witchcraft, of superstition, of wood sprites, of those sects that live in the same state of ages ago, and for whom Petrograd means nothing. On the other hand, in passing, "the factory became resurrected" owing to the activity of groups of provincial workers. "Is there not a poem here, a hundred-fold greater than the resurrection of Lazarus?"

The city is robbed in the year 1918–1919, and Pilnyak hails this, because it suddenly appears that even he has "no use for Petrograd." On the other hand, still in passing, the Bolsheviks, the men in leather jackets, are "the pick of the flabby and uncouth Russian people. In leather jackets—you can't dampen them. This we know, this we want; this we have decided, and no turning back." But Bolshevism is the product of a city culture. Without Petrograd there would have been no selection from the "uncouth people." The witches' rites, the folk-songs, the age-old words are the foundation. But the "Gviu, the Glavbum, the Guvuz! Oh, what a blizzard! How stormy it is! How good it is!" It is very good, but ends do not meet, and that is not so good.

Indeed, Russia is full of contradictions and of the most extreme contradictions at that. Side by side with sorcerers' incantations is the Glavbum. How the little literary men turn up their noses contemptuously at this new syllabic formation, and Pilnyak repeats: "Guvuz, Glavbum...how nice!" In these unusual temporary words—temporary as a camp, or as a bonfire on a river bank (for a camp is not a house and a bonfire is not a hearth)—Pilnyak sees reflected the spirit of his times. "How nice!" It is good that Pilnyak sees this. But how shall one deal with the city, which the Revolution, though city born, has damaged so heavily? Here lies Pilnyak's failure. He has not decided, either intellectually or emotionally, what he will choose out of the chaos of contradictions. But one must choose. The Revolution has cut time in half. And though in present-day Russia, the sorcerers' incantations exist side by side with the Gviu and the Glavbum, they are not on the same historic plane. The Gviu and the Glavbum, no matter how imperfect, tend forward, while the incantations, no matter how "folklike," are the dead weight of history. The sectarian Donat is splendid. He is a stumpy peasant and a horse thief with strict rules (he does not drink tea). He, if you please, is not in need of Petrograd. The Bolshevik Archipov is also very fine. He manages the district and at daybreak memorizes foreign words from a book and he is clever and strong and says, "foonction energetically," but what is more important, he himself functions energetically. But in which one of them is the Revolution? Donat belongs to the unhistoric, to the "green" Russia, to the undigested seventeenth century. Archipov, on the contrary, belongs to the twenty-first century, even though he does not know his foreign words well. If Donat proves the stronger, and if this sedate pious horse thief carries away both capital and railroad, then it will be the end of the Revolution and at the same time the end of Russia. Time has been cut in two, one-half is living and the other half is dead, and one has to choose the living half. Pilnyak cannot decide and hesitates to make his choice, and for the sake of conciliation, he puts a Pugachev beard on the Bolshevik Archipov. But these are all theatricals. We have seen Archipov—he shaves.

The sorcerer Egorka says: "'Russia is wise in herself. The German is clever, but his mind is foolish...' 'And how about the Karl Marxes?' one asks. 'He is a German,' I say, 'and therefore a fool.'—and Lenin?—'Lenin,' I say, 'is a peasant, a Bolshevik, and you must be communists...'" Pilnyak himself is hiding behind the sorcerer Egorka, and it is very disturbing that when he speaks for the Bolsheviks he speaks openly and when he speaks against the Bolsheviks, it is in the half-witted tongue of a sorcerer. What has he that is deeper and more real? Might not this "fellow traveler" change at one of the stations into the train going the other way!

The political danger here produces an immediate artistic one. If Pilnyak should insist on resolving the Revolution into peasant revolts and peasant life—it would mean a further simplifying of his artistic methods. Even now Pilnyak does not present a picture of the Revolution, but only its base and background. He has laid on the base with good, bold strokes, but what a pity if the master should decide that the base is the whole picture. The October Revolution is an urban one, a Petrograd and Moscow one. "The Revolution is still going on," Pilnyak remarks in passing. The entire future work of the Revolution will be directed toward the industrializing and modernizing of our economy, toward making more precise the processes and methods of reconstruction in all fields, toward uprooting the idiocy of village life, toward making human personality more complex and enriching it. The proletarian revolution can be technically and culturally completed and justified only through electrification, and not through a return to the candle, through the materialistic philosophy of a working optimism, and not through woodland superstitions and stagnant fatalism. It would be too bad if Pilnyak should want to become the poet of the candle with the pretensions of a revolutionist! This, of course, is no political harm—no one would think of dragging Pilnyak into politics—but a most real and genuine artistic danger. The fault lies in an historic approach, which comes from a false point of view and from a crying dualism. This results in a deviation from the most important aspects of reality, and in a reduction of everything to the primitive, to the socially barbaric, to the further roughening of artistic methods, to naturalistic excesses, insolent but not courageous, for they are not carried to the end. Further on, before you know it, it will lead to mysticism and to mystic hypocrisy (as per the passport of a romanticist), which is the complete and final death.

Even now Pilnyak shows his romanticist passport every time he is in difficulty. This is especially true when he has to show his acceptance of the Revolution, not in vague and ambiguous terms, but quite clearly. Then he makes immediately (in the manner of Andrey Biely) a typographical recession of several quads and in quite a new tone announces: Do not forget, please, that I am a romanticist. Drunkards very frequently have to display great solemnity, but also sober people have often to pretend that they are drunk to escape from difficult situations. Does not Pilnyak belong to the latter? When he insistently calls himself a romanticist and asks that this should not be forgotten, does not the frightened realist who is lacking horizon speak in him? The Revolution is not at all a torn boot, plus romanticism. The art of the Revolution does not at all consist in not seeing the truth or in transforming the stern reality by an effort of the imagination into the vulgarity of the "legend in the making" for oneself, and for one's own use. The psychology of "the legend in the making" is contrary to the Revolution. With it, and with its mysticism and its mystifications, began the counter-revolutionary period that came after 1905.

To accept the workers' Revolution in the name of a high ideal means not only to reject it, but to slander it. All the social illusions that mankind has raved about in religion, poetry, morals, or philosophy, served only the purpose of deceiving and blinding the oppressed. The Socialist Revolution tears the cover off "illusions," off "elevating," as well as off humiliating deceptions, and washes off reality's makeup in blood. The Revolution is strong to the extent to which it is realistic, rational, strategic, and mathematical. Can it be that the Revolution, the same one that is now before us, the first since the earth began, needs the seasoning of romantic outbursts, as a cat ragout needs hare sauce? Leave that to the Bielys. Let them chew to the very end the philistine cat ragout with Anthroposophic sauce.

For all the significance and freshness of Pilnyak's manner, his mannerisms, because they are frequently imitative, are trouble-some. It is difficult to understand how Pilnyak could have fallen into artistic dependence on Biely, and on Biely's worst sides at that. There is the tiresome subjectivism that takes the form of fre-quently repeated nonsensical lyrical interpositions; the rabid and irrational literary argumentation that swings back and forth from ultrarealism to unexpected psychophilosophical discourses; the arrangement of the text in typographic terraces; the unrelated quotations that are brought in by mechanical association; all of which are unnecessary, boring and imitative. But Andrey Biely is cunning. He covers the holes in his teaching with a lyrical hyste-ria. Biely is an Anthroposophist, he acquired wisdom from Rudolph Steiner, he kept vigil in the German mystic temple in Switzerland, he drank coffee and ate sausages. And as his mystic philosophy is meager and pitiful, a half sincere (hysterical) char-latanism and a charlatanism strictly according to the dictionary have crept into his literary methods, for the sake of covering this up—and the farther he advances, the more this is true. But why should Pilnyak find this necessary, or can it be that Pilnyak is also preparing to teach us the tragi-consoling philosophy of redemp-tion with a sauce made of Peter's chocolate? Does not Pilnyak take the world as it is in its corporeality and value it for that? Why, then, this dependence on Biely? Evidently, like a curved mirror, it reflects Pilnyak's inner need of a synthetic picture of the Revolution. The gaps in Pilnyak's spiritual grasp cause his weak-ness for Biely, the verbal decorator of spiritual failures. But for Pilnyak, this is a road downward, and it would be good for him if he could throw off the semi-buffoonish manner of the Russian Steinerite, and would move upward on his own road.

Pilnyak is a young writer, but, nonetheless, he is not a youth. He has entered the most critical age, and his great danger lies in a premature and sudden venerability. He hardly ceased to be prom-ising when he became an oracle. He writes like an oracle; he is ambiguous, he is obscure, he hints like a priest, he instructs, though really it is he who needs to study and to study very hard, because his ends are not socially or artistically correlated. His technique is unstable and uneconomical, his voice breaks, his plagiarisms strike the eye. Perhaps all these are the inevitable ail-ments of growth, but there must be one condition—no venerabil-ity. Because if self-satisfaction and pedantry lurk behind the broken voice, then, even his big talent will not save him from an inglorious end. Even in pre-revolutionary days, this was the fate of many of our promising authors, who plunged at once into venerability and were smothered in it. The example of Leonid Andreyev should be entered into the primers for promising writers.

Pilnyak is talented, but his difficulties are also great. One needs to wish him success.

The Rustic or Peasant-Singing Writers

It is impossible to understand, to accept, or to picture the Revolution, even partially, if one does not see it in its entirety, with the objective historic tasks that are the goal of its leading forces. If this is missed, then the pivot and the Revolution are gone. The latter disintegrates into episodes and anecdotes that are either heroic or evil. It is possible to make rather clever pictures, but it is impossible to recreate the Revolution, and it is, of course, impossible to reconcile oneself to it—because, if there is no purpose in the unheard-of sacrifices and privations, then history is a madhouse.

Pilnyak and Vsevolod Ivanov and Yessenin seem to try to drown themselves in a whirlpool without reflection and without responsibility. They do not dissolve themselves, in the sense of becoming unseen. This would be something to praise them for, not reproach them with, but they do not deserve praise. On the contrary, they are too well seen—Pilnyak, with his coquettishness and mannerisms, Vsevolod Ivanov, with his suffocating lyricism; Yessenin, with his overweighted "arrogance." The trouble is that between them and the Revolution, as the subject matter of their work, there is no ideological distance that would secure artistic perspective. The want of both desire and capacity on the part of the literary "fellow travelers" to grasp the Revolution by merging with it, and yet not to dissolve in it, to grasp it not only as an elemental power, but also as a purposeful process, is a social and not an individual trait. The peasant-singing intelligentsia forms the majority of "fellow travelers." The intelligentsia cannot accept the Revolution by leaning on the peasant without being silly. That is why the "fellow travelers" are not revolutionists, but fools of the Revolution. Until the alarm is sounded, it is unclear to what they are reconciling themselves—to the Revolution as a starting point of a persistent movement forward, or because in some respects it has moved us back. For there are facts enough for either category. The peasant, as is known, tried to accept the Bolshevik and to reject the communist. This meant that the *kulak,* the richer peasant, tried to rob both history and the Revolution by trampling under him the middle peasant. After driving out the landlord, he wanted to carry off the city piecemeal, and to turn his broad back to the State. The kulak does not need Leningrad (at least, not in the beginning) and if the capital becomes "mangy" (Pilnyak) then it serves her right. Not alone the peasant pressure on the landlord—immeasurably significant and invaluable in its historic consequences as it is—but also the peasant's pressure on the city, is a necessary element of the Revolution. However, this is not the entire Revolution. The city lives and leads. If you give up the city, that is, if you let it be torn to pieces economically by the kulak and artistically by Pilnyak, then there will remain no Revolution, but a violent and bloody process of retrogression. Peasant Russia, deprived of the leadership of the city, not only will never get to socialism, but will not be able to maintain itself for two months, and will become the manure and the peat of world imperialism. Is this a political question? It is a question of a life attitude, therefore also a question of great art, and on this question one must pause.

Not so long ago Chukovsky urged Alexey Tolstoy to reconcile himself with revolutionary Russia or with Russia, regardless of the Revolution. And Chukovsky's main argument was that Russia is the same as she always was, and that the Russian peasant will not exchange his icons or his roaches for any historical gingerbread. Chukovsky evidently feels that in this phrase there is a very large sweep of the national spirit and an evidence of its ineradicability. The experiment of the brother-housekeeper in the monastery who passed out a roach in the bread for a raisin is extended by Chukovsky to all Russian culture. The roach as the "raisin" of the national spirit! What a low national inferiority this is in fact, and what a contempt for a living people! It would be well enough if Chukovsky himself believed in icons. But no, he does not, for if he did he would not be mentioning them in the same breath with roaches, though in the village hut the roach hides willingly behind the icon. But as Chukovsky has his roots entirely in the past, and as his past in its turn maintained itself on the moss-covered and superstitious peasant, Chukovsky makes the old national roach that lives behind the icon the reconciling principle between himself and the Revolution. What a shame and a disgrace! What a disgrace and a shame! These intellectuals studied their books (on the neck of that same peasant), they scribbled in magazines, they lived through various "eras," they created "movements," but when the Revolution came in earnest, they found refuge for the national spirit in the darkest corner of the peasant hut where the roach lives.

Chukovsky is merely less ceremonious, but all the rustic writers tend in the direction of a primitive nationalism smelling of the roach. Undoubtedly there are processes in this same Revolution that touch nationalism at various points. The economic decline, the strengthening of provincialism, the *revanche* of the bast shoe over the boot, home brew, and drink—all these are pulling (one can even say, have pulled) backward into the depths of centuries. And parallel with this can be seen a conscious return to the "folk" motif in literature. Blok's great development of the city couplets ("The Twelve"), the notes of folk song (in Akhmatova, and with more mannerisms in Tsvetaeva), the wave of localism (Ivanov), the quite mechanical putting in of couplets, of rituals, and so forth, in the text of Pilnyak's stories—all this has been undoubtedly called forth by the Revolution, that is, by the fact that the masses, just as they are, have taken the foremost place in life. One can point out other manifestations of a return to the "national," which are pettier, more accidental, and more superficial. For instance, our military uniforms, though they have something from French and from the disgusting Gallifet, begin to approach the medieval tunic and our old military cap. Though in other fields, fashion has not yet come forward because of the general poverty, there are grounds to assume a certain trend toward folk patterns, which, even there, the Lord knows, are not so very profound. In the broad sense of the word fashion was foreign to us, and extended only to the possessing classes, thereby implying a sharp line of social demarcation. The advent of the workers as a ruling class caused an inevitable reaction against the borrowing of bourgeois patterns in various fields of life.

It is quite evident that the return to bast shoes, to homemade rope, and to home brew is not a social revolution, but an economic reaction, which is the main obstacle to revolution. Insofar as a conscious turn to the past and to the "folk" is concerned, everything that has been done is extremely unstable and superficial. It would be unreasonable to expect the development of a new literary form from a city couplet or from a peasant song; it cannot go much beyond a "trickling in." Literature will throw out excessive local words. The medieval tunic is already considerably internationalized now on the ground of economy in cloth. The originality of our new national life and of our new art will be less striking but much more profound, and will show itself much later. Essentially, the Revolution means the people's final break with the Asiatic, with the seventeenth century, with Holy Russia, with icons, and with roaches. It does not mean a return to the pre-Peter era, but on the contrary, it means a communion of the entire people with civilization and a reconstruction of the material foundations of civilization in accordance with the interests of the people. The Peter era was only a first step in the historic climb toward October and through October it will go further on and higher up. In this sense Blok has seen more deeply than Pilnyak. In Blok the revolutionary tendency is expressed in the finished verse:*

At Holy Russia let's fire a shot.

At hutted Russia
Thick-rumped and solid,
Russia, the stolid,
Eh, eh, unhallowed, unblessed.

The break with the seventeenth century, with the Russia of the peasant hut, appears to the mystic Blok as a holy affair, even as a state for the conciliation with Christ. In this archaic form the thought is expressed that the break is not imposed from without, but is the result of national development and corresponds to the profoundest needs of the people. Without this break, the people would have rotted away. The same idea that the Revolution is

---

*"The Twelve," Alexander Blok. Translated by Babette Deutsch and Abraham Yarmolinsky. [Trans. note.]

national in character is expressed in Briusov's interesting poem about the old women; "On the Baptismal Day in October:"

> On the square I was told
> There where the Kremlin stood as a target,
> They cut the thread and brought fresh hemp for the yarn.

What is the meaning of "national"? Here one must go back to the ABCs. Pushkin did not believe in icons and did not live with roaches and was not national. Nor was Belinsky national. One could name a few others without touching the contemporaries. Pilnyak considers the seventeenth century national. Peter is anti-national. It follows that the national is only that which represents the dead weight of evolution, from which the spirit of action has flown and which the national organism in the past centuries has digested and thrown off. It follows, then, that only the excrements of history are national. But we think it is quite the opposite. The barbarian Peter was more national than the whole bearded and overdecorated past that opposed him. The Decembrists were more national than the official statehood of Nicholas the First with its serfdom, its bureaucratic icons, and its state roaches. Bolshevism is more national than the monarchist and other émigrés, and Budenny is more national than Wrangel, whatever the ideologists, mystics, and poets of national excrements may say. The life and movement of a nation take their course through the contradictions that are embodied in classes, parties, and groups. Dynamically the national and class elements coincide. In all the critical periods of its development, that is, in all the most responsible periods, the nation is broken into two halves—and national is that which raises the people to a higher economic and cultural plane.

The Revolution has issued from the national "element," but that does not mean that only the elemental in the Revolution is the vital and the national, as those acquiescent poets of the Revolution seem to think.

To Blok the Revolution is a rebellious element: "Wind, wind—in all God's world!" Vsevolod Ivanov seems never to rise above the peasant element. To Pilnyak the Revolution is a blizzard. To Kliuev and to Yessenin it is a Pugachev or a Stenka Razin insurrection. Elements, blizzard, flame, maelstrom, whirlpool. But Chukovsky—he who was ready to make his peace via the roach—declared that the October Revolution was not real because its flames were too few.

And even that phlegmatic snob, Zamyatin, discovered an insufficiency of temperature in our Revolution. Here is the whole gamut from tragedy to horseplay. But in fact both the tragedy and the horseplay show the same passive, contemplative, and philistine romantic attitude toward the Revolution as toward a national elemental power unleashed.

But the Revolution is not at all only a blizzard. The revolutionary element of the peasant is represented by Pugachev, Stenka Razin, and in part by Makhno. The revolutionary element of the city is represented by Father Gapon and partly by Khrustalev and even by Kerensky. This, however, is not yet the Revolution, but only riot or disorder on top of riot, as in the case of Kerensky. The Revolution is above all the struggle of the working class for power, for the establishment of power, for the reconstruction of society. It passes through the highest points, through the most acute paroxysms of bloody fighting, but it remains one and indivisible throughout its whole course—from its first shy beginnings to its final ideal moment when the state organized by the Revolution will become dissolved into a communist society.

The poetry of the Revolution is not in the booming of machine guns, nor in the struggle behind barricades; it is not in the heroism of the fallen, nor in the triumph of the victorious, because all these moments are found in a war of violence also. There, too, bloodshed will be found even more abundant; there, too, the machine guns will crackle; there, too, are victors and vanquished. The pathos and poetry of the Revolution consist in the fact that a new revolutionary class becomes master of all these instruments of struggle, and in the name of a new ideal to enrich man and to form a new man, it carries on a struggle with the old world, falling and rising until its final victorious moment. The poetry of the Revolution is synthetic. It cannot be changed into small coin for the temporary lyrical use of sonnet-makers. The poetry of the Revolution is not portable. It is in the difficult struggle of the working class, in its growth, in its persistence, in its defeats, in its repeated efforts, in the cruel expenditure of energy that pays for every conquered inch, in the growing will and intensity of the struggle, in the triumph of its victories, as well as in its calculated retreats, in its watchfulness, in its assaults, in the elemental flood of mass rebellion, in the exact computation of forces, and in the chess-like movements of strategy. The Revolution began to grow with the first factory wheelbarrow in which the embittered slaves carried out their foreman; with the first strike in which they denied their hands to their master; with the first underground circle where Utopian fanaticism and revolutionary idealism fed on the reality of social wounds. It flowed and ebbed, swung by the rhythm of the economic situation, by its high points and by its crises. With a battering ram of bleeding bodies it bursts open for itself the arena of the legal system of the exploiters, puts its antenna through and gives them, when necessary, a protective coloring. It builds trade unions, insurance societies, cooperatives, and self-educational circles. It penetrates into hostile parliaments, creates newspapers, agitates, and at the same time makes an indefatigable selection of the best, of the most courageous, of the consecrated elements of the working class, and builds its own party. The strikes are more frequently defeats than half-victories; the demonstrations are marked by new victims and by new blood—but all these form notches in the class memory, which strengthen and temper the union of the select, the party of the Revolution.

It does not act on a vacant stage of history, and it is therefore not free to choose its ways and its times. In the course of events, it will find itself forced to begin decisive action before it has the opportunity to gather the necessary forces; such was the case in 1905. From the height to which it is carried by self-sacrificing courage and by the clarity of its aims, it is doomed to be precipitated downward for the lack of an organized mass support. The fruits of many years' efforts are torn from its hands. The organization that seemed omnipotent is broken and shattered. The best are annihilated, jailed, dispersed, and scattered. It seems as if all is at an end. And the little poets who tinkled pathetically about it in the moment of its temporary triumph, begin to tune their lyres to a pitch of pessimism, mysticism, and eroticism. The proletariat itself seems discouraged and demoralized. But after all, there has been cut into his memory a new and very important notch from which there is no turning back. And the defeat turns out to be a step toward victory. New efforts come with gritting of teeth and new sacrifices. Bit by bit the advance guard gathers its scattered forces, and the best elements of the new generation that are awakened by the defeat of the old, join it. The Revolution, bleeding but not vanquished, lives on in the dumb hatred that dwells in the workers' quarters and in the villages, which are suppressed but not dispersed. It lives in the clear consciousness of the small but tried old guard, which, unfrightened by defeat, immediately takes an account of it, analyzes it, estimates it, weighs it, defines the new points of departure, detects the general line of development, and points out the road. Five years after its defeat, the movement breaks forth again in the spring floods of 1912.

Out of the Revolution grew the materialist method, which permits one to gauge one's strength, to foresee changes, and to direct events. This is the greatest fulfillment of the Revolution, and in this lies its highest poetry. A wave of strikes grows up with an irresistible design, in which the deeper foundation of the masses and the experience of the Revolution of 1905 are immediately felt. But the War, which was the logical outcome of all these developments and was also foreseen, intersects the line of the growing Revolution. Nationalism drowns everything. Thundering militarism expresses the will of the Nation. Socialism seems buried forever. But just at the moment of its imminent fall, the Revolution forms its most daring prognosis—to turn the imperialistic war into a civil one, and to have the working classes take over the power. Amidst the noise of the armored cars on the stone streets, and amidst the ravings of chauvinism in all languages, the Revolution gathers its strength at the bottom of the trenches, in the factories and in the villages. The masses grasp for the first time with poignant sagacity the inner relation of historical events. February 1917 is a great victory for the Revolution in Russia. Yet this victory apparently condemns the revolutionary demands of the proletariat as destructive and hopeless. It leads to the era of Kerensky, of Tseretelli, of patriotic revolutionary colonels and lieutenants, of the many-worded, cross-eyed, suffocating, stupid, scoundrelly Chernovs. Oh, the sainted faces of the young village teachers and of the village scribes charmed by the tenor notes of Avksentiev! Oh, the deep revolutionary laughter of the democrats, and the mad howl of rage that followed it as answer to the speeches of the "tiny handful" of Bolsheviks! Yet the fall of the power of the "revolutionary democracy" was foreordained by the deeper correlation of social forces, by the growing mood of the masses, by the foresight and activity of the revolutionary vanguard. The poetry of the Revolution lay not alone in the elemental rise of the October tide, but in the clear consciousness and in the tense will of the leading Party. In July 1917, when we were crushed and driven out, when we were jailed and proclaimed spies of the Hohenzollerns, when we were deprived of fire and water, when the democratic press buried us under mounds of slander, we felt, though we were underground or in jail, that it was we who were the victors and the masters of the situation. In this predestined dynamics of the Revolution, in this her political geometry, lay her greatest poetry.

October was only a crowning of these, and at once it brought with it immense new tasks and immeasurable difficulties. The ensuing struggle called for the most varied methods and means, for mad assaults by the Red Guard, for the formula of "No war, no peace," and for temporary capitulation before the ultimatum of the enemy. But even in Brest-Litovsk, when first we refused the Hohenzollern his peace, and later signed it without reading it, the revolutionary party did not feel itself vanquished, but rather the master of tomorrow. It helped the revolutionary logic of events by its diplomatic pedagogics. November 1918 was the answer it received. True, historic foresight cannot have mathematical precision. Now it exaggerates, now it underrates. But the conscious will of the vanguard becomes a greater and greater factor in the events that prepare the future. The responsibility of the revolutionary party deepens and becomes more complex. The Party organs penetrate into the thick of the people, feel, evaluate, foresee, prepare, and direct developments. True, the Party retreats more often during this period than it attacks. But its retreats do not change the general line of its historic action. They are the episodes, the curves of the great road. Is the NEP "prosaic"? Of course! Participation in Rodzianko's Duma, submission to the bell of Chkheidze and of Dan in the first Soviet, the negotiations with von Kullmann at Brest-Litovsk, were also not very attractive. But Rodzianko and his Duma have gone. Chkheidze and Dan have been overthrown, just as von Kullmann and his master. The NEP came. Came, and will go away. The artist, for whom the Revolution loses its aroma, because it does not remove the smells of the Sucharevka market, is empty-headed and small. Given all other necessary conditions, he only will become the poet of the Revolution who will learn to grasp it in its entirety, to regard its defeats as steps toward victory, to penetrate into the plans of its retreats, and who will be able to see in the intense preparation of forces, during the ebb tide of the elements, the undying pathos and the poetry of the Revolution.

The October Revolution is profoundly national. But it is not only a national element—it is a national academy. The art of the Revolution must pass through this academy. And it is a very difficult course.

Because of its peasant foundation, and because of its vast spaces and its patches of culture, the Russian Revolution is the most chaotic and formless of all revolutions. But in its leadership, in the method of its orientation, in its organization, in its aims and tasks, it is the most "correct," the most planful and the most finished of all revolutions. In the combination of these two extremes lies the soul, the internal character of our Revolution.

In his pamphlet on the Futurists, Chukovsky, who has on his tongue what the more cautious ones have on their mind, names the fundamental weakness of the October Revolution: "In externals it is violent and catastrophic, but in essence it is calculating, brainy, and shrewd." They would have recognized in the end a revolution that is only violent, only catastrophic. They, or their direct descendants, would probably have founded their pedigree from it, for a revolution that is not calculating and not brainy never would have carried its business to the end, that is, it never would have carried out the victory of the exploited over the exploiters, and never would have destroyed the material basis that is at the bottom of the retainer's art and the retainer's criticism. In all former revolutions, the masses were violent and catastrophic, and it was the bourgeoisie who was calculating and shrewd and who, thanks to this, reaped the fruits of victory. The gentlemen aesthetes, romantics, elementals, mystics, and agile critics would have accepted without difficulty a revolution in which the masses showed enthusiasm and self-sacrifice, but no political calculation. They would have canonized such a revolution according to a well-established romantic ritual. A vanquished workers' revolution would have found a magnanimous aesthetic recognition on the part of that art that would have come in the train of the victor. A very comforting perspective, indeed. But we prefer a victorious revolution, though deprived of artistic recognition by that art which is now in the camp of the vanquished.

Herzen said that Hegel's doctrine is the algebra of revolution. This definition can even more correctly be applied to Marxism. The materialistic dialectics of the class struggle is the true algebra of revolution. In the arena visible to the external eye are chaos and floods, formlessness and boundlessness. But it is a counted and measured chaos, whose successive stages are foreseen. The regularity of their succession is anticipated and enclosed in steel-like formulas. In elemental chaos there is an abyss of blindness. But clear-sightedness and vigilance exist in a directing politics. Revolutionary strategy is not formless like an element, it is finished like a mathematical formula. For the first time in history, we see the algebra of revolution in action.

But these most important traits—clarity, realism, the physical power of thought, a merciless consistency, a lucidity and solidity of line, which come not from the village, but from industry, from the city, from the last word of its spiritual development—are the fundamental traits of the October Revolution, and they are entirely foreign to the "fellow travelers." And this is why they are only "fellow travelers." And one has to say it to them in the interest of that very clarity and lucidity of line that is in the Revolution.

The Insinuating "Changing Landmarks" Group

In *Russia*, a journal that is supposed to be the organ of the "Changing Landmarks" group, Lezhnev attacks, with all the might that is in him, and that is not much, the whole "Changing Landmarks" group in general. He accuses them, not without reason, of a belated Slavophilism. True, they do sin a little in this respect. The effort of the "Changing Landmarks" group to become related to the Revolution is very praiseworthy, but the ideologic crutches that they use for this are very clumsy. One would think that this somewhat unexpected campaign of Lezhnev would be welcomed. But it is not. The "Changing Landmarks" group, though hobbling helplessly and clumsily, is changing color and seems to be coming nearer to the Revolution, while Lezhnev bravely and boldly goes further and further away from it. If he is embarrassed by the Slavophilism of Kluchnikov and Potechin, which is tardy and not carefully thought out, it is not because it is Slavophilism, but because it is ideology. He wants to free himself from all ideology whatever. He calls this acknowledging the rights of life.

The whole article is constructed very diplomatically, and is thought out to the very end. The author liquidates the Revolution, and with it, in passing, also the generation that made it. He constructs his philosophy of history as if it were a question of defending the new generation that is now growing up in Soviet Russia against the old people, against the idealistic democrats, the doctrinaires, and so forth, among whom Lezhnev also includes the Constitutional Democrats, the Social Revolutionists, and the Mensheviks. But what is the new generation that he accepts and takes under his wing? At first it seems that it is the very same generation that abruptly cut off democratic ideology and all its fictions, that established the Soviet regime, and that, well or badly, is leading the Revolution further. It seems so at first, and Lezhnev suggests this impression for a subtle psychologic reason; it is easier this way to enter into the confidence of the reader, so that afterwards he can take him into his own hands. In the second part of the article there appear not two generations, but three; the generation that prepared the Revolution, but that, in accordance with the general rule, proved incapable of accomplishing it; the generation that accomplished its "heroic" and "destructive" aspects, and the third that is called upon not to destroy the law, but to fulfill it. This new generation is characterized somewhat indefinitely, but all the more insinuatingly. They are the strong, the builders without prejudices, and without anything superfluous. In Lezhnev's opinion all ideology is superfluous. Revolution, don't you know, like life in general, "is made just as a river flows, just as a bird sings, and is not in itself teleological." This philosophic vulgarity is accompanied by nods in the direction of the doctrinaires of the Revolution, among whom are all and everyone who is armed with a theoretic doctrine of revolution, and who sees definite aims and creative tasks ahead of the Revolution. In fact, what does it mean that life "in itself" is not teleological, and that it is created just as a river flows? About what life is here the question? If the question is about physiologic metabolism, then it is more or less correct, though here man has recourse to teleology in the form of the culinary art, of hygiene, of medicine, etc. In this lies the difference between his life and a flowing river. But life consists also of something that is higher than physiology. Human labor, that very thing that distinguishes man from the animal, is thoroughly teleological; outside of the rationally directed expenditures of energy there is no labor. And labor occupies a place in human life. Art, even the "purest," is thoroughly teleological, because if it breaks with great aims, no matter how unconsciously felt by the artist, it degenerates into a mere rattle. Politics is embodied teleology. And revolution is condensed politics, bringing into action a mass of many millions. How, then, is revolution possible without teleology?

In connection with this, Lezhnev's relation to Pilnyak is significant in the highest degree. Lezhnev declares Pilnyak to be a true artist, almost the artistic creator of the Revolution. "He perceived it, he carried and he carries it within himself.".... In vain, says Lezhnev, is Pilnyak accused of dissolving the Revolution into the elemental. In this very thing, it seems, lies Pilnyak's power as an artist. Pilnyak "grasped the Revolution, not from without, but from within, gave it dynamics, disclosed its organic nature." But what does it mean to understand the Revolution from within? It would mean to look at it with the eyes of its greatest dynamic force, of the working class, of its conscious vanguard. And what does it mean to look at the Revolution from without? It would mean to see in the Revolution only an element, a blind process, a blizzard, a chaos of facts, of people, and of shadows. This is what it would mean to look at it from without. And it is in this way that Pilnyak looks at it.

In contrast to us who think abstractly, Pilnyak supposedly gave "an artistic synthesis of Russia and of the Revolution." But in what way is a "synthesis" of Russia and of the Revolution possible? Did the Revolution appear from without, or from the side? Is not the Revolution the property of Russia? Is it possible to separate them, and then contrast Russia to the Revolution, and so synthesize them? This is equivalent to speaking of a synthesis of man and his age, or of a synthesis of woman and the birth process. Whence this monstrous combination of words and concepts? It comes from this very approach to the Revolution, from without and from the side. The Revolution, to them, is a gigantic but an unexpected event. Russia is not the real Russia, with her past and with that future that she had in her, but the habitual and possible Russia, which was deposited in their conservative consciousness, and which does not reconcile itself to the Revolution that has fallen upon them. And these people need the effort of logic and psychology, and a very big effort at that, to "synthetize" Russia with the Revolution and not damage their spiritual economy. An artist like Pilnyak, with his deficiencies and his weaknesses, is just made for them. To reject revolutionary teleology is, in reality, to reduce the Revolution to a temporary peasant revolt. Here lies the conscious and unconscious approach to the Revolution of the majority of those writers whom we have called "fellow travelers." Pushkin said that our popular movement is a revolt, irrational and cruel. Of course this is a nobleman's definition, but within the limitations of a nobleman's point of view, it is profound and apt. As long as the revolutionary movement retains its peasant character, it is "not teleological," to use Lezhnev's phrase, nor "irrational," if one prefers Pushkin's. The peasantry has never in history risen independently to general political aims, and peasant movements have resulted either in a Pugachev or a Stenka Razin, and were repressed throughout all history, or they served as a basis for the struggle of other classes. A purely peasant revolution has never been anywhere. Whenever a peasantry were without leadership, either of the bourgeois democracy, as in the old revolutions, or of the proletariat, as with us, its movement only beat on the existing regime and shook it up, but it never ended in planful reorganization. A revolutionary peasantry was never capable of creating a government. In its struggle it built guerrilla bands, but it never created a centralized revolutionary army. That is why it suffered defeats. How significant that all our revolutionary poets, almost without exception, come back to Pugachev and Stenka Razin! Vasili Kamensky is Stenka Razin's poet; while Yessenin is Pugachev's. Of course it is not bad that the poets are inspired by these dramatic moments of Russian history, but it is bad and it is criminal that they cannot make their approach to the present Revolution otherwise than by dissolving it into blind revolts, into elemental uprisings, and so wipe out one hundred or one hundred and fifty years of Russian history, as if they had never been. As Pilnyak says, "peasant life is known—it is to eat in order to work, to work in order to eat, and besides that, to be born, to bear, and to die." Of course this is a vulgarization of peasant life. However, artistically it is a legitimate vulgarization. For what is our Revolution, if it is not a mad rebellion in the name of the conscious, rational, purposeful, and dynamic principle of life, against the elemental, senseless, biologic automatism of life, that is, against the peasant roots of our old Russian history, against its aimlessness, its non-teleological character, against the "holy" and idiotic philosophy of Tolstoy's Karataiev in *War and Peace*? If we take this away from the Revolution, then the Revolution is not worth the candles that were burned for it, and, as is known, much more than candles were burned for it.

However, it would be libelous, not only to the Revolution, but also to the peasant, to say that Pilnyak's or, what is more, Lezhnev's point of view is the true peasant approach to the Revolution. No, our great historic conquest consists in the fact that the peasant himself, clumsily and almost like a bear, with stops and retreats, is separating himself from the old, irrational, and meaningless life, and is gradually being drawn into the sphere of conscious reconstruction. It will take decades before the philosophy of Karataiev will be burned and leave no trace of itself, but this process has already been begun, and has been begun well. Lezhnev's point of view is not the peasant's: it is the point of view of a philistine intellectual, who is hiding behind the back of the peasant of yesterday, because he does not want to show his own back of today. It is not very artistic.

"Neo-Classicism"

Art, don't you see, means prophecy. Works of art are the embodiments of presentiments; therefore pre-revolutionary art is the real art of the Revolution. In the almanac *Shipovnik*, which is filled with reactionary ideas, this philosophy is worked out by Muratov, and by Efros, each one in his own way, but their conclusions are the same. It is absolutely unquestionable that the War and the Revolution were prepared in the material conditions and in the consciousness of the classes. It is also unquestionable that this preparation was reflected in different ways in art. But this, at any rate, was pre-revolutionary art, the art of the languishing bourgeois intelligentsia before the storm. We are talking, however, about the art of the Revolution, which was created by the Revolution and from which it draws its new "presentiments" and which in its turn it now feeds. This art is not behind us, but ahead of us.

The Futurists and the Cubists, who reigned almost unchallenged over the desert-like field of art in the first years of the Revolution, found themselves driven from the positions they first occupied. This was so not only because the Soviet budget was reduced, but because they did not have, and in their very essence could not have had, sufficient resources to solve their vast artistic problems. And now we hear that Classicism is on the way. And what is more, we hear that the art of Classicism is the art of the Revolution. And still more, Classicism is "the child and essence of the Revolution." (Efros.) Of course these are very cheerful notes. The one thing that is strange is, why Classicism should remember its kinship to the Revolution only after four years of reflection? This is a classic caution. But is it so true that the neo-Classicism of Akhmatova, Verkhovsky, Grossman, and Efros is "the child and essence of the Revolution"? In so far as the "essence" is concerned, this is going too far. But is not neo-Classicism a "child of the Revolution," in the same sense in which the NEP is? This question may seem somewhat unexpected, and even out of place. And yet it is most appropriate. The NEP has found an echo abroad in the form of the "Changing Landmarks" group, and we are told the good news that the theorists of change accept the "essence" of the Revolution. They want to strengthen and to order its conquests, and their slogan is "revolutionary conservatism." For us the NEP is a turn of the revolutionary trajectory, which, in its general direction, is going upward; for them, the turn is in the entire direction of the trajectory. We consider that the historic train has just begun to move, and that this is only a brief stop at a station for the purpose of taking on water and getting up steam. They think, on the contrary, that what ought to be preserved is this state of rest after the disorder of movement has finally stopped. The NEP has produced the "Changing Landmarks" group, and it is the NEP that has caused the discovery that neo-Classicism is the "child of the Revolution." "We are alive; in our arteries, our pulse is whole and strong; its beat is in harmony with the rhythm of the current day, we have lost neither sleep nor appetite, because the past has

passed.".... This is very well said. Perhaps even a little better than
the author himself intended. The children of the Revolution who,
as you see, have not lost their appetite because the past has
passed! Children with an appetite, one cannot help saying. But
the Revolution is not at all so easily satisfied that it will recognize
as its own those poets who, in spite of the Revolution, have lost
no sleep, and have not run away across the border. Akhmatova
has some strong lines on why she did not go away. It is very good
that she did not go away. But Akhmatova herself hardly thinks
that her songs are of the Revolution, and the author of the neo-
Classic manifesto is in too much of a hurry. Not to lose sleep because of the Revolution is not the same as grasping its "essence."
It is true that Futurism has not mastered the Revolution, but it
has an internal striving, which, in a certain sense, is parallel to it.
The best of the Futurists were on fire, and perhaps are still so.
But neo-Classicism is not merely losing its appetite. Neo-Classicism is very similar to the poetry of the "Changing Landmarks"
group, that foster-sister of the NEP.

And this is only natural, after all. If Futurism was attracted
toward the chaotic dynamics of the Revolution, tried to express
itself in the chaotic dynamics of words, then neo-Classicism expressed the need of peace, of stable forms, and of correct punctuation. In the language of the "Changing Landmarks" group, this
may be called "revolutionary conservatism."

Marietta Shaginyan

Shaginyan's benevolent and even "sympathetic" attitude toward the Revolution, as is now evident, has its source in the most
unrevolutionary, Asiatic, passive, Christian, and non-resistant
point of view. Shaginyan's recently published novel, *Our Destiny*,
serves as an explanatory note to this point of view. Here all is
psychology, and transcendental psychology at that, with roots
that go off into religion. There is character "in general," spirit
and soul, destiny noumenal and destiny phenomenal, psychologic riddles throughout, and to make the piling up of all this
seem not too monstrous, the novel takes place in a sanatorium
for psychopathics. There is the very splendid professor, a most
keen-minded psychiatrist, who is also the noblest husband and

father, and a most unusual Christian; the wife is a little simpler, but her union with her husband, in sublimation to Christ, is complete; the daughter tries to rebel, but later humiliates herself in the name of the Lord; a young psychiatrist, in whose name the story is told, is entirely in accord with this family. He is intelligent, soft, and pious. There is a technician, with a Swedish name, who is unusually noble, good, wise in his simplicity, all forbearing and submissive to God. There is the priest Leonid, unusually keen, unusually pious, and, of course, according to his avocation, submissive to God. And all about them are crazy and half-crazy people, by whom on the one hand is revealed the understanding and profundity of the professor, and, on the other hand, the necessity of obeying God, who did not succeed in building a world without crazy people. There is another young psychiatrist, who comes here as an atheist, and of course also submits to God. These heroes discuss among themselves whether the professor recognizes the devil, or whether he considers evil impersonal, and they are inclined to get along without the devil. On the cover is written, 1923, Moscow and Petrograd! What wonders in a sieve —truly!

Shaginyan's keen-minded, good, and pious heroes do not call forth sympathy, but complete indifference, which at moments passes into nausea. And this is so, in spite of the fact that a clever author is evident, for all the cheap language and all too provincial humor. There is falseness even in Dostoyevsky's pious and submissive figures, for one feels that they are strangers to the author. He created them in large degree as an antithesis to himself, because Dostoyevsky was passionate and bad-tempered in everything, even in his perfidious Christianity. But Shaginyan seems really to be good, though with a domestic goodness only. She has enclosed the abundance of her knowledge and her extraordinary psychological penetration in the framework of her domestic point of view. She herself recognizes it, and speaks of it openly. But the Revolution is not at all a domestic event. That is why Shaginyan's fatalistic submission is so strikingly incongruous to the spirit and meaning of our times. And that is why her very wise and pious people, if you will forgive the word, stink of bigotry.

In her literary diary, Shaginyan speaks of the necessity of struggling for culture everywhere and always; if people blow their noses into their five fingers, teach them the use of the handkerchief. This is correct, and strikes a bold note, especially today when, for the first time, the real bulk of the people are beginning consciously to reconstruct culture. But the semi-illiterate proletarian who is unused to the handkerchief (having never owned one), who has done with the idiocy of divine commandments once and for all, and who is seeking a way for the building of correct human relationships, is infinitely more cultured than those educated reactionaries (of both sexes) who blow their noses philosophically into their mystic handkerchief, and who complicate this unaesthetic gesture by the most complex artistic tricks, and by stealthy and cowardly borrowings from science.

Shaginyan is anti-revolutionary in her very essence. It is her fatalistic Christianity, her household indifference to everything that is not of the household, that reconciles her to the Revolution. She has simply changed her seat from one car into another, carrying with her hand baggage and her philosophic artistic handwork. It may possibly seem to her that she has retained her individuality more surely this way. But not a single thread points upward from this individuality.

CHAPTER THREE

Alexander Blok

Blok belonged entirely to pre-October literature. Blok's impulses—whether toward tempestuous mysticism, or toward revolution—arise not in empty space, but in the very thick atmosphere of the culture of old Russia, of its landlords and intelligentsia. Blok's symbolism was a reflection of this immediate and disgusting environment. A symbol is a generalized image of a reality. Blok's lyrics are romantic, symbolic, mystic, formless, and unreal. But they presuppose a very real life with definite forms and relationships. Romantic symbolism is only a going away from life, in the sense of an abstraction from its concreteness, from individual traits, and from its proper names; at bottom, symbolism is a means of transforming and sublimating life. Blok's starry, stormy, and formless lyrics reflect a definite environment and period, with its manner of living, its customs, its rhythms, but outside of this period, they hang like a cloud-patch. This lyric poetry will not outlive its time or its author.

Blok belonged to pre-October literature, but he overcame this, and entered into the sphere of October when he wrote "The Twelve." That is why he will occupy a special place in the history of Russian literature.

One should not allow Blok to be obscured by those petty poetic and semi-poetic demons who whirl around his memory, and who to this very day (the pious idiots!) cannot understand how Blok recognized Mayakovsky as a great talent, and yawned frankly over Gumilev. Blok, the "purest" of lyricists, did not speak of pure art, and did not place poetry above life. On the contrary, he recognized the fact that "art, life, and politics were indivisible and inseparable." "I am accustomed," writes Blok in his preface to "Retaliation," written in 1919, "to put together the facts accessible to my eye in a given time in every field of life, and I am sure that all together they always create one musical chord." This is much bigger and stronger and deeper than a self-sufficient aestheticism, than all the nonsense about art being independent of social life.

Blok knew the value of the intelligentsia: "I am none the less a blood-relation of the intelligentsia," he said, "but the intelligentsia has always been negative. If I did not go over to the Revolution, it is still less worth while to go over to the War." Blok did not "go over to the Revolution," but he took his spiritual course from it. Already the approach of the Revolution of 1905 opened up the factory to Blok, and for the first time raised his art above lyrical nebulousness. The first Revolution entered his soul and tore him away from individualistic self-contentment and mystic quietism. Blok felt the reaction between the two Revolutions to be an emptiness of spirit, and the aimlessness of the epoch he felt to be a circus, with cranberry sauce for blood. Blok wrote of "the true mystic twilight of the years that preceded the first Revolution" and of "the untrue mystic after-effect that immediately followed it" ("Retaliation"). The second Revolution gave him a feeling of wakening, of movement, of purpose, and of meaning. Blok was not the poet of the Revolution. Blok caught hold of the wheel of the Revolution as he lay perishing in the stupid cul-de-sac of pre-revolutionary life and art. The poem called "The Twelve," Blok's most important work, and the only one that will live for ages, was the result of this contact.

As he himself said, Blok carried chaos within himself all his life. His manner of saying this was formless, just as his philosophy of life and his lyrics were on the whole formless. What he felt to be chaos was his incapacity to combine the subjective and the objective, his cautious and watchful lack of willpower, in an epoch that saw the preparation and afterwards the letting loose of the greatest events. Throughout all his changes, Blok remained a true decadent, if one were to take this word in a large historic sense, in the sense of the contrast between decadent individualism and the individualism of the rising bourgeoisie.

Blok's anxious state of chaos gravitated into two main directions, the mystic and the revolutionary. But in neither direction did it resolve itself to the end. His religion was unclear and infirm, not imperative like his lyrics. The Revolution, which descended on the poet like a hail of facts, like a geologic avalanche of events, refuted or rather swept away the pre-revolutionary Blok, who was wasting himself in languor and presentiments. It drowned the tender, gnat-like note of individualism in the roaring and heaving music of destruction. And here one had to choose. Of course, the parlor poets could continue their chirping without choosing, and needed merely to add their complaints about the difficulties of life. But Blok, who was carried away by the period, and who translated it into his own inner language, had to choose, and he chose by writing "The Twelve."

This poem is unquestionably Blok's highest achievement. At bottom it is a cry of despair for the dying past, and yet a cry of despair that rises in a hope for the future. The music of the terrible events inspired Blok. It seemed to say to him: "Everything which you have written up to now is not right. New people are coming. They bring new hearts. They do not need this. Their victory over the old world signifies a victory over you, over your lyrics, which voiced only the torment of the old world before its death." Blok heard this, and accepted it, and because it was hard to accept, and because he sought support for his lack of faith in his revolutionary faith, and because he wanted to fortify and convince himself, he expressed his acceptance of the Revolution in the most extreme images, that the bridges behind him might be burned. Blok does not make even a shadow of an attempt to sugar the revolutionary change. On the contrary, he takes it in its most uncouth forms and only in its uncouth forms—a strike of prostitutes, for instance, the murder of Katka by a Red guard, the pillage of a bourgeois home—and, he says, I accept this, and he sanctifies all this provocatively with the blessings of Christ, and perhaps tries even to save the artistic image of Christ by propping it up with the Revolution.

But nonetheless, "The Twelve" is not a poem of the Revolution. It is the swan song of the individualistic art that went over to the Revolution. And this poem will remain. The twilight lyrics of Blok are gone into the past, and will never return, for such times will not come again, but "The Twelve" will remain with its cruel wind, with its placard, with Katka lying on the snow, with the revolutionary step, and with the old world like a mangy cur.

The fact that Blok wrote "The Twelve" and that he became silent after "The Twelve," that he stopped hearing music, is due as much to Blok's character as to the very extraordinary "music" that he grasped in 1918. The convulsive and pathetic break with the whole past became, for the poet, a fatal rupture. Aside from the destructive processes that were going on in his organism, Blok could have been kept going perhaps only by a continual development of revolutionary events, by a powerful spiral of shocks that would embrace the whole world. But the march of history is not adapted for the psychic needs of a romanticist who is struck by the Revolution. And to be able to maintain oneself on the temporary sandbanks, one has to have a different training, a different faith in the Revolution, an understanding of its sequential rhythms, and not only an understanding of the chaotic music of its tides. Blok did not and could not have all this. The leaders of the Revolution were all people whose psychology and behavior were strange to him. That is why he withdrew into himself, and became silent after "The Twelve." And those with whom he had lived spiritually, the wise men and the poets, the same who are always "negative," turned away from him with malice and with hate. They could not forgive him his phrase, the mangy cur. They stopped shaking hands with Blok, as with a traitor, and only after his death did they "make peace with him," and tried to show that "The Twelve" contained nothing unexpected, and that it was not of October, but of the old Blok, and that all the elements of "The Twelve" had their roots in the past, and let not the Bolsheviks imagine that Blok was one of theirs. This contention is not hard to gather from Blok's various other works. There are rhythms, alliterations, strophes that find their full development in "The Twelve." But one can find in the individualist Blok other rhythms and moods also; and it was this same Blok who, just in 1918, found in himself (certainly not on the pavement, but in himself) the broken music of "The Twelve." The pavement of

October was needed for this. Others escaped abroad from this pavement, or moved into interior islands. Here is the crux of the matter and this is what they do not forgive Blok for!

> Thus rave all the fed,
> Thus longs the satisfaction of important bellies,
> Their trough is overturned,
> And confusion is in their foul pen.
>   (Alexander Blok, "The Fed")

But just the same, "The Twelve" is not a poem of the Revolution; because, after all, the meaning of the Revolution as an element (if one were to consider it as an element only) does not consist in releasing individualism that had been driven into a blind alley. The inner meaning of the Revolution remains somewhere outside the poem. The poem itself is eccentric in the sense of the word as it is used in physics. That is why Blok crowns his poem with Christ. But Christ belongs in no way to the Revolution, only to Blok's past.

When Eichenvald, expressing the bourgeois attitude toward "The Twelve," says openly and most maliciously, that the acts of Blok's heroes are characteristic of the "comrades," he fulfills the task he has set himself, namely, to slander the Revolution. A Red guard kills Katka, for jealousy. Is this possible, or is it impossible? It is entirely possible. But had such a Red guard been caught, he would have been sentenced to be shot by the Revolutionary Tribunal. The Revolution, which applies the frightful sword of Terrorism, guards it severely as a State right. Were Terror used for personal ends, the Revolution would be threatened by inevitable destruction. As early as the beginning of 1918, the Revolution put an end to anarchistic unruliness, and carried on a merciless and victorious struggle with the disintegrating methods of guerrilla warfare.

"Open up the cellars; the sansculottes are now having their holiday." And this happened. But what bloody collisions took place for this very reason between the Red guards and the hooligans! "Soberness" was written on the banner of the Revolution. The Revolution was ascetic, especially in this most intense period. Therefore Blok does not give a picture of the Revolution, and certainly not of the work of its vanguard, but of its accompanying phenomena that were called forth by it, but which were in essence contrary to it. The poet seems to want to say that he feels the Revolution in this also, that he feels its sweep, the terrible commotion in the heart, the awakening, the bravery, the risk, and that even in these disgusting, senseless, and bloody manifestations is reflected the spirit of the Revolution, which, to Blok, is the spirit of Christ rampant.

Of all the things that have been written about Blok and about "The Twelve," perhaps the most impossible are the writings of Mr. Chukovsky. His booklet about Blok is not worse than his other books. They reveal an external vivacity combined with an inability to bring the least order into his thoughts, an unevenness of exposition, a provincial newspaper rhythm, as well as a meager pedantism and a tendency to generalize on the basis of external antitheses. And Chukovsky always discovers what no one else has ever seen. Has anyone ever considered "The Twelve" as the poem of the Revolution, that very Revolution that took place in October? Heaven forbid! Chukovsky will immediately explain all about it, and will reconcile Blok with "public opinion." "The Twelve" does not sing the Revolution, but Russia, in spite of the Revolution: "Here is an obstinate nationalism which, unembarrassed by anything, wants to see holiness even in ugliness, as long as this ugliness is Russia." (K. Chukovsky, *A Book About Alexander Blok*). Blok then accepts Russia, in spite of the Revolution, or, to be more exact, in spite of the ugliness of the Revolution. This seems to be his reasoning; that much seems definite. At the same time, however, it turns out that Blok was always (!) the poet of the Revolution, "but not of the Revolution which is taking place now, but of another revolution, national and Russian...." This is jumping from the frying pan into the fire. Thus Blok in "The Twelve" did not sing of Russia in spite of the Revolution, but sang of a revolution, not of the one that has taken place, but of another one, the exact address of which is fully known to Chukovsky. This is the way this talented fellow says it: "The Revolution he sang of was not the Revolution which was taking place around him, but another one, a true one, a flaming one." But we just heard that he sang of ugliness, and not of a burning flame, and he sang of this ugliness because it was a Russian one, and not because it was revolutionary. And now we discover that he did not make his peace with the ugliness of the true revolution at all, just because that ugliness was Russian, but that he sang exaltingly of a revolution, of another one, a true and flaming one, only because that revolution was directed against an existing ugliness.

Vanka kills Katka with the rifle that was given him by his class to defend the Revolution. We say that this is incidental to the Revolution, but not of the Revolution. Blok means his poem to say: I accept this also, because here, also, I hear the dynamics of events, and the music of the storm. Now comes his interpreter Chukovsky, and explains it. The murder of Katka by Vanka is the ugliness of the Revolution. Blok accepts Russia, even with this ugliness, because it is Russian. But at the same time when he sings of the murder of Katka by Vanka and of the pillaging of the houses, Blok sings of a revolution, but not of this ugly present-day real Russian Revolution, but of another, a truer, flaming one. The address of this true and flaming revolution Chukovsky will tell us soon, right away.

But if the Revolution to Blok is Russia herself, just as she is, then what is the meaning of the "orator," who looks upon the Revolution as treason? What is the meaning of the priest who walks by the side? What is the meaning of "the old world like a mangy cur"? What is the meaning of Denikin, Miliukov, Chernov, and the émigrés? Russia has been split in half. That is the Revolution. Blok called one-half a mangy cur, and the other half he blessed with the blessings at his command, that is, with verses and with Christ. But Chukovsky declares all this to be a mere misunderstanding. What charlatanism of words, what an indecent slovenliness of thought, what a spiritual devastation, what a cheap and mean and shameful jabber of speech!

To be sure, Blok is not one of ours, but he reached toward us. And in doing so, he broke down. But the result of his impulse is the most significant work of our epoch. His poem, "The Twelve," will remain forever.

CHAPTER FOUR

Futurism

Futurism is a European phenomenon, and it is interesting because, in spite of the teachings of the Russian Formalist School, it did not shut itself within the confines of art, but from the first, especially in Italy, it connected itself with political and social events.

Futurism reflected in art the historic development that began in the middle of the 1890s, and that became merged in the World War. Capitalist society passed through two decades of unparalleled economic prosperity, which destroyed the old concepts of wealth and power, and elaborated new standards, new criteria of the possible and of the impossible, and urged people toward new exploits.

At the same time, the social movement lived on officially in the automatism of yesterday. The armed peace, with its patches of diplomacy, the hollow parliamentary systems, the external and internal politics based on the system of safety valves and brakes, all this weighed heavily on poetry at a time when the air, charged with accumulated electricity, gave sign of impending great explosions. Futurism was the "foreboding" of all this in art.

A phenomenon was observed that has been repeated in history more than once, namely, that the backward countries that were without any special degree of spiritual culture, reflected in their ideology the achievements of the advanced countries more brilliantly and strongly. In this way, German thought of the eighteenth and nineteenth centuries reflected the economic achievements of England and the political achievements of France. In the same way, Futurism obtained its most brilliant expression, not in

112

America and not in Germany, but in Italy and in Russia.

With the exception of architecture, art is based on technique only in its last analysis, that is, only to the extent to which technique is the basis of all cultural superstructures. The practical dependence of art, especially of the art of words, upon material technique is insignificant. A poem that sings the skyscrapers, the dirigibles, and the submarines can be written in a faraway corner of some Russian province on yellow paper and with a broken stub of a pencil. In order to inflame the bright imagination of that province, it is quite enough if the skyscrapers, the dirigibles, and the submarines are in America. The human word is the most portable of all materials.

Futurism originated in an eddy of bourgeois art, and could not have originated otherwise. Its violent oppositional character does not contradict this in the least.

The intellectuals are extremely heterogeneous. At the same time, each recognized school of art is a well paid school. It is headed by mandarins with their many little balls. As a general rule, these mandarins of art develop the methods of their schools to the greatest subtlety, while at the same time they use up their whole supply of powder. Then some objective change, such as a political upheaval or a social storm, arouses the literary Bohemia, the youth, the geniuses who are of military age, who, cursing the satiated and vulgar bourgeois culture, secretly dream of a few little balls for themselves, and gilded ones, too, if possible.

When investigators define the social nature of early Futurism and ascribe a decisive significance to the violent protests against bourgeois life and art, they simply do not know the history of literary tendencies well enough. The French romanticists, as well as the German, always spoke scathingly of bourgeois morality and philistine life. More than that, they wore long hair, flirted with a green complexion, and for the ultimate shaming of the bourgeoisie, Theophile Gautier put on a sensational red vest. The Futurist yellow blouse is undoubtedly a grandniece to this romantic vest, which inspired such horror to the papas and mamas. As is known, nothing cataclysmic followed these rebellious protests of the long hair or the red vest of romanticism, and bourgeois public opinion safely adopted these gentlemen romantics and canonized them in their school textbooks.

It is extremely naive to contrast the dynamics of Italian Futurism and its sympathies to the Revolution, with the "decadent" character of the bourgeoisie. One ought not to represent the bourgeoisie as a withered old cat. No, the beast of imperialism is bold, flexible, and has claws. Or is the lesson of 1914 already forgotten? For its war, the bourgeoisie used extensively the feelings and moods that were destined by their nature to feed rebellion. In France, the War was pictured as the final completion of the work of the Great Revolution. And did not the belligerent bourgeoisie actually arrange revolutions in other lands? In Italy, the interventionists (that is, those in favor of intervention in the War) were the "revolutionists," that is, the Republicans, Free Masons, social chauvinists, and Futurists. Last of all, did not Italian fascism come into power by "revolutionary" methods, by bringing into action the masses, the mobs, and the millions, and by tempering and arming them? It is not an accident, it is not a misunderstanding, that Italian Futurism has merged into the torrent of fascism; it is entirely in accord with the law of cause and effect.

Russian Futurism was born in a society that passed through the preparatory class of fighting the priest Rasputin, and was preparing for the democratic Revolution of February, 1917.* This gave our Futurism certain advantages. It caught rhythms of movement, of action, of attack, and of destruction that were as yet vague. It carried its struggle for a place in the sun more sharply, more resolutely, and more noisily than all preceding schools, which was in accordance with its activist moods and points of view. To be sure, a young Futurist did not go to the factories and to the mills, but he made a lot of noise in cafes, he banged his fist upon music stands, he put on a yellow blouse, he painted his cheeks and threatened vaguely with his fist.

The workers' Revolution in Russia broke loose before Futurism had time to free itself from its childish habits, from its yellow blouses, and from its excessive excitement, and before it could be officially recognized, that is, made into a politically harmless artistic school whose style is acceptable. The seizure of power by the proletariat caught Futurism still in the stage of being a persecuted group.

And this fact alone pushed Futurism toward the new mas-

---

*New Style, March 1917. (Trans. note.)

ters of life, especially since the contact and rapprochement with the Revolution was made easier for Futurism by its philosophy, that is, by its lack of respect for old values and by its dynamics. But Futurism carried the features of its social origin, bourgeois Bohemia, into the new stage of its development.

In the advance guard of literature, Futurism is no less a product of the poetic past than any other literary school of the present day. To say that Futurism has freed art of its thousand-year-old bonds of bourgeoisdom is to estimate thousands of years very cheaply. The call of the Futurists to break with the past, to do away with Pushkin, to liquidate tradition, etc., has a meaning in so far as it is addressed to the old literary caste, to the closed-in circle of the intelligentsia. In other words, it has a meaning only insofar as the Futurists are busy cutting the cord that binds them to the priests of bourgeois literary tradition.

But the meaninglessness of this call becomes evident as soon as it is addressed to the proletariat. The working class does not have to, and cannot break with literary tradition, because the working class is not in the grip of such tradition. The working class does not know the old literature, it still has to commune with it, it still has to master Pushkin, to absorb him, and so overcome him. The Futurist break with the past is, after all, a tempest in the closed-in world of the intelligentsia, which grew up on Pushkin, Fet, Tiutschev, Briusov, Balmont, and Blok, and who are passive, not because they are infected with a superstitious veneration for the forms of the past, but because they have nothing in their soul that calls for new forms. They simply have nothing to say. They sing the old feelings over again with slightly new words. The Futurists have done well to push away from them. But it is not necessary to make a universal law of development out of the act of pushing away.

A Bohemian nihilism exists in the exaggerated Futurist rejection of the past, but not a proletarian revolutionism. We Marxists live in traditions, and we have not stopped being revolutionists on account of it. We elaborated and lived through the traditions of the Paris Commune, even before our first revolution. Then the traditions of 1905 were added to them, by which we nourished ourselves and by which we prepared the second revolution. Going farther back, we connected the Commune with the June days of 1848, and with the great French Revolution. In the field of theory, we based ourselves, through Marx, on Hegel and on English classical political economy. We were educated, and we entered the struggle during an organic epoch, and we lived on revolutionary traditions. More than one literary tendency was born under our eyes, which declared a merciless war upon "bourgeoisdom," and which looked upon us as not quite whole. Just as the wind always returns to its own circles, so these literary revolutionists and destroyers of traditions found their way to the Academy. The October Revolution appeared to the intelligentsia, including its literary left wing, as a complete destruction of its known world, of that very world from which it broke away from time to time, for the purpose of creating new schools, and to which it invariably returned. To us, on the contrary, the Revolution appeared as the embodiment of a familiar tradition, internally digested. From a world that we rejected theoretically, and that we undermined practically, we entered into a world that was already familiar to us, as a tradition and a vision. Here lies the incompatibility of psychologic type between the communist, who is a political revolutionist, and the Futurist, who is a revolutionary innovator of form. This is the source of the misunderstandings between them. The trouble is not that Futurism "denies" the holy traditions of the intelligentsia. On the contrary, it lies in the fact that it does not feel itself to be part of the revolutionary tradition. We stepped into the Revolution while Futurism fell into it.

But the situation is not at all hopeless. Futurism will not go back "to its circles" because these circles do not exist any longer. And this not insignificant circumstance gives Futurism the possibility of a rebirth, of entering into the new art, not as an all determining current, but as an important component part.

■   ■   ■

Russian Futurism is composed of several elements, which are quite independent from one another, and are often contradictory; philologic constructions and surmises considerably imbued with the archaic (Khlebnikov, Kruchenikh), which at any rate lie outside the sphere of poetry; a poetics, that is, a doctrine about the methods and processes of wordmaking; a philosophy of art, in fact two whole philosophies, a formalistic one (Shklovsky), and another one, more Marxist (Arvatov, Chuzhak, etc.); finally, poetry itself, the living work. We are not considering their literary insolence as an independent element, because it is generally combined with one of these fundamental elements. When Kruchenikh says that the meaningless syllables, "Dir, bul, tschil," contain more poetry than all of Pushkin (or something to this effect) it is something midway between philologic poetics, and the insolence of bad manners. In a more sober form, Kruchenikh's idea may mean that the orchestration of verse in the key of "Dir, bul, tschil" suits the structure of the Russian language and the spirit of its sounds more than Pushkin's orchestration, which is unconsciously influenced by the French language. Whether this is correct or incorrect, it is evident that "Dir, bul, tschil" is not a poetic extract from a Futurist work—so there is really nothing for one to compare. Perhaps it is possible that someone will write poems in this musical and philologic key that will be greater than Pushkin's. But we have to wait.

Khlebnikov's and Kruchenikh's word-forms also lie outside poetry. They are philology of a doubtful character, poetics in part, but not poetry. It is absolutely unquestionable that language lives and develops, creating new words from within, and discarding antiquated ones. But a language does this extremely cautiously and calculatingly, and according to the strictest need. Every new great epoch gives an impetus to language. The latter hurriedly absorbs a large number of neologisms, and then reregisters them in its own way, discarding all that are unnecessary and foreign. Khlebnikov's or Kruchenikh's making ten or one hundred new derivative words out of existing roots may have a certain philological interest; they may, in a certain though very modest degree, facilitate the development of the living and even of the poetic language, and forecast a time when the evolution of speech will be more consciously directed. But this very work, whose character is subsidiary to art, is outside of poetry.

One need not fall into a state of pious adoration at the sound of superrational poetry, which resembles verbal musical scales and exercises and that is perhaps useful to pupils, but entirely inappropriate to the platform. At any rate, it is quite clear that to substitute the exercises of the "superreason" for poetry would stifle poetry. But Futurism will not go along this line. Mayakovsky, who is unquestionably a poet, takes his words generally from a standard dictionary and very rarely from Khlebnikov or

Kruchenikh, and as time goes on, Mayakovsky uses arbitrary word-forms and neologisms more and more rarely.

The problems raised by the theorists of the "Lef" group about art and a machine industry, about art that does not embellish life, but forms it, about conscious influence upon the development of language and systematic formation of words, about biomechanics as the education of the activities of man in the spirit of the greatest rationality, and therefore of the greatest beauty—are all problems that are extremely significant and interesting from the point of view of building a socialist culture.

Unfortunately, the "Lef" colors these problems by a Utopian sectarianism. Even when they mark out correctly the general trend of development in the field of art or life, the theorists of "Lef" anticipate history and contrast their scheme or their prescription with that which is. They thus have no bridge to the future. They remind one of anarchists who anticipate the absence of government in the future, and who contrast their scheme with the politics, parliaments, and several other realities that the present ship of State must, in their imagination, of course, throw overboard. In practice, therefore, they bury their noses before they have hardly freed their tails. Mayakovsky proves, by complicated and rhymed verses, the superfluousness of verse and rhyme, and promises to write mathematical formulas, though we have mathematicians for that purpose. When the passionate experimenter, Meyerhold, the furious Vissarion Belinsky of the stage, produces on the stage the few semi-rhythmic movements he has taught those actors who are weak in dialogue, and calls this biomechanics, the result is—abortive. To tear out of the future that which can only develop as an inseparable part of it, and to hurriedly materialize this partial anticipation in the present day dearth and before the cold footlights, is only to make an impression of provincial dilettantism. And there is nothing more inimical to a new art than provincialism and dilettantism.

The new architecture will be made up of two halves; of new problems and of a new technical means of mastering both new and old material. The new problem will not be the building of a temple, or a castle, or a private mansion, but rather a people's home, a hotel for the masses, a commons, a community house, or a school of gigantic dimensions. The materials and the method of using them will be determined by the economic condition of the country at the moment when architecture will have become ready to solve its problems. To tear architectural construction out of the future is only arbitrariness, clever and individual. However, a new style cannot be reconciled to individual arbitrariness. The writers of the "Lef" themselves correctly point out that a new style develops where the machine industry produces for an impersonal consumer. The telephone apparatus is an example of a new style. The sleeping cars, the staircases and the stations of the subway, the elevators, all these are undoubtedly elements of a new style, just as were metallic bridges, covered markets, skyscrapers, and cranes. Thus beyond a practical problem and the steady work of solving this problem, one cannot create a new architectural style. The effort to reason out such a style by the method of deduction from the nature of the proletariat, from its collectivism, activism, atheism, and so forth, is the purest idealism, and will give nothing but an ingenious expression of one's ego, an arbitrary allegorism, and the same old provincial dilettantism.

The error of the "Lef," at least of some of its theorists, appears to us in its most generalized form, when they make an ultimatum for the fusion of art with life. It is not to be argued that the separation of art from other aspects of social life was the result of the class structure of society, that the self-sufficient character of art is merely the reverse side of the fact that art became the property of the privileged classes, and that the evolution of art in the future will follow the path of a growing fusion with life, that is, with production, with popular holidays, and with the collective group life. It is good that the "Lef" understands this and explains it. But it is not good when they present a short time ultimatum on the basis of the present-day art, when they say: leave your "lathe" and fuse with life. In other words, the poets, the painters, the sculptors, the actors must cease to reflect, to depict, to write poems, to paint pictures, to carve sculptures, to speak before the footlights, but they must carry their art directly into life. But how, and where, and through what gates? Of course, one may hail every attempt to carry as much rhythm and sound and color as is possible into popular holidays and meetings and processions. But one must have a little historic vision, at least, to understand that between our present-day economic and cultural poverty and the time of the fusion of art with life, that is, between the time when life will reach such proportions that it will be entirely formed by art, more than one generation will have come and gone. Whether for good or for bad, the "lathelike" art will remain for many years more, and will be the instrument of the artistic and social development of the masses and their aesthetic enjoyment, and this is true not only of the art of painting, but of lyrics, novels, comedies, tragedies, sculpture, and symphony. To reject art as a means of picturing and imaging knowledge because of one's opposition to the contemplative and impressionistic bourgeois art of the last few decades is to strike from the hands of the class that is building a new society its most important weapon. Art, it is said, is not a mirror, but a hammer: it does not reflect, it shapes. But at present even the handling of a hammer is taught with the help of a mirror, a sensitive film that records all the movements. Photography and motion-picture photography, owing to their passive accuracy of depiction, are becoming important educational instruments in the field of labor. If one cannot get along without a mirror, even in shaving oneself, how can one reconstruct oneself or one's life, without seeing oneself in the "mirror" of literature? Of course no one speaks about an exact mirror. No one even thinks of asking the new literature to have a mirror-like impassivity. The deeper literature is, and the more it is imbued with the desire to shape life, the more significantly and dynamically it will be able to "picture" life.

What does it mean to "deny experiences," that is, deny individual psychology in literature and on the stage? This is a late and long outlived protest of the left wing of the intelligentsia against the passive realism of the Chekhov school and against dreamy symbolism. If the experiences of Uncle Vanya have lost a little of their freshness—and this sin has actually taken place—it is nonetheless true that Uncle Vanya is not the only one with an inner life. In what way, on what grounds, and in the name of what, can art turn its back to the inner life of present-day man who is building a new external world, and thereby rebuilding himself? If art will not help this new man to educate himself, to strengthen and refine himself, then what is it for? And how can it organize the inner life, if it does not penetrate it and reproduce it? Here Futurism merely repeats its own ABCs, which are now quite behind the times.

The same may be said about institutional life. Futurism arose as a protest against the art of petty realists who sponged on life. Literature suffocated and became stupid in the stagnant little world of the lawyer, the student, the amorous lady, the district civil servant, and of all their feelings, their joys and their sorrows. But should one carry one's protest against sponging on life to the extent of separating literature from the conditions and forms of human life? If the Futurist protest against a shallow realism had its historic justification, it was only because it made room for a new artistic recreating of life, for destruction and reconstruction on new pivots.

It is curious that while denying that it is the mission of art to picture life, the "Lef" points to *Nepoputschitsa* of Brick as a model of prose. What is this work, if not a picture of life, in the form of an almost communist 'change? The trouble does not lie in the fact that the communists are not pictured here sweet as sugar or hard as steel, but in the fact that between the author and the vulgar environment that he describes, there isn't an inch of perspective. But for art to be able to transform as well as to reflect, there must be a great distance between the artist and life, just as there is between the revolutionist and political reality.

In reply to criticisms against the "Lef," which are often more insulting than convincing, the point is emphasized that the "Lef" is still constantly seeking. Undoubtedly the "Lef" seeks more than it has found. But this is not a sufficient reason why the Party cannot do that which is persistently recommended, and canonize the "Lef" or even a definite wing of it, as "Communist Art." It is as impossible to canonize seekings as it is impossible to arm an army with an unrealized invention.

But does this mean that the "Lef" stands absolutely on a false road, and that we can have nothing to do with it? No, it does not mean this. The situation is not that the Party has definite and fixed ideas on the question of art in the future, and that a certain group is sabotaging them. This is not the case at all. The Party has not, and cannot have, ready-made decisions on versification, on the evolution of the theater, on the renovation of the literary language, on architectural style, etc., just as in another field the Party has not and cannot have ready-made decisions on the best kind of fertilization, on the most correct organization of transport, and on the most perfect machine guns. But as regards machine guns and transportation and fertilization, the practical decisions are needed immediately. What does the Party do then? It assigns certain Party workers to the task of considering and mastering these problems, and it checks up these Party workers by the practical results of their achievements. In the field of art the question is both simpler and more complex. As far as the political use of art is concerned, or the impossibility of allowing such use by our enemies, the Party has sufficient experience, insight, decision, and resource. But the actual development of art, and its struggle for new forms are not part of the Party's tasks, nor is it its concern. The Party does not delegate anyone for such work. At the same time, a certain point of contact exists between the problems of art, politics, technique, and economics. It is necessary for the inner interdependence of these problems. This is what the group of the "Lef" is concerned with. This group plays tricks, plunges to this side and that, and—let them not be offended by this—does a good deal of theoretical bluffing. But did we not, and are we not also bluffing in fields much more vitally important? In the second place, did we try seriously to correct errors of theoretic approach or of partisan enthusiasm in practical work? We have no reason to doubt that the "Lef" group is striving seriously to work in the interest of socialism, that it is profoundly interested in the problems of art, and that it wants to be guided by a Marxian criterion. Why, then, do they begin with a rupture, and not with an effort to influence and to assimilate? The question is not at all so imminent. The Party, has plenty of time for an examining, for a careful influencing and a selection. Or have we so much skilled strength that we can so lightheartedly be wasteful of it? But the center of gravity lies, after all, not in the theoretic elaboration of the problems of the new art, but in its poetic expression. What is the situation as regards the artistic expression of Futurism and its gropings and accomplishments? Here there is even less ground for haste and intolerance.

Today, one can hardly deny entirely the Futurist achievements in art, especially in poetry. With very few exceptions, all our present-day poetry has been influenced by Futurism, directly or indirectly. One cannot dispute Mayakovsky's influence on a whole series of proletarian poets. Constructivism has also made significant conquests, though not at all in the direction it had marked out for itself. Articles are continually being published on the complete futility and on the counterrevolutionary character

of Futurism between covers made by the hand of the Constructivist. In the most official editions, Futurist poems are published
side by side with the most destructive summings up of Futurism.
The Proletkult [the organization for proletarian culture] is united
to the Futurists by living cords. *Gorn* is edited at present in a
quite clear spirit of Futurism. To be sure, there is no use exaggerating the significance of these facts, because they take place, as in
the great majority of all our groups of art, in an upper, and for
the time being quite superficial stratum, and are very feebly connected with the working masses. But it would be stupid to close
one's eyes to these facts, and to treat Futurism as a charlatan invention of a decadent intelligentsia. Even if tomorrow the fact
will be disclosed that the strength of Futurism is declining—and I
do not consider this quite impossible—today, at any rate, the
strength of Futurism is greater than all those tendencies at whose
expense Futurism is spreading.

The original Futurism of Russia, as has already been said,
was the revolt of Bohemia, that is, of the semi-pauperized left
wing of the intelligentsia, against the closed-in and caste-like aesthetics of the bourgeois intelligentsia. Through the outer layer of
this poetic revolt was felt the pressure of deep social forces,
which Futurism itself did not quite understand. The struggle
against the old vocabulary and syntax of poetry, regardless of all
its Bohemian extravagances, was a progressive revolt against
a vocabulary that was cramped and selected artificially with
the view of being undisturbed by anything extraneous; a revolt
against impressionism, which was sipping life through a straw; a
revolt against symbolism, which had become false in its heavenly
vacuity, against Zinaida Hippius and her kind, and against all the
other squeezed lemons and picked chicken bones of the little
world of the liberal-mystic intelligentsia. If we survey attentively
the period left behind, we cannot help but realize how vital and
progressive was the work of the Futurists in the field of philology.
Without exaggerating the dimensions of this "revolution" in language, we must realize that Futurism has pushed out of poetry
many worn words and phrases, and has made them full-blooded
again and, in a few cases, has happily created new words and
phrases that have entered, or are entering, into the vocabulary
of poetry and that can enrich the living language. This refers
not only to the separate word, but also to its place among other

words, that is, to syntax. In the field of word combinations, as well as in the field of word formations, Futurism truly has gone somewhat beyond the limits that a living language can hold. The same thing, however, has happened with the Revolution; and is the "sin" of every living movement. It is true, the Revolution, especially its conscious vanguard, shows more self-criticism than the Futurists, but in return for this, the Revolution has also had more resistance from the outside, and, one may hope, will receive more in the future. The superfluous will fall and does fall away, but the fundamentally purifying and truly revolutionizing work that is done in the field of poetic language will remain.

Nor can one help recognize and value the progressive and creative work of Futurism in the field of rhythm and rhyme. The indifferent and those who merely tolerate these things because they are bequeathed to us by our ancestors may regard all Futurist innovations as a troublesome business that demands a certain expenditure of attention. In connection with this, one can raise the question in general: are rhythm and rhyme necessary at all? Quite curiously enough, Mayakovsky himself proves from time to time, in lines that have a very complex rhythm, that rhythm is unnecessary. A purely logical approach destroys the question of artistic form. One must judge this question not with one's reason, which does not go beyond formal logic, but with one's whole mind, which includes the irrational, in so far as it is alive and vital. Poetry is not a rational but an emotional thing, and human psychology, which has absorbed biologic rhythms, the rhythms and rhythmic combinations related to collective work, seeks to express them in an idealized form in sound and song and in artistic words. As long as such a need is a vital one, the Futurist rhythms and rhymes that are more flexible, bolder and more varied, represent a surer and more valuable acquisition. And this acquisition has already had its influence outside the purely Futurist groups.

In the orchestration of verse, the conquests of the Futurists are just as indisputable. One must not forget that the sound of a word is an acoustic accompaniment of its sense. If the Futurists have sinned, and still sin by their almost monstrous bias for sound as against sense, it is only the enthusiasm of the "infantile sickness of leftism," which, of course, must be rejected as the ravings of a new poetic school, which has felt in a new way and with a fresh ear, sound as opposed to the sleek routine of words. Of course, the overwhelming majority of the working class today are not interested in these questions. The greater part of the vanguard of the working class is too busy for them—it has other, more urgent tasks. But there is also the tomorrow. That tomorrow will demand a much more attentive and accurate attitude, a much more masterly and artistic one toward language, as the fundamental instrument of culture—not only toward the language of verse, but also of prose, and especially of prose. A word never covers a concept precisely in the whole concrete meaning with which it is taken in each given case. On the other hand, a word has sound and outline, not only to our ear and for our eye, but also for our logic and imagination. It is possible to make thought more precise through a careful selection of words, only if the latter are weighed from all sides, which means acoustically as well, and only if they are combined in the most thought-out manner. Here haphazard methods will not do; micro-metric instruments are necessary. Routine, tradition, habit, and carelessness must all make room for thoughtful systematic work. On its best side Futurism is a protest against the haphazard, which forms a powerful literary school of its own, and which has very influential representatives in every field.

In Gorlov's unpublished work, which, in my opinion, traces incorrectly the international origin of Futurism, and which violates a historic perspective and identifies Futurism with proletarian poetry, the achievements of Futurism in art and form are very thoughtfully and weightily summarized. Gorlov points out correctly that the Futurist revolution in form, which grew out of the revolt against the old aesthetics, reflects in the plane of theory the revolt against the stagnant and smelly life which produced that aesthetics. And that this caused in Mayakovsky, who is the greatest poet of the school, and in his most intimate friends, a revolt against the social order that produced that discarded life with its discarded aesthetics. That is why these poets are organically connected with October. Gorlov's outline is correct, but it must be made more precise and more definite. It is true that new words and new word combinations, new rhythms and new rhymes were necessary, because Futurism, in its feeling for the world, re-arranged events and facts, and established, that is, discovered, for itself new relationships between them.

Futurism is against mysticism, against the passive deification of nature, against the aristocratic and every other kind of laziness, against dreaminess, and against lachrymosity—and stands for technique, for scientific organization, for the machine, for planfulness, for willpower, for courage, for speed, for precision, and for the new man, who is armed with all these things. The connection of the aesthetics "revolt" with the moral and social revolt is direct; both enter entirely and fully into the life experience of the active, new, young, and untamed section of the intelligentsia of the Left, the creative Bohemia. Disgust against the limitations and the vulgarity of the old life produces a new artistic style as a way of escape, and thus the disgust is liquidated. In different combinations, and on different historic bases, we have seen the disgust of the intelligentsia form more than one new style. But that was always the end of it. This time, the proletarian Revolution caught Futurism in a certain stage of its growth and pushed it forward. Futurists became communists. By this very act they entered the sphere of more profound questions and relationships, which far transcended the limits of their own little world, and which were not quite worked out organically in their soul. That is why Futurists, even including Mayakovsky, are weakest artistically at those points where they finish as communists. This is more the result of their spiritual past than of their social origin. The Futurist poets have not mastered the elements of the communist point of view and world-attitude sufficiently to find an organic expression for them in words; they have not entered, so to speak, into their blood. That is why they are frequently subject to artistic and psychologic defeats, to stilted forms and to making much noise about nothing. In its most revolutionary and compelling works, Futurism becomes stylization. Nevertheless, the young poet Bezimensky, who is so much obligated to Mayakovsky, gives a really true artistic expression of the communist point of view; the reason being that Bezimensky was not a poet already formed when he came to communism, but was spiritually born in communism.

It is possible to argue, and it has been argued more than once, that even the proletarian doctrine and program were made by members of the bourgeois and democratic intelligentsia. There is a great difference here. The economic and historico-philosophic doctrine of the proletariat consists of objective knowledge. If that cabinetmaker, Bebel, who was ascetically economical in life and thought, and who had a mind as keen as a razor, had been the creator of the theory of surplus value, and not that universally educated doctor of philosophy, Karl Marx, he would have formulated it in a much more accessible and simple and one-sided work. The wealth and variety of thoughts, of arguments, of images, and of quotations in *Capital,* undoubtedly reveal the "intellectualist" background of this great book. But, as the question here concerns objective knowledge, the essence of *Capital* came to Bebel as his property, and to thousands and millions of other proletarians. In the field of poetry we deal with the process of feeling the world in images, and not with the process of knowing the world scientifically. The life, the personal environment, the cycle of personal experience exercises, therefore, a determining influence upon artistic creation. To reshape the world of feelings, which one has absorbed from one's childhood, by means of a scientific program, is the most difficult inner labor. Not everyone is capable of it. That is why there are many people in this world who think as revolutionists and who feel as Philistines. And that is why we feel, in Futurist poetry, even in that section that has given itself entirely to the Revolution, a revolutionism that is more Bohemian than proletarian.

■　　■　　■

Mayakovsky is a big, or, as Blok defines him, an enormous talent. He has the capacity of turning things that we have seen many times around in such a way that they seem new. He handles words and the dictionary like a bold master who works according to his own laws, regardless of whether his artisanship pleases or not. Many of his images and phrases and expressions have entered literature, and will remain in it for a long time, if not forever. He has his own construction, his own imaging, his own rhythm, and his own rhyme.

Mayakovsky's artistic design is almost always significant, and sometimes grandiose. The poet gathers into his own circle war and revolution, heaven and hell. Mayakovsky is hostile to mysticism, to every kind of hypocrisy, to the exploitation of man by man; his sympathies are entirely on the side of the struggling proletariat. He does not claim to be the priest of art, at least, not a priest with principles; on the contrary, he is entirely ready to place his art at the service of the Revolution.

But even in this big talent, or, to be more correct, in the entire creative personality of Mayakovsky, there is no necessary correlation between its component parts; there is no equilibrium, not even a dynamic one. Mayakovsky shows the greatest weakness where a sense of proportion and a capacity for self-criticism are needed.

It was more natural for Mayakovsky to accept the Revolution than for any other Russian poet, because it was in accordance with his entire development. Many roads lead the intelligentsia to the Revolution (not all of them lead to the goal) —and therefore it is important to define and to estimate Mayakovsky's line of approach more accurately. There is the road of the rustic school of the intelligentsia and of the capricious "fellow travelers" (we have already spoken of them); there is the road of the mystics, who seek higher "music" (A. Blok); there is the road of the "Changing Landmarks" group, and of those who have merely reconciled themselves (Shkapskaya, Shaginyan); there is the road of the rationalists and of the eclectics (Briusov, Gorodetsky, and Shaginyan again). There are many other roads; they cannot all be named. Mayakovsky came by the shortest route, by that of the rebellious persecuted Bohemia. For Mayakovsky, the Revolution was a true and profound experience, because it descended with thunder and lightning upon the very things that Mayakovsky, in his own way, hated, with which he had not as yet made his peace. Herein lies his strength. Mayakovsky's revolutionary individualism poured itself enthusiastically into the proletarian Revolution, but did not blend with it. His subconscious feeling for the city, for nature, for the whole world, is not that of a worker, but of a Bohemian. "The bald-headed street lamp which pulls the stocking off from the street" —this striking image alone, which is extremely characteristic of Mayakovsky, throws more light upon the Bohemian and city quality of the poet than all possible discussion. The impudent and cynical tone of many images, especially of those of the first half of his creative career, betrays the all-too-clear stamp of the artistic cabaret, of the cafe, and of all the rest of it.

Mayakovsky is closer to the dynamic quality of the Revolution and to its stern courage than to the mass character of its heroism, deeds, and experiences. Just as the ancient Greek was an anthropomorphist and naively thought of the forces of nature as resembling himself, so our poet is a Mayakomorphist and fills the squares, the streets, and fields of the Revolution with his own personality. True, extremes meet. The universalization of one's ego breaks down, to some extent, the limits of one's individuality, and brings one nearer to the collectivity—from the reverse end. But this is true only to a certain degree. The individualistic and Bohemian arrogance—in contrast, not to humility, which no one wants, but to a necessary sense of the measure of things—runs through everything written by Mayakovsky. He has frequently a very high degree of pathos in his works, but there is not always strength behind it. The poet is too much in evidence. He allows too little independence to events and facts, so that it is not the Revolution that is struggling with obstacles, but it is Mayakovsky who does athletic stunts in the arena of words. Sometimes he performs miracles indeed, but every now and then he makes a heroic effort and lifts a hollow weight.

At every step Mayakovsky speaks about himself, now in the first person, and now in the third, now individually, and now dissolving himself in mankind. When he wants to elevate man, he makes him be Mayakovsky. He assumes a familiarity to the greatest events of history. This is the most intolerable, as well as the most dangerous thing in his works. One can't speak about stilts or buskins in his case; such props are too poor. Mayakovsky has one foot on Mont Blanc and the other on Elbrus. His voice drowns thunder; can one wonder that he treats history familiarly, and is on intimate terms with the Revolution? But this is most dangerous, for given such gigantic standards, everywhere and in everything, such thunderous shouts (the poet's favorite word) against the horizon of Elbrus and Mont Blanc—the proportions of our worldly affairs vanish, and it is impossible to establish the difference between a little thing and a big. That is why Mayakovsky speaks of the most intimate thing, such as love, as if he were speaking about the migration of nations. For the same reason he cannot find different words for the Revolution. He is always shooting at the edge, and, as every artilleryman knows, such gunning gives a minimum of hits and tells most heavily on the guns.

It is true that hyperbolism reflects to a certain degree the rage of our times. But this does not offer a wholesale justification of art. It is hard to shout louder than the War or the Revolution, and it is easy to break down. A sense of measure in art is the same as having a sense of realism in politics. The principal fault of Futurist poetry, even in its best examples, lies in this absence of a sense of measure; it has lost the measure of the salon, and it has not yet found the measure of the street. But one has to find it. If you force your voice in the street, it will become hoarse and shriek and break, and the impression of the word will be lost. You must speak in the voice given you by nature, and not in a voice that is louder than you have. But if you know how, you can use your voice to the fullest extent. Mayakovsky shouts too often, where he should merely speak; that is why his shouting, in those places where he ought to shout, seems insufficient. The poet's pathos is destroyed by shouting and hoarseness.

Mayakovsky's weighty images, though frequently splendid, quite often disintegrate the whole, and paralyze the action. The poet evidently feels this himself; that is why he is yearning for another extreme, for the language of "mathematical formulas," a language unnatural to poetry. It makes one think that the self-sufficient imagery that Imagism has in common with Futurism (which is beginning to resemble our peasant-singing Imagism!) has its roots in the village background of our culture. It is more related to the church of Vassili the Blessed than to a steel bridge, but, whatever may be the historic and cultural explanation of this, the fact remains that the thing that is most lacking in Mayakovsky's works is action. This may look like a paradox, for Futurism is entirely founded on action. But here enters the unimpeachable dialectics; an excess of violent imagery results in quiescence. Action must correspond to the mechanics of our perception and to the rhythm of our feelings, if it is to be perceived artistically, and even physically. A work of art must show the gradual growth of an image, of a mood, of a plot, or of an intrigue to its climax, and must not throw the reader about from one end to another end, no matter if it is done by the most skillful boxing blows of Imagery. Each phrase, each expression, each image of Mayakovsky's works tries to be the climax. That is why the whole "piece" has no climax. The spectator has a feeling that he has to spend himself in parts, and the whole eludes him. To climb a mountain is difficult but worthwhile, but a walk across plowed-up country is no less fatiguing and gives much less joy.

Mayakovsky's works have no peak; they are not disciplined internally. The parts refuse to obey the whole. Each part tries to be separate. It develops its own dynamics, without considering the welfare of the whole. That is why it is without entity or dynamics. The Futurists have not yet found a synthetic expression of words and images in their work.

"The 150 Million" was supposed to be the poem of the Revolution. But it is not. The whole of this work, which is big in its design, is devoured by the weakness and defects of Futurism. The author wanted to write an epic of mass suffering, of mass heroism, of an impersonal revolution of the 150 million Ivans. And the author did not sign it. "No one is the author of this poem of mine." But this state of impersonal ownership does not change the situation. The poem is profoundly personal and individualistic, and in the bad sense of the term. It contains too much purposeless arbitrariness of art. The poem has these images: "Wilson swimming in fat," "In Chicago every inhabitant has the title of a general, at least," "Wilson gobbles, grows fat, his bellies grow story on story,"—and other such. Such images are very simple and very rude, but they are not at all popular; at any rate, they are not the images that belong to the present-day masses. The worker, at least the worker who will read Mayakovsky's poem, has seen Wilson's photograph. Wilson is thin, though we may readily believe that he swallows a sufficient quantity of proteins and fats. The worker has also read Upton Sinclair, and knows that Chicago has stockyard workers besides "generals." In spite of their loud hyperbolism, one feels a certain lisp in these purposeless and primitive images, of the kind grownups use with children. The simplicity that looks at us from these images does not come from a gross and wholesale and popular imagination, but it comes from a Bohemian silliness. Wilson has a ladder—"If you walk on foot, start walking young, and you will hardly reach the end by the time you are old!" Ivan marches upon Wilson, "the championship (!) of the world's class struggle" takes place, and Wilson has "pistols with four cocks, and a sword bent in seventy sharp points," but Ivan has "a hand and another hand, and that is stuck in his belt." The unarmed Ivan with his hand in his belt against the infidel armed with pistols is an old Russian motif! Is not Ilya Murometz before us? Or maybe it is Ivan the Fool who is stepping forward barefoot against the shrewd German mechanicians. Wilson struck Ivan with his sword: "He cut him for four versts....But a man crawled forth suddenly from the wound." And so on, and in the same way. How out of place, and particularly how frivolous do these primitive ballads and fairytales sound when hurriedly adapted to Chicago mechanics and to the class struggle. All this was meant to be titanic, but, as a matter of fact, it is only athletic, and very uncertain athletics, a sort of parody with inflated balls. "The championship of the world's class struggle!" Champ-i-on-ship! Self-criticism, where art thou? Championship is a holiday spectacle, quite often combined with charlatanism. Neither the image nor the word are appropriate here. Instead of a really titanic struggle of 150 millions, there is a parody of a ballad, and a championship of a ballad-like circus. The parody is unintentional, but this does not make it lighter.

The purposeless images, that is, those that have not been worked out internally, devour the idea without leaving a crumb and spoil it artistically, as well as politically. Why does Ivan hold one hand in his belt against swords and pistols? Why such contempt for technique? It is true that Ivan is less armed than Wilson. But that is just why he has to work with both hands. And if he does not fall stricken, it is because there are workers in Chicago, as well as generals, and because a considerable part of these workers are against Wilson, and for Ivan. But the poem doesn't show this. While running down a supposedly monumental image, the author strikes down its very essence.

Hurriedly and in passing, that is, without purpose, the author divides the whole world into two classes: on the one hand, there is Wilson, floating in fat, and with him are ermines, beavers, and large heavenly stars, and on the other hand, there is Ivan, and with him are blouses and the millions of the Milky Way. "To the beavers—the little lines of the decadence of the whole world, to the blouses the iron lines of the Futurists." But in general, though the poem has a richness of expression and quite a few strong apt lines and brilliant images, it has in truth no iron lines for the blouses. Is this for want of talent? No, for want of an image of the Revolution worked over by nerves and brain, an image to which the craftsmanship of words is subordinate. The author plays the strong man, catching and throwing about one image and then another. "We shall finish you, romanticist world!" Mayakovsky threatens. That is right. One has to put an end to the romanticism of Oblomov and of Tolstoy's Karataiev. But how? "He is old—kill him and make an ashtray of his skull."

But this is the most real and most negative romanticism! Ashtrays made of skulls are inconvenient and unhygienic. And its savagery is after all…meaningless? By making such an unnatural use of the skull bones, the poet becomes caught in romanticism; at any rate, he has not worked out his images, nor has he unified them. "Pocket the wealth of all the worlds!" In this familiar tone Mayakovsky speaks of socialism. But to pocket means to put it into one's pocket like a thief. Is this word suitable when the matter hinges on the collective expropriation of the land and the factories? It is strikingly unsuitable. The author uses such vulgarisms so that he could be pals with socialism and with the Revolution. But when he pokes the 150 million Ivans familiarly "under the ribs," it doesn't make the poet grow to titanic dimensions, but only reduces Ivan to an eighth part of a page. Familiarity is not at all an expression of an inner intimacy, for frequently it is merely an evidence of political or moral slovenliness. An internally developed bond with the Revolution would exclude a familiar tone, and would bring forth what the Germans call the pathos of distance.

The poem has striking lines, bold images, and very apt words. The final "triumphal requiem of peace" is perhaps the strongest part of it. But the whole has been struck fatally, because of a lack of inner movement. There is no condensing of contradictions in order to resolve them later. Here is a poem about the Revolution lacking in movement! The images live separately, they collide and they bounce off one another. The hostility of the images is not an outgrowth of the historic materials but is the result of an internal disharmony with the revolutionary philosophy of life. However, when not without difficulty one reads the poem to the very end, one says to oneself: a great work could have been composed out of these elements, had there been measure and self-criticism! Perhaps these fundamental defects are not to be explained by Mayakovsky's personal qualities, but by the fact that he works in an isolated little world; nothing is so adverse to self-criticism and measure as living in a small group.

Mayakovsky's satirical things also lack profound penetration into the essence of things and relationships. His satire is racy and superficial. It takes more than the mastery of a pencil for a cartoonist to be significant. The world he exposes must be familiar to him through and through and inside out. Saltikov knew the bureaucracy and the nobility well! An approximate caricature (and such, alas, are ninety-nine Soviet caricatures out of one hundred) is like a bullet that misses the bull's-eye by the width of a finger, or even by a hair; it has almost hit the mark, but still, it missed. Mayakovsky's satire is approximate; his racy observations from the side miss the mark, sometimes by the width of a finger, and sometimes by the width of the whole palm. Mayakovsky seriously thinks that the "comic" can be withdrawn from its matter and be reduced to a form. In the preface to his volume of satires, he even presents "an outline of laughter." If in reading this "outline" there is something that can call forth a perplexed smile, it is the fact that in this outline of laughter there is absolutely nothing funny. But even if one could make a happier "outline" than Mayakovsky has succeeded in making, the difference between laughter called forth by a satire that hits the mark, and giggling, which results from a verbal tickling, will not disappear.

Mayakovsky has risen from the Bohemia that brought him forth to extraordinarily significant creative achievements. But the rod on which he has raised himself is individualistic. The poet is in revolt against the condition of his life, against the material and moral dependence in which his life, and above all, his love, is placed; and suffering and indignant against the masters of life who have deprived him of his beloved one, he rises to an appeal for revolution and to a forecast that it will fall upon the society that does not allow free space to Mayakovsky's individuality. After all, his poem, "A Cloud in Trousers," a poem of unrequited love, is artistically his most significant and creatively his boldest and most promising work. It is even difficult to believe that a thing of such intense strength and independence of form was written by a youth of twenty-two or twenty-three years of age. His "War and Peace," "Mystery Bouffe," and "150 Million" are much weaker, for the reason that here Mayakovsky leaves his individualist orbit and tries to enter the orbit of the Revolution. One may hail the efforts of the poet, for in general no other road exists for him. "About This" is a return to the theme of personal love, but is several steps behind "A Cloud," and not ahead. Only his wider grasp, and a deeper artistic volume, help him to maintain his creative equilibrium on a much higher level. But one cannot help seeing that his conscious turning to a new and essentially social direction is a very difficult thing. Mayakovsky's technique in these years has undoubtedly become more skilled, but also more stereotyped. The "Mystery Bouffe" and the "150 Million" have splendid lines side by side with fatal failures filled with rhetoric and with verbal tightrope walking. The organic quality, the sincerity, the cry from within which we heard in "A Cloud" are no longer there. "Mayakovsky is repeating himself," some say; "Mayakovsky has written himself out," others add; "Mayakovsky has become official," others say maliciously. But is that so? We are in no haste to make pessimistic prophecies. Mayakovsky is not a youth, but he is still young. However, let us not close our eyes to the difficulties of the road before him. That creative spontaneity that beats like a living fountain from "A Cloud" cannot be regained. But one need not regret this. The youthful talent that beats like a fountain is replaced in maturer years by a self-reliant mastery, which signifies not only a mastery of the word, but also a broad historical and experiential grasp, a penetration into the mechanism of the live collective and personal forces, ideas, temperaments, and passions. Such mature artisanship cannot go hand in hand with social dilettantism, with shouting, with a lack of self-respect and a tiresome boastfulness, with playing the genius with the left hand, and with the other making tricks and signs from the cafes of the intelligentsia. If the poet's crisis—and there is such a crisis—will be solved with a wise insight that knows the particular and the general, then the historian of literature will say that the "Mystery" and the "150 Million" were merely the inevitable and temporary decline on the turn of the road toward the creative peak. We sincerely wish that Mayakovsky will give the future historian the right to make such a summing up.

▨   ▨   ▨

When one breaks a hand or a leg, the bones, the tendons, the muscles, the arteries, the nerves, and the skin do not break and tear in one line, nor afterwards do they grow together and heal at the same time. So, in a revolutionary break in the life of society, there is no simultaneousness and no symmetry of processes either in the ideology of society, or in its economic structure. The ideologic premises that are needed for the revolution are formed before the revolution, and the most important ideological deductions from the revolution appear only much later. It would be extremely flippant to establish by analogies and comparisons the identity of Futurism and communism, and so form the deduction that Futurism is the art of the proletariat. Such pretensions must be rejected. But this does not signify a contemptuous attitude toward the work of the Futurists. In our opinion they are the necessary links in the forming of a new and great literature. But they will prove to be only a significant episode in its evolution. To prove this, one has to approach the question more concretely and historically. The Futurists in their way are right when, in answer to the reproach that their works are above the heads of the masses, they say that Marx's *Capital* is also above their heads. Of course the masses are culturally and aesthetically unprepared, and will rise only slowly. But this is only one of the causes of it being above their heads. There is another cause. In its methods and in its forms, Futurism carries within itself clear traces of that world, or rather, of that little world in which it was born, and which—psychologically and not logically—it has not left to this very day. It is just as difficult to strip Futurism of the robe of the intelligentsia as it is to separate form from content. And when this happens, Futurism will undergo such a profound qualitative change that it will cease to be Futurism. This is going to happen, but not tomorrow. But even today one can say with certainty that much in Futurism will be useful and will serve to elevate and to revive art, if Futurism will learn to stand on its own legs, without any attempt to have itself decreed official by the government, as happened in the beginning of the Revolution. The new forms must find for themselves, and independently, an access into the consciousness of the advanced elements of the working class as the latter develop culturally. Art cannot live and cannot develop without a flexible atmosphere of sympathy around it. On this road, and on no other, does the process of complex interrelation lie ahead. The cultural growth of the working class will help and influence those innovators who really hold something in their bosom. The mannerisms that inevitably crop out in all small groups will fall away, and from the vital sprouts will come fresh forms for the solution of new artistic tasks. This process implies, first of all, an accumulation of material culture, a growth of prosperity, and a development of technique. There is no other road. It is impossible to think seriously that history will simply conserve the works of the Futurists, and will serve them up to the masses after many years, when the masses will have become ripe for them. This, of course, would be *passéism* of the purest kind. When that time, which is not immediate, comes, and the cultural and aesthetics education of the working masses will destroy the wide chasm between the creative intelligentsia and the people, art will have a different aspect from what it has today. In the evolution of that art, Futurism will prove to have been a necessary link. And is this so very little?

CHAPTER FIVE

The Formalist School
of Poetry and Marxism

Leaving out of account the weak echoes of pre-revolutionary ideological systems, the only theory which has opposed Marxism in Soviet Russia these years is the Formalist theory of art. The paradox consists in the fact that Russian Formalism connected itself closely with Russian Futurism, and that while the latter was capitulating politically before communism, Formalism opposed Marxism with all its might theoretically.

Victor Shklovsky is the theorist of Futurism, and at the same time the head of the Formalist school. According to his theory, art has always been the work of self-sufficient pure forms, and it has been recognized by Futurism for the first time. Futurism is thus the first conscious art in history, and the Formalist school is the first scientific school of art. Owing to the efforts of Shklovsky —and this is not an insignificant virtue!—the theory of art, and partly art itself, have at last been raised from a state of alchemy to the position of chemistry. The herald of the Formalist school, the first chemist of art, gives a few friendly slaps in passing to those Futurist "conciliators" who seek a bridge to the Revolution, and who try to find this bridge in the materialistic conception of history. Such a bridge is unnecessary; Futurism is entirely sufficient unto itself.

There are two reasons why it is necessary to pause a little before this Formalist school. One is for its own sake; in spite of the superficiality and reactionary character of the Formalist theory of art, a certain part of the research work of the Formalists is useful. The other reason is Futurism itself; however unfounded the claims of the Futurists to a monopolistic representation of the new art may be, one cannot thrust Futurism out of that process which is preparing the art of the future.

What is the Formalist school?

As it is represented at present by Shklovsky, Zhirmunsky, Jakobson, and others, it is extremely arrogant and immature. Having declared form to be the essence of poetry, this school reduces its task to an analysis (essentially descriptive and semi-statistical) of the etymology and syntax of poems, to the counting of repetitive vowels and consonants, of syllables and epithets. This analysis, which the Formalists regard as the essence of poetry, or poetics, is undoubtedly necessary and useful, but one must understand its partial, scrappy, subsidiary, and preparatory character. It can become an essential element of poetic technique and of the rules of the craft. Just as it is useful for a poet or a writer to make lists of synonyms for himself and increase their number so as to expand his verbal keyboard, so it is useful, and quite necessary, for a poet, to estimate a word not only in accord with its inner meaning, but also in accord with its acoustics, because a word is passed on from man to man, first of all by acoustics. The methods of Formalism, confined within legitimate limits, may help to clarify the artistic and psychological peculiarities of form (its economy, its movement, its contrasts, its hyperbolism, etc.). This, in turn, may open a path—one of the paths—to the artist's feeling for the world, and may facilitate the discovery of the relations of an individual artist, or of a whole artistic school, to the social environment. In so far as we are dealing with a contemporary and living school that is still developing, there is an immediate significance in our transitional stage in probing it by means of a social probe and in clarifying its class roots, so that not only the reader, but the school itself could orient itself, that is, know itself, purify and direct itself.

But the Formalists are not content to ascribe to their methods a merely subsidiary, serviceable, and technical significance—similar to that which statistics has for social science, or the microscope for the biological sciences. No, they go much further. To them verbal art ends finally and fully with the word, and depictive art with color. A poem is a combination of sounds, a painting is a combination of color spots, and the laws of art are the laws of verbal combinations and of combinations of color spots. The social and psychological approach, which, to us, gives a meaning to the microscopic and statistical work done in connection with verbal material, is, for the Formalists, only alchemy.

"Art was always free of life, and its color never reflected the color of the flag which waved over the fortress of the City" (Shklovsky). "Adjustment to the expression, the verbal mass, is the one essential element of poetry" (R. Jakobson, in his "Recent Russian Poetry"). "With a new form comes a new content. Form thus determines content" (Kruchenikh). "Poetry means the giving of form to the word, which is valuable in itself" (Jakobson), or, as Khlebnikov says, "The word which is something in itself," etc.

True, the Italian Futurists have sought in the word a means of expressing the locomotive, the propeller, electricity, the radio, etc., for their own age. In other words, they sought a new form for the new content of life. But it turned out that "this was a reform in the field of reporting, and not in the field of poetic language" (Jakobson). It is quite different with Russian Futurism; it carries to the end "the adjustment to verbal mass." For Russian Futurism, form determines content.

True, Jakobson is compelled to admit that "a series of new poetic methods finds application (?) for itself in urbanism" (in the culture of the city). But this is his conclusion: "Hence the urban poems of Mayakovsky and Khlebnikov." In other words: not city culture, which has struck the eye and the ear of the poet and which has re-educated them, has inspired him with new form, with new images, new epithets, new rhythm, but, on the contrary, the new form, originating arbitrarily, forced the poet to seek appropriate material and so pushed him in the direction of the city! The development of the "verbal mass" went on arbitrarily from the "Odyssey" to "A Cloud in Trousers;" the torch, the wax candle, the electric lamp, had nothing to do with it! One has only to formulate this point of view clearly to have its childish inadequacy strike the eye. But Jakobson tries to insist; he replies in advance that the same Mayakovsky has such lines as these: "Leave the cities, you silly people." And the theorist of the Formalist school reasons profoundly: "What is this, a logical contradiction? But let others fasten on the poet thoughts expressed in his works. To incriminate a poet with ideas and feelings is just as absurd as the behavior of the medieval public which beat the actor who played Judas." And so on.

It is quite evident that all this was written by a very capable high-school boy who had a very evident and quite "self-signifi-cant" intention to "stick the pen into our teacher of literature, a notable pedant." At sticking the pen, our bold innovators are masters, but they do not know how to use their pen theoretically or grammatically. This is not hard to prove.

Of course Futurism felt the suggestions of the city—of the tram-car, of electricity, of the telegraph, of the automobile, of the propeller, of the night cabaret (especially of the night cabaret) much before it found its new form. Urbanism (city culture) sits deep in the subconsciousness of Futurism, and the epithets, the etymology, the syntax, and the rhythm of Futurism are only an attempt to give artistic form to the new spirit of the cities that has conquered consciousness. And when Mayakovsky exclaims: "Leave the cities, you silly people," it is the cry of a man citified to the very marrow of his bones, who shows himself strikingly and clearly a city person, especially when he is outside the city, that is, when he "leaves the city" and becomes an inhabitant of a summer resort. It is not at all a question of "incriminating" (this word misses something!) a poet with the ideas and feelings that he expresses. Of course the way he expresses them makes the poet. But after all, a poet uses the language of the school that he has accepted or that he has created to fulfill tasks that lie outside of him. And this is even true also when he limits himself to lyri-cism, to personal love and personal death. Though individual shadings of poetic form correspond to individual makeup, they do go hand in hand with imitation and routine, in the feeling it-self, as well as in the method of its expression. A new artistic form, taken in a large historic way, is born in reply to new needs. To take an example from intimate lyric poetry, one may say that between the physiology of sex and a poem about love there lies a complex system of psychological transmitting mechanisms in which there are individual, racial, and social elements. The racial foundation, that is, the sexual basis of man, changes slowly. The social forms of love change more rapidly. They affect the psycho-logical superstructure of love, they produce new shadings and in-tonations, new spiritual demands, a need of a new vocabulary, and so they present new demands on poetry. The poet can find material for his art only in his social environment and transmits the new impulses of life through his own artistic consciousness. Language, changed and complicated by urban conditions, gives the poet a new verbal material, and suggests or facilitates new word combinations for the poetic formulation of new thoughts or of new feelings, which strive to break through the dark shell of the subconscious. If there were no changes in psychology produced by changes in the social environment, there would be no movement in art; people would continue from generation to generation to be content with the poetry of the Bible, or of the old Greeks.

But the philosopher of Formalism jumps on us, and says it is merely a question of a new form "in the field of reporting and not in the field of poetic language." There he struck us! If you will, poetry is reporting, only in a peculiar, grand style.

The quarrels about "pure art" and about art with a tendency took place between the liberals and the "populists." They do not become us. Materialistic dialectics are above this; from the point of view of an objective historical process, art is always a social servant and historically utilitarian. It finds the necessary rhythm of words for dark and vague moods, it brings thought and feeling closer or contrasts them with one another, it enriches the spiritual experience of the individual and of the community, it refines feeling, makes it more flexible, more responsive, it enlarges the volume of thought in advance and not through the personal method of accumulated experience, it educates the individual, the social group, the class, and the nation. And this it does quite independently of whether it appears in a given case under the flag of a "pure" or of a frankly tendentious art. In our Russian social development tendentiousness was the banner of the intelligentsia that sought contact with the people. The helpless intelligentsia, crushed by Tsarism and deprived of a cultural environment, sought support in the lower strata of society and tried to prove to the "people" that it was thinking only of them, living only for them, and that it loved them "terribly." And just as the "populists" who went to the people were ready to do without clean linen and without a comb and without a toothbrush, so the intelligentsia was ready to sacrifice the "subtleties" of form in its art, in order to give the most direct and spontaneous expression to the sufferings and hopes of the oppressed. On the other hand, "pure" art was the banner of the rising bourgeoisie, which could not openly declare its bourgeois character, and which at the same time tried to keep the intelligentsia in its service. The Marxist point of view is far removed from these tendencies, which were historically necessary, but which have become historically passé. Keeping on the plane of scientific investigation, Marxism seeks with the same assurance the social roots of the "pure" as well as of the tendentious art. It does not at all "incriminate" a poet with the thoughts and feelings that he expresses, but raises questions of a much more profound significance, namely, to which order of feelings does a given artistic work correspond in all its peculiarities? What are the social conditions of these thoughts and feelings? What place do they occupy in the historic development of a society and of a class? And, further, what literary heritage has entered into the elaboration of the new form? Under the influence of what historic impulse have the new complexes of feelings and thoughts broken through the shell that divides them from the sphere of poetic consciousness? The investigation may become complicated, detailed, or individualized, but its fundamental idea will be that of the subsidiary role that art plays in the social process.

Each class has its own policy in art, that is, a system of presenting demands on art, which changes with time; for instance, the Macaenas-like protection of court and grand *seigneur*, the automatic relationship of supply and demand that is supplemented by complex methods of influencing the individual, and so forth, and so on. The social and even the personal dependence of art was not concealed, but was openly announced as long as art retained its court character. The wider, more popular, anonymous character of the rising bourgeoisie led, on the whole, to the theory of "pure art," though there were many deviations from this theory. As indicated above, the tendentious literature of the "populist" intelligentsia was imbued with a class interest; the intelligentsia could not strengthen itself and could not conquer for itself a light to play a part in history without the support of the people. But in the revolutionary struggle, the class egotism of the intelligentsia was turned inside out, and in its left wing, it assumed the form of highest self-sacrifice. That is why the intelligentsia not only did not conceal art with a tendency, but proclaimed it, thus sacrificing art, just as it sacrificed many other things.

Our Marxist conception of the objective social dependence and social utility of art, when translated into the language of politics, does not at all mean a desire to dominate art by means of decrees and orders. It is not true that we regard only that art as new and revolutionary that speaks of the worker, and it is nonsense to say that we demand that the poets should describe inevitably a factory chimney, or the uprising against capital! Of course the new art cannot but place the struggle of the proletariat in the center of its attention. But the plough of the new art is not limited to numbered strips. On the contrary, it must plow the entire field in all directions. Personal lyrics of the very smallest scope have an absolute right to exist within the new art. Moreover, the new man cannot be formed without a new lyric poetry. But to create it, the poet himself must feel the world in a new way. If Christ alone or Sabaoth himself bends over the poet's embraces (as in the case of Akhmatova, Tsvetaeva, Schkapskaya, and others), then this only goes to prove how much behind the times his lyrics are and how socially and aesthetically inadequate they are for the new man. Even where such terminology is not a survival of experience so much as of words, it shows psychological inertia and therefore stands in contradiction to the consciousness of the new man. No one is going to prescribe themes to a poet or intends to prescribe them. Please write about anything you can think of! But allow the new class that considers itself, and with reason, called upon to build a new world, to say to you in any given case: It does not make new poets of you to translate the philosophy of life of the seventeenth century into the language of the Acméists. The form of art is to a certain and very large degree independent, but the artist who creates this form, and the spectator who is enjoying it, are not empty machines, one for creating form and the other for appreciating it. They are living people, with a crystallized psychology representing a certain unity, even if not entirely harmonious. This psychology is the result of social conditions. The creation and perception of art forms is one of the functions of this psychology. And no matter how wise the Formalists try to be, their whole conception is simply based upon the fact that they ignore the psychological unity of the social man, who creates and who consumes what has been created.

The proletariat has to have in art the expression of the new spiritual point of view that is just beginning to be formulated within him, and to which art must help him give form. This is not a state order, but a historic demand. Its strength lies in the objectivity of historic necessity. You cannot pass this by, nor escape its force.

The Formalist school seems to try to be objective. It is disgusted, and not without reason, with the literary and critical arbitrariness that operates only with tastes and moods. It seeks precise criteria for classification and valuation. But owing to its narrow outlook and superficial methods, it is constantly falling into superstitions, such as graphology and phrenology. These two "schools" have also the task of establishing purely objective tests for determining human character; such as the number of the flourishes of one's pen and their roundness, and the peculiarities of the bumps on the back of one's head. One may assume that pen flourishes and bumps do have some relation to character; but this relation is not direct, and human character is not at all exhausted by them. An apparent objectivism based on accidental, secondary, and inadequate characteristics leads inevitably to the worst subjectivism. In the case of the Formalist school it leads to the superstition of the word. Having counted the adjectives, and weighed the lines, and measured the rhythms, a Formalist either stops silent with the expression of a man who does not know what to do with himself, or throws out an unexpected generalization that contains 5 percent of Formalism and 95 percent of the most uncritical intuition.

In fact, the Formalists do not carry their idea of art to its logical conclusion. If one is to regard the process of poetic creation only as a combination of sounds or words, and to seek along these lines the solution of all the problems of poetry, then the only perfect formula of "poetics" will be this: Arm yourself with a dictionary and create by means of algebraic combinations and permutations of words all the poetic works of the world that have been created and that have not yet been created. Reasoning "formally" one may produce *Eugene Onegin* in two ways: either by subordinating the selection of words to a preconceived artistic idea (as Pushkin himself did), or by solving the problem algebraically. From the "Formal" point of view, the second method is more correct, because it does not depend upon mood, inspiration, or other unsteady things, and has besides the advantage that while leading to *Eugene Onegin* it may bring one to an incalculable number of other great works. All that one needs is infinity in time, called eternity. But as neither mankind nor the individual poet have eternity at their disposal, the fundamental source of poetic words will remain, as before, the preconceived artistic idea understood in the broadest sense, as an accurate thought and as a clearly expressed personal or social feeling and as a vague mood. In its striving toward artistic materialization, this subjective idea will be stimulated and jolted by form and may be sometimes pushed on to a path that was entirely unforeseen. This simply means that verbal form is not a passive reflection of a preconceived artistic idea, but an active element that influences the idea itself. But such an active mutual relationship—in which form influences and at times entirely transforms content—is known to us in all fields of social and even biologic life. This is no reason at all for rejecting Darwinism and Marxism and for the creation of a Formalist school either in biology or sociology.

Victor Shklovsky, who flits lightly from verbal Formalism to the most subjective valuations, assumes a very uncompromising attitude toward the historico-materialistic theory of art. In a booklet that he published in Berlin, under the title of *The March of the Horse,* he formulates in the course of three small pages— brevity is a fundamental and, at any rate, an undoubted merit of Shklovsky—five (not four and not six, but five) exhaustive arguments against the materialist conception of art. Let us examine these arguments, because it won't harm us to take a look and see what kind of chaff is handed out as the last word in scientific thought (with the greatest variety of scientific references on these same three microscopic pages).

"If the environment and the relations of production," says Shklovsky, "influenced art, then would not the themes of art be tied to the places that would correspond to these relations? But themes are homeless." Well, and how about butterflies? According to Darwin, they also "correspond" to definite relations, and yet they flit from place to place, just like an unweighted litterateur.

It is not easy to understand why Marxism should be supposed to condemn themes to a condition of serfdom. The fact that different peoples and different classes of the same people make use of the same themes, merely shows how limited the human imagination is, and how man tries to maintain an economy of energy in every kind of creation, even in the artistic.

Every class tries to utilize, to the greatest possible degree, the material and spiritual heritage of another class. Shklovsky's argument could be easily transferred into the field of productive technique. From ancient times on, the wagon has been based on one and the same theme, namely, axles, wheels, and a shaft. However, the chariot of the Roman patrician was just as well adapted to his tastes and needs as was the carriage of Count Orlov, fitted out with inner comforts, to the tastes of this favorite of Catherine the Great. The wagon of the Russian peasant is adapted to the needs of his household, to the strength of his little horse, and to the peculiarities of the country road. The automobile, which is undoubtedly a product of the new technique, shows, nevertheless, the same "theme," namely, four wheels on two axles. Yet every time a peasant's horse shies in terror before the blinding lights of an automobile on the Russian road at night, a conflict of two cultures is reflected in the episode.

"If environment expressed itself in novels," so runs the second argument, "European science would not be breaking its head over the question of where the stories of *A Thousand and One Nights* were made, whether in Egypt, India, or Persia." To say that man's environment, including the artist's, that is, the conditions of his education and life, find expression in his art also, does not mean to say that such expression has a precise geographic, ethnographic, and statistical character. It is not at all surprising that it is difficult to decide whether certain novels were made in Egypt, India, or Persia, because the social conditions of these countries have much in common. But the very fact that European science is "breaking its head" trying to solve this question from these novels themselves, shows that these novels reflect an environment, even though unevenly. No one can jump beyond himself. Even the ravings of an insane person contain nothing that the sick man had not received before from the outside world. But it would be an insanity of another order to regard his ravings as the accurate reflection of an external world. Only an experienced and thoughtful psychiatrist, who knows the past of the patient, will be able to find the reflected and distorted bits of reality in the contents of his ravings. Artistic creation, of course, is not a raving, though it is also a deflection, a changing and a transformation of reality, in accordance with the peculiar laws of art. However fantastic art may be, it cannot have at its disposal any other material except that which is given to it by the world of three dimensions and by the narrower world of class society. Even when the artist creates heaven and hell, he merely transforms the experience of his own life into his phantasmagorias, almost to the point of his landlady's unpaid bill.

"If the features of class and caste are deposited in art," continues Shklovsky, "then how does it come that the various tales of the Great Russians about their nobleman are the same as their fairy tales about their priest?"

In essence, this is merely a paraphrase of the first argument. Why cannot the fairy tales about the nobleman and about the priest be the same, and how does this contradict Marxism? The proclamations that are written by well-known Marxists not infrequently speak of landlords, capitalists, priests, generals, and other exploiters. The landlord undoubtedly differs from the capitalist, but there are cases when they are considered under one head. Why, then, cannot folk art in certain cases treat the nobleman and the priest together, as the representatives of the classes that stand above the people and that plunder them? In the cartoons of Moor and of Deni, the priest often stands side by side with the landlord, without any damage to Marxism.

"If ethnographic traits were reflected in art," Shklovsky goes on, "the folklore about the peoples beyond the border would not be interchangeable and could not be told by any one folk about another."

As you see, there is no letting up here. Marxism does not maintain at all that ethnographic traits have an independent character. On the contrary, it emphasizes the all-determining significance of natural and economic conditions in the formation of folklore. The similarity of conditions in the development of the herding and agricultural and primarily peasant peoples, and the similarity in the character of their mutual influence upon one another, cannot but lead to the creation of a similar folklore. And from the point of view of the question that interests us here, it makes absolutely no difference whether these homogeneous themes arose independently among different peoples, as the reflection of a life-experience that was homogeneous in its fundamental traits and that was reflected through the homogeneous prism of a peasant imagination, or whether the seeds of these fairy tales were carried by a favorable wind from place to place, striking root wherever the ground turned out to be favorable. It is very likely that, in reality, these methods were combined.

And finally, as a separate argument—"The reason (i.e., Marxism) is incorrect in the fifth place"—Shklovsky points to the theme of abduction that goes through Greek comedy and reaches Ostrovsky. In other words, our critic repeats, in a special form, his very first argument (as we see, even insofar as formal logic is concerned, all is not well with our Formalist). Yes, themes migrate from people to people, from class to class, and even from author to author. This means only that the human imagination is economical. A new class does not begin to create all of culture from the beginning, but enters into possession of the past, assorts it, touches it up, rearranges it, and builds on it further. If there were no such utilization of the "secondhand" wardrobe of the ages, historic processes would have no progress at all. If the theme of Ostrovsky's drama came to him through the Egyptians and through Greece, then the paper on which Ostrovsky developed his theme came to him as a development of the Egyptian papyrus through the Greek parchment. Let us take another and closer analogy: the fact that the critical methods of the Greek Sophists, who were the pure Formalists of their day, have penetrated the theoretic consciousness of Shklovsky, does not in the least change the fact that Shklovsky himself is a very picturesque product of a definite social environment and of a definite age.

Shklovsky's destruction of Marxism in five points reminds us very much of those articles that were published against Darwinism in the magazine *The Orthodox Review* in the good old days. If the doctrine of the origin of man from the monkey were true, wrote the learned Bishop Nikanor of Odessa thirty or forty years ago, then our grandfathers would have had distinct signs of a tail, or would have noticed such a characteristic in their grandfathers and grandmothers. Second, as everybody knows, monkeys can only give birth to monkeys....Fifth, Darwinism is incorrect, because it contradicts Formalism—I beg your pardon, I meant to say the formal decisions of the universal church conferences. The advantage of the learned monk consisted, however, in the fact that he was a frank *passéist* and took his cue from the Apostle Paul and not from physics, chemistry, or mathematics, as the Futurist, Shklovsky, does.

It is unquestionably true that the need for art is not created by economic conditions. But neither is the need for food created by economics. On the contrary, the need for food and warmth creates economics. It is very true that one cannot always go by the principles of Marxism in deciding whether to reject or to accept a work of art. A work of art should, in the first place, be judged by its own law, that is, by the law of art. But Marxism alone can explain why and how a given tendency in art has originated in a given period of history; in other words, who it was who made a demand for such an artistic form and not for another, and why.

It would be childish to think that every class can entirely and fully create its own art from within itself, and, particularly, that the proletariat is capable of creating a new art by means of closed art guilds or circles, or by the Organization for Proletarian Culture, etc. Generally speaking, the artistic work of man is continuous. Each new rising class places itself on the shoulders of its preceding one. But this continuity is dialectic, that is, it finds itself by means of internal repulsions and breaks. New artistic needs or demands for new literary and artistic points of view are stimulated by economics, through the development of a new class, and minor stimuli are supplied by changes in the position of the class, under the influence of the growth of its wealth and cultural power. Artistic creation is always a complicated turning inside out of old forms, under the influence of new stimuli that originate outside of art. In this large sense of the word, art is a handmaiden. It is not a disembodied element feeding on itself, but a function of social man indissolubly tied to his life and environment. And how characteristic it is—if one were to reduce every social superstition to its absurdity—that Shklovsky has come to the idea of art's absolute independence from the social environment at a period of Russian history when art has revealed with such utter frankness its spiritual, environmental, and material dependence upon definite social classes, subclasses, and groups!

Materialism does not deny the significance of the element of form, either in logic, jurisprudence, or art. Just as a system of jurisprudence can and must be judged by its internal logic and consistency, so art can and must be judged from the point of view of its achievements in form, because there can be no art without them. However, a juridical theory that attempted to establish the independence of law from social conditions would be defective at its very base. Its moving force lies in economics—in class contradictions. The law gives only a formal and an internally harmonized expression of these phenomena, not of their individual peculiarities, but of their general character, that is, of the elements that are repetitive and permanent in them. We can see now with a clarity that is rare in history how new law is made. It is not done by logical deduction, but by empirical measurement and by adjustment to the economic needs of the new ruling class. Literature, whose methods and processes have their roots far back in the most distant past and represent the accumulated experience of verbal craftsmanship, expresses the thoughts, feelings, moods, points of view, and hopes of the new epoch and of its new class. One cannot jump beyond this. And there is no need of making the jump, at least, for those who are not serving an epoch already past nor a class that has already outlived itself.

The methods of formal analysis are necessary, but insufficient. You may count up the alliterations in popular proverbs, classify metaphors, count up the number of vowels and consonants in a wedding song. It will undoubtedly enrich our knowledge of folk art, in one way or another; but if you don't know the peasant system of sowing, and the life that is based on it, if you don't know the part the scythe plays, and if you have not mastered the meaning of the church calendar to the peasant, of the time when the peasant marries, or when the peasant women give birth, you will have only understood the outer shell of folk art, but the kernel will not have been reached. The architectural scheme of the Cologne cathedral can be established by measuring the base and the height of its arches, by determining the three dimensions of its naves, the dimensions and the placement of the columns, etc. But without knowing what a medieval city was like, what a guild was, or what was the Catholic Church of the Middle Ages, the Cologne cathedral will never be understood. The effort to set art free from life, to declare it a craft self-sufficient unto itself, devitalizes and kills art. The very need of such an operation is an unmistakable symptom of intellectual decline.

The analogy with the theological arguments against Darwinism that was made above may appear to the reader external and anecdotal. That may be true, to some extent. But a much deeper connection exists. The Formalist theory inevitably reminds a Marxist who has done any reading at all of the familiar tunes of a very old philosophic melody. The jurists and the moralists (to recall at random the German Stammler, and our own subjectivist Mikhailovsky) tried to prove that morality and law could not be determined by economics, because economic life was unthinkable outside of juridical and ethical norms. True, the formalists of law and morals did not go so far as to assert the complete independence of law and ethics from economics. They recognized a certain complex mutual relationship of "factors," and these "factors," while influencing one another, retained the qualities of independent substances, coming no one knew whence. The assertion of complete independence of the aesthetic "factor" from the influence of social conditions, as is made by Shklovsky, is an instance of specific hyperbole whose roots, by the way, lie in social conditions too; it is the megalomania of aesthetics turning our hard reality on its head. Apart from this peculiarity, the constructions of the Formalists have the same kind of defective methodology that every other kind of idealism has. To a materialist, religion, law, morals, and art represent separate aspects of one and the same process of social development. Though they differentiate themselves from their industrial basis, become complex, strengthen, and develop their special characteristics in detail, politics, religion, law, ethics, and aesthetics remain, nonetheless, functions of social man and obey the laws of his social organization. The idealist, on the other hand, does not see a unified process of historic development that evolves the necessary organs and functions from within itself, but a crossing or combining and interacting of certain independent principles —the religious, political, juridical, aesthetic, and ethical substances, which find their origin and explanation in themselves. The (dialectic) idealism of Hegel arranges these substances (which are the eternal categories) in some sequence by reducing them to a genetic unity. Regardless of the fact that this unity with Hegel is the absolute spirit, which divides itself in the process of its dialectic manifestation into various "factors," Hegel's system, because of its dialectic character, not because of its idealism, gives an idea of historic reality that is just as good as the idea of a man's hand that a glove gives when turned inside out. But the Formalists (and their greatest genius was Kant) do not look at the dynamics of development, but at a cross section of it, on the day and at the hour of their own philosophic revelation. At the crossing of the line they reveal the complexity and multiplicity of the object (not of the process, because they do not think of processes). This complexity they analyze and classify. They give names to the elements, which are at once transformed into essences, into sub-absolutes, without father or mother; to wit, religion, politics, morals, law, art. Here we no longer have a glove of history turned inside out, but the skin torn from the separate fingers, dried out to a degree of complete abstraction, and this hand of history turns out to be the product of the "interaction" of the thumb, the index, the middle finger, and all the other "factors." The aesthetic "factor" is the little finger, the smallest, but not the least beloved.

In biology, vitalism is a variation of the same fetish of presenting the separate aspects of the world-process, without understanding its inner relation. A creator is all that is lacking for a super-social, absolute morality or aesthetics, or for a super-physical absolute "vital force." The multiplicity of independent factors, "factors" without beginning or end, is nothing but a masked polytheism. Just as Kantian idealism represents historically a translation of Christianity into the language of rationalistic philosophy, so all the varieties of idealistic formalization, either openly or secretly, lead to a God, as the Cause of all causes. In comparison with the oligarchy of a dozen sub-absolutes of the idealistic philosophy, a single personal Creator is already an element of order. Herein lies the deeper connection between the Formalist refutations of Marxism and the theological refutations of Darwinism.

The Formalist school represents an abortive idealism applied to the question of art. The Formalists show a fast ripening religiousness. They are followers of Saint John. They believe that "In the beginning was the Word." But we believe that in the beginning was the deed. The word followed, as its phonetic shadow.

CHAPTER SIX

Proletarian Culture
and Proletarian Art

Every ruling class creates its own culture, and consequently, its own art. History has known the slave-owning cultures of the East and of classic antiquity, the feudal culture of medieval Europe, and the bourgeois culture, which now rules the world. It would follow from this that the proletariat has also to create its own culture and its own art.

The question, however, is not as simple as it seems at first glance. Societies in which slave owners were the ruling class, existed for many and many centuries. The same is true of feudalism. Bourgeois culture, if one were to count only from the time of its open and turbulent manifestation, that is, from the period of the Renaissance, has existed five centuries, but it did not reach its greatest flowering until the nineteenth century, or, more correctly, the second half of it. History shows that the formation of a new culture that centers around a ruling class demands considerable time and reaches completion only at the period preceding the political decadence of that class.

Will the proletariat have enough time to create a "proletarian" culture? In contrast to the regime of the slave owners and of the feudal lords and of the bourgeoisie, the proletariat regards its dictatorship as a brief period of transition. When we wish to denounce the all-too-optimistic views about the transition to socialism, we point out that the period of the social revolution, on a world scale, will last not months and not years, but decades—decades, but not centuries, and certainly not thousands of years. Can the proletariat in this time create a new culture? It is legitimate to doubt this, because the years of social revolution will be

154

years of fierce class struggles in which destruction will occupy more room than new construction. At any rate, the energy of the proletariat itself will be spent mainly in conquering power, in retaining and strengthening it, and in applying it to the most urgent needs of existence and of further struggle. The proletariat, however, will reach its highest tension and the fullest manifestation of its class character during this revolutionary period and it will be within such narrow limits that the possibility of planful, cultural reconstruction will be confined. On the other hand, as the new regime will be more and more protected from political and military surprises and as the conditions for cultural creation will become more favorable, the proletariat will be more and more dissolved into a socialist community and will free itself from its class characteristics and thus cease to be a proletariat. In other words, there can be no question of the creation of a new culture, that is, of construction on a large historic scale during the period of dictatorship. The cultural reconstruction that will begin when the need of the iron clutch of a dictatorship unparalleled in history will have disappeared, will not have a class character. This seems to lead to the conclusion that there is no proletarian culture and that there never will be any and in fact there is no reason to regret this. The proletariat acquires power for the purpose of doing away forever with class culture and to make way for human culture. We frequently seem to forget this.

The formless talk about proletarian culture, in antithesis to bourgeois culture, feeds on the extremely uncritical identification of the historic destinies of the proletariat with those of the bourgeoisie. A shallow and purely liberal method of making analogies of historic forms has nothing in common with Marxism. There is no real analogy between the historic development of the bourgeoisie and of the working class.

The development of bourgeois culture began several centuries before the bourgeoisie took into its own hands the power of the state by means of a series of revolutions. Even when the bourgeoisie was a third estate, almost deprived of its rights, it played a great and continually growing part in all the fields of culture. This is especially clear in the case of architecture. The Gothic churches were not built suddenly, under the impulse of a religious inspiration. The construction of the Cologne cathedral, its architecture and its sculpture, sum up the architectural experience of mankind from the time of the cave and combine the elements of this experience in a new style that expresses the culture of its own epoch that is, in the final analysis, the social structure and technique of this epoch. The old pre-bourgeoisie of the guilds was the factual builder of the Gothic. When it grew and waxed strong, that is, when it became richer, the bourgeoisie passed through the Gothic stage consciously and actively and created its own architectural style, not for the church, however, but for its own palaces. With its basis on the Gothic, it turned to antiquity, especially to Roman architecture and the Moorish, and applied all these to the conditions and needs of the new city community, thus creating the Renaissance (Italy at the end of the first quarter of the fifteenth century). Specialists may count the elements that the Renaissance owes to antiquity and those it owes to the Gothic and may argue as to which side is the stronger. But the Renaissance only begins when the new social class, already culturally satiated, feels itself strong enough to come out from under the yoke of the Gothic arch, to look at Gothic art and on all that preceded it as material for its own disposal, and to use the technique of the past for its own artistic aims. This refers also to all the other arts, but with this difference, that because of their greater flexibility, that is, of their lesser dependence upon utilitarian aims and materials, the "free" arts do not reveal the dialectics of successive styles with such firm logic as does architecture.

From the time of the Renaissance and of the Reformation, which created more favorable intellectual and political conditions for the bourgeoisie in feudal society, to the time of the Revolution, which transferred power to the bourgeoisie (in France), there passed three or four centuries of growth in the material and intellectual force of the bourgeoisie. The great French Revolution and the wars that grew out of it temporarily lowered the material level of culture. But later the capitalist regime became established as the "natural" and the "eternal."

Thus the fundamental processes of the growth of bourgeois culture and of its crystallization into style were determined by the characteristics of the bourgeoisie as a possessing and exploiting class. The bourgeoisie not only developed materially within feudal society, entwining itself in various ways with the latter and attracting wealth into its own hands, but it weaned the intelligentsia to its side and created its cultural foundation (schools, universities, academies, newspapers, magazines) long before it openly took possession of the state. It is sufficient to remember that the German bourgeoisie, with its incomparable technology, philosophy, science, and art, allowed the power of the state to lie in the hands of a feudal bureaucratic class as late as 1918 and decided, or, more correctly, was forced to take power into its own hands only when the material foundations of German culture began to fall to pieces.

But one may answer: It took thousands of years to create the slave-owning art and only hundreds of years for the bourgeois art. Why, then, could not proletarian art be created in tens of years? The technical bases of life are not at all the same at present and therefore the tempo is also different. This objection, which at first sight seems convincing, in reality misses the crux of the question. Undoubtedly, in the development of the new society, the time will come when economics, cultural life, and art will receive the greatest impulse forward. At the present time we can only create fancies about their tempo. In a society that will have thrown off the pinching and stultifying worry about one's daily bread, in which community restaurants will prepare good, wholesome, and tasteful food for all to choose, in which communal laundries will wash clean everyone's good linen, in which children, all the children, will be well fed and strong and gay, and in which they will absorb the fundamental elements of science and art as they absorb albumen and air and the warmth of the sun, in a society in which electricity and the radio will not be the crafts they are today, but will come from inexhaustible sources of super-power at the call of a central button, in which there will be no "useless mouths," in which the liberated egotism of man—a mighty force!—will be directed wholly toward the understanding, the transformation, and the betterment of the universe—in such a society the dynamic development of culture will be incomparable with anything that went on in the past. But all this will come only after a climb, prolonged and difficult, which is still ahead of us. And we are speaking only about the period of the climb.

But is not the present moment dynamic? It is in the highest degree. But its dynamics are centered in politics. The War and the Revolution were dynamic, but very much at the expense of technology and culture. It is true that the War has produced a long series of technical inventions. But the poverty that it has produced has put off the practical application of these inventions for a long time and with this their possibility of revolutionizing life. This refers to radio, to aviation, and to many mechanical discoveries. On the other hand, the Revolution lays out the ground for a new society. But it does so with the methods of the old society, with the class struggle, with violence, destruction, and annihilation. If the proletarian Revolution had not come, mankind would have been strangled by its own contradictions. The Revolution saved society and culture, but by means of the most cruel surgery. All the active forces are concentrated in politics and in the revolutionary struggle, everything else is shoved back into the background and everything that is a hindrance is cruelly trampled under foot. In this process, of course, there is an ebb and flow; military communism gives place to the NEP, which, in its turn, passes through various stages. But in its essence, the dictatorship of the proletariat is not an organization for the production of the culture of a new society, but a revolutionary and military system struggling for it. One must not forget this. We think that the historian of the future will place the culminating point of the old society on the 2nd of August, 1914, when the maddened power of bourgeois culture let loose upon the world the blood and fire of an imperialistic war. The beginning of the new history of mankind will be dated from November 7, 1917. The fundamental stages of the development of mankind we think will be established somewhat as follows: pre-historic "history" of primitive man; ancient history, whose rise was based on slavery; the Middle Ages, based on serfdom; capitalism, with free wage exploitation; and finally, socialist society, with, let us hope, its painless transition to a stateless Commune. At any rate, the twenty, thirty, or fifty years of proletarian world revolution will go down in history as the most difficult climb from one system to another, but in no case as an independent epoch of proletarian culture.

At present, in these years of respite, some illusions may arise in our Soviet Republic as regards this. We have put the cultural questions on the order of the day. By projecting our present-day problems into the distant future, one can think himself through a long series of years into proletarian culture. But no matter how important and vitally necessary our culture building may be, it is entirely dominated by the approach of European and world revolution. We are, as before, merely soldiers in a campaign. We are bivouacking for a day. Our shirt has to be washed, our hair has to be cut and combed and, most important of all, the rifle has to be cleaned and oiled.

Our entire present-day economic and cultural work is nothing more than a bringing of ourselves into order between two battles and two campaigns. The principal battles are ahead and may be not so far off. Our epoch is not yet an epoch of new culture, but only the entrance to it. We must, first of all, take possession, politically, of the most important elements of the old culture, to such an extent, at least, as to be able to pave the way for a new culture.

This becomes especially clear when one considers the problem as one should, in its international character. The proletariat was, and remains, a non-possessing class. This alone restricted it very much from acquiring those elements of bourgeois culture that have entered into the inventory of mankind forever. In a certain sense, one may truly say that the proletariat also, at least the European proletariat, had its epoch of reformation. This occurred in the second half of the nineteenth century, when, without making an attempt on the power of the state directly, it conquered for itself under the bourgeois system more favorable legal conditions for development. But, in the first place, for this period of "reformation" (parliamentarism and social reforms), which coincides mainly with the period of the Second International, history allowed the working class approximately as many decades as it allowed the bourgeoisie centuries. In the second place, the proletariat, during this preparatory period, did not at all become a richer class and did not concentrate in its hands material power. On the contrary, from a social and cultural point of view, it became more and more unfortunate. The bourgeoisie came into power fully armed with the culture of its time. The proletariat, on the other hand, comes into power fully armed only with the acute need of mastering culture. The problem of a proletariat that has conquered power consists, first of all, in taking into its own hands the apparatus of culture—the industries, schools, publications, press, theaters, etc.—which did not serve it before, and thus to open up the path of culture for itself.

Our task in Russia is complicated by the poverty of our entire cultural tradition and by the material destruction wrought by the events of the last decade. After the conquest of power and after almost six years of struggle for its retention and consolidation, our proletariat is forced to turn all its energies toward the creation of the most elementary conditions of material existence and of contact with the ABC of culture—ABC in the true and literal sense of the word. It is not for nothing that we have put to ourselves the task of having universal literacy in Russia by the tenth anniversary of the Soviet regime.

Someone may object that I take the concept of proletarian culture in too broad a sense. That if there may not be a fully and entirely developed proletarian culture, yet the working class may succeed in putting its stamp upon culture before it is dissolved into a communist society. Such an objection must be registered first of all as a serious retreat from the position that there will be a proletarian culture. It is not to be questioned but that the proletariat, during the time of its dictatorship, will put its stamp upon culture. However, this is a far cry from a proletarian culture in the sense of a developed and completely harmonious system of knowledge and of art in all material and spiritual fields of work. For tens of millions of people for the first time in history to master reading and writing and arithmetic is in itself a new cultural fact of great importance. The essence of the new culture will be not an aristocratic one for a privileged minority, but a mass culture, a universal and popular one. Quantity will pass into quality; with the growth of the quantity of culture will come a rise in its level and a change in its character. But this process will develop only through a series of historic stages. In the degree to which it is successful it will weaken the class character of the proletariat and in this way it will wipe out the basis of a proletarian culture.

But how about the upper strata of the working class? About its intellectual vanguard? Can one not say that in these circles, narrow though they are, a development of proletarian culture is already taking place today? Have we not the Socialist Academy? Red professors? Some are guilty of putting the question in this very abstract way. The idea seems to be that it is possible to create a proletarian culture by laboratory methods. In fact, the texture of culture is woven at the points where the relationships and interactions of the intelligentsia of a class and of the class itself meet. The bourgeois culture—the technical, political, philosophical, and artistic—was developed by the interaction of the bourgeoisie and its inventors, leaders, thinkers, and poets. The reader created the writer and the writer created the reader. This is true in an immeasurably greater degree of the proletariat, because its economics and politics and culture can be built only on the basis of the creative activity of the masses. The main task of the proletarian intelligentsia in the immediate future is not the abstract formation of a new culture regardless of the absence of a basis for it, but definite culture-bearing, that is, a systematic, planful and, of course, critical imparting to the backward masses of the essential elements of the culture that already exists. It is impossible to create a class culture behind the backs of a class. And to build culture in cooperation with the working class and in close contact with its general historic rise, one has to build socialism, even though in the rough. In this process, the class characteristics of society will not become stronger, but, on the contrary, will begin to dissolve and to disappear in direct ratio to the success of the Revolution. The liberating significance of the dictatorship of the proletariat consists in the fact that it is temporary—for a brief period only—that it is a means of clearing the road and of laying the foundations of a society without classes and of a culture based upon solidarity.

In order to explain the idea of a period of culture-bearing in the development of the working class more concretely, let us consider the historic succession not of classes, but of generations. Their continuity is expressed in the fact that each one of them, given a developing and not a decadent society, adds its treasure to the past accumulations of culture. But before it can do so, each new generation must pass through a stage of apprenticeship. It appropriates existing culture and transforms it in its own way, making it more or less different from that of the older generation. But this appropriation is not, as yet, a new creation, that is, it is not a creation of new cultural values, but only a premise for them. To a certain degree, that which has been said may also be applied to the destinies of the working masses, which are rising toward epoch-making creative work. One has only to add that before the proletariat will have passed out of the stage of cultural apprenticeship, it will have ceased to be a proletariat. Let us also not forget that the upper layer of the bourgeois third estate passed its cultural apprenticeship under the roof of feudal society; that while still within the womb of feudal society it surpassed the old ruling estates culturally and became the instigator of culture before it came into power. It is different with the proletariat in general and with the Russian proletariat in particular. The proletariat is forced to take power before it has appropriated the fundamental elements of bourgeois culture; it is forced to overthrow bourgeois society by revolutionary violence for the very reason that society does not allow it access to culture. The working class strives to transform the state apparatus into a powerful pump for quenching the cultural thirst of the masses. This is a task of immeasurable historic importance. But, if one is not to use words lightly, it is not as yet a creation of a special proletarian culture. "Proletarian culture," "proletarian art," etc., in three cases out of ten is used uncritically to designate the culture and the art of the coming communist society, in two cases out of ten to designate the fact that special groups of the proletariat are acquiring separate elements of pre-proletarian culture, and finally, in five cases out of ten, it represents a jumble of concepts and words out of which one can make neither head nor tail.

Here is a recent example, one of a hundred, where a slovenly, uncritical and dangerous use of the term "proletarian culture" is made. "The economic basis and its corresponding system of super-structures," writes Sizov, "form the cultural characteristics of an epoch (feudal, bourgeois, or proletarian)." Thus the epoch of proletarian culture is placed here on the same plane as that of the bourgeois. But that which is here called the proletarian epoch is only a brief transition from one social-cultural system to another, from capitalism to socialism. The establishment of the bourgeois regime was also preceded by a transitional epoch. But the bourgeois Revolution tried, successfully, to perpetuate the domination of the bourgeoisie, while the proletarian Revolution has for its aim the liquidation of the proletariat as a class in as brief a period as possible. The length of this period depends entirely upon the success of the Revolution. Is it not amazing that one can forget this and place the proletarian cultural epoch on the same plane with that of feudal and bourgeois culture?

But if this is so, does it follow that we have no proletarian science? Are we not to say that the materialistic conception of history and the Marxist criticism of political economy represent invaluable scientific elements of a proletarian culture?

Of course, the materialistic conception of history and the labor theory of value have an immeasurable significance for the arming of the proletariat as a class and for science in general. There is more true science in the *Communist Manifesto* alone than in all the libraries of historical and historico-philosophical compilations, speculations, and falsifications of the professors. But can one say that Marxism represents a product of proletarian culture? And can one say that we are already making use of Marxism, not in political battles only, but in broad scientific tasks as well?

Marx and Engels came out of the ranks of the petty bourgeois democracy and, of course, were brought up on its culture and not on the culture of the proletariat. If there had been no working class, with its strikes, struggles, sufferings, and revolts, there would, of course, have been no scientific communism, because there would have been no historical necessity for it. But its theory was formed entirely on the basis of bourgeois culture both scientific and political, though it declared a fight to the finish upon that culture. Under the pressure of capitalistic contradictions, the universalizing thought of the bourgeois democracy, of its boldest, most honest, and most far-sighted representatives, rises to the heights of a marvelous renunciation, armed with all the critical weapons of bourgeois science. Such is the origin of Marxism.

The proletariat found its weapon in Marxism not at once, and not fully even to this day. Today this weapon serves political aims almost primarily and exclusively. The broad realistic application and the methodological development of dialectic materialism are still entirely in the future. Only in a socialist society will Marxism cease to be a one-sided weapon of political struggle and become a means of scientific creation, a most important element and instrument of spiritual culture.

All science, in greater or lesser degree, unquestionably reflects the tendencies of the ruling class. The more closely science attaches itself to the practical tasks of conquering nature (physics, chemistry, natural science in general), the greater is its non-class and human contribution. The more deeply science is connected with the social mechanism of exploitation (political economy), or the more abstractly it generalizes the entire experience of man-kind (psychology, not in its experimental, physiological sense but in its so-called "philosophic sense"), the more does it obey the class egotism of the bourgeoisie and the less significant is its con-tribution to the general sum of human knowledge. In the domain of the experimental sciences, there exist different degrees of scien-tific integrity and objectivity, depending upon the scope of the generalizations made. As a general rule, the bourgeois tendencies have found a much freer place for themselves in the higher spheres of methodological philosophy, of *Weltanschauung*. It is therefore necessary to clear the structure of science from the bot-tom to the top, or, more correctly, from the top to the bottom, because one has to begin from the upper stories. But it would be naive to think that the proletariat must revamp critically all science inherited from the bourgeoisie, before applying it to so-cialist reconstruction. This is just the same as saying with the Utopian moralists: before building a new society, the proletariat must rise to the heights of communist ethics. As a matter of fact, the proletariat will reconstruct ethics as well as science radically, but he will do so after he will have constructed a new society, even though in the rough. But are we not traveling in a vicious circle? How is one to build a new society with the aid of the old science and the old morals? Here we must bring in a little dialec-tics, that very dialectics which we now put so uneconomically into lyric poetry and into our office bookkeeping and into our cabbage soup and into our porridge. In order to begin work, the proletarian vanguard needs certain points of departure, certain scientific methods that liberate the mind from the ideological yoke of the bourgeoisie; it is mastering these; in part has already mastered them. It has tested its fundamental method in many battles, under various conditions. But this is a long way from proletarian science. A revolutionary class cannot stop its struggle, because the Party has not yet decided whether it should or should not accept the hypothesis of electrons and ions, the psychoanalyt-ical theory of Freud, the new mathematical discoveries of relativ-ity, etc. True, after it has conquered power, the proletariat will find a much greater opportunity for mastering science and for re-vising it. This is more easily said than done. The proletariat can-not postpone socialist reconstruction until the time when its new scientists, many of whom are still running about in short trousers, will test and clean all the instruments and all the channels of knowledge. The proletariat rejects what is clearly unnecessary, false and reactionary, and in the various fields of its reconstruction makes use of the methods and conclusions of present-day science, taking them necessarily with the percentage of reactionary class alloy that is contained in them. The practical result will justify itself generally and on the whole, because such a use when controlled by a socialist goal will gradually manage and select the methods and conclusions of the theory. And by that time there will have grown up scientists who are educated under the new conditions. At any rate, the proletariat will have to carry its socialist reconstruction to quite a high degree, that is, provide for real material security and for the satisfaction of society culturally before it will be able to carry out a general purification of science from top to bottom. I do not mean to say by this anything against the Marxist work of criticism, which many in small circles and in seminars are trying to carry through in various fields. This work is necessary and fruitful. It should be extended and deepened in every way. But one has to maintain the Marxian sense of the measure of things to count up the specific gravity of such experiments and efforts today in relation to the general scale of our historic work.

Does the foregoing exclude the possibility that even in the period of revolutionary dictatorship, there might appear eminent scientists, inventors, dramatists, and poets out of the ranks of the proletariat? Not in the least. But it would be extremely light-minded to give the name of proletarian culture, even to the most valuable achievements of individual representatives of the working class. One cannot turn the concept of culture into the small change of individual daily living and determine the success of a class culture by the proletarian passports of individual inventors or poets. Culture is the organic sum of knowledge and capacity that characterizes the entire society, or at least its ruling class. It embraces and penetrates all fields of human work and unifies them into a system. Individual achievements rise above this level and elevate it gradually.

Does such an organic interrelation exist between our present-day proletarian poetry and the cultural work of the working class in its entirety? It is quite evident that it does not. Individual workers or groups of workers are developing contacts with the art that was created by the bourgeois intelligentsia and are making use of its technique, for the time being, in quite an eclectic manner. But is it for the purpose of giving expression to their own internal proletarian world? The fact is that it is far from being so. The work of the proletarian poets lacks an organic quality, which is produced only by a profound interaction between art and the development of culture in general. We have the literary works of talented and gifted proletarians, but that is not proletarian literature. However, they may prove to be some of its springs.

It is possible that in the work of the present generation many germs and roots and springs will be revealed to which some future descendant will trace the various sectors of the culture of the future, just as our present-day historians of art trace the theater of Ibsen to the church mystery, or Impressionism and Cubism to the paintings of the monks. In the economy of art, as in the economy of nature, nothing is lost, and everything is connected in the large. But factually, concretely, vitally, the present-day work of the poets who have sprung from the proletariat is not developing at all in accordance with the plan that is behind the process of preparing the conditions of the future socialist culture, that is, the process of elevating the masses.

The proletarian poets were greatly pained and aroused against Dubovskoy because of an article in which he expressed— side by side with ideas that seem to be doubtful—a series of truths that are a little bitter, but fundamentally indisputable. Dubovskoy's conclusion is that proletarian poetry does not lie in the "Kuznitsa" group, but in the local factory newspapers, written by anonymous authors. The thought here is true though it is expressed paradoxically. One might with as much reason say that the proletarian Shakespeares and Goethes are running about barefoot somewhere today in the elementary schools. Undoubtedly the work of the factory poets is much more organic, in the sense of its being connected with the life, environment, and interests of the working masses. Nonetheless, it is not proletarian literature, but it expresses in writing the molecular process of the cultural rise of the proletariat. We have already explained above that this is not one and the same thing. The letters of the workers, the local poets, the complainants, are carrying on a great cultural work, breaking up the ground and preparing it for future sowing. But a cultural and artistic harvest of full value will be—happily!—socialist and not "proletarian."

Pletnov, in an interesting article on the methods of proletarian poetry, expresses the thought that the works of the proletarian poets, apart from their artistic value, are significant because of their direct contact with the life of a class. By giving examples of proletarian poetry Pletnov shows convincingly the changes in the moods of the worker poets and their relation to the general development of the life and struggles of the proletariat. Pletnov proves irrefutably by this that the products of proletarian poetry —not all, but many—are significant cultural and historical documents. But this does not at all mean that they are artistic documents. "Let us suppose, if you please, that these poems are weak, old in form, illiterate," says Pletnov, in characterizing one of the worker poets, who rose from a prayerful mood to a militant revolutionary one—"but do they not mark just the same the growth of the proletarian poet?" Undoubtedly; the weak, the colorless, and even the illiterate poems may reflect the path of the political growth of a poet and of a class and may have an immeasurable significance as a symptom of culture. But weak and, what is more, illiterate poems do not make up proletarian poetry, because they do not make up poetry at all. It is extremely interesting that, while tracing the political evolution of the worker poets, which went hand in hand with the revolutionary growth of the class, Pletnov justly points out that among the proletarian writers there has been a breaking away from their class during the latter years, especially since the beginning of the New Economic Policy. Pletnov explains "the crisis of proletarian poetry" and the simultaneous trend toward Formalism and toward Philistinism by the neglect of the poets by the Party. From this it has resulted that the poets "have not resisted the colossal pressure of bourgeois ideology and have given way, or are giving way." The explanation is clearly insufficient. What kind of colossal pressure of bourgeois ideology exists among us? One should not exaggerate. Let us not quarrel about whether the Party could have done more for proletarian poetry than it has done. But this alone no more covers the question of why this poetry lacks the power of resistance than does the violent "class" gesture (in the manner of the manifesto of "Kuznitsa") compensate it for its insufficient power of resistance. The fact is that in the pre-revolutionary period, and during the first period of the Revolution, the proletarian poets regarded versification not as an art that had its own laws, but as one of the means of complaining of one's sad fate, or of expressing one's revolutionary mood. The proletarian poets approached poetry as an art and as a craft only during these latter years, after the tension of the civil war was relaxed. Then it became clear that the proletariat had not yet created a cultural background in art, but that the bourgeois intelligentsia had such a background for better or for worse. It is not the fact that the Party or its leaders did "not help sufficiently," but that the masses were not artistically prepared; and art, just as science, demands preparation. Our proletariat has its political culture, within limits sufficient for securing its dictatorship, but it has no artistic culture. While the proletarian poets marched in the general ranks of the military, their poems, as was said above, retained the importance of revolutionary documents. But when these poets were faced with the problems of craftsmanship and art, they began to seek for themselves willy-nilly a new environment. It is, therefore, not a matter of their being neglected—the cause lies in a deeper historic condition. However, this does not mean that the worker poets who are passing through a crisis have been lost entirely for the proletariat. Let us hope that some, at least, will come out stronger from this crisis. Still, it doesn't look as if the present groups of worker poets are destined to lay immutable foundations for a new great poetry. Most likely this will be the privilege of distant generations, which, too, will have to pass through crises. For there will be plenty of ideological and cultural deviations, waverings, and errors for a long time to come, the cause of which will lie in the cultural immaturity of the working class.

The study of literary technique alone is a necessary stage and it is not a brief one. Technique is noticed most markedly in the case of those who have not mastered it. One can say with full justice about many of the young proletarian writers that it is not they who are the masters of technique, but that the technique is their master. For the more talented, this is merely a disease of growth. But they who refuse to master technique will come to look "unnatural," imitative, and even buffoon-like. It would be monstrous to conclude from this that the technique of bourgeois art is not necessary to the workers. Yet there are many who fall into this error. "Give us," they say, "something even pockmarked, but our own." This is false and untrue. A pockmarked art is no art and is therefore not necessary to the working masses. Those who believe in a "pockmarked" art are imbued to a considerable extent with contempt for the masses and are like the breed of politicians who have no faith in class power but who flatter and praise the class when "all is well." On the heels of the demagogues come the sincere fools who have taken up this simple formula of a pseudo-proletarian art. This is not Marxism, but reactionary populism, falsified a little to suit a "proletarian" ideology. Proletarian art should not be second-rate art. One has to learn regardless of the fact that learning carries within itself certain dangers because out of necessity one has to learn from one's enemies. One has to learn and the importance of such organizations as the Proletkult [the Organization for Proletarian Culture] cannot be measured by the rapidity with which they create a new literature, but by the extent to which they help elevate the literary level of the working class, beginning with its upper strata.

Such terms as "proletarian literature" and "proletarian culture" are dangerous, because they erroneously compress the culture of the future into the narrow limits of the present day. They falsify perspectives, they violate proportions, they distort standards, and they cultivate the arrogance of small circles, which is most dangerous.

But if we are to reject the term "proletarian culture," what shall we do with the Proletkult? Let us agree, then, that the Proletkult means to work for proletarian culture, that is, to struggle obstinately to raise the cultural level of the working class. In truth, such an interpretation will not diminish the importance of the Proletkult by one iota.

In their manifesto already mentioned, the proletarian writers of "Kuznitsa" declare that "style is class," and that therefore the writers who are outsiders socially are unable to create a style of art that would correspond to the nature of the proletariat. It would follow from this that the "Kuznitsa" group is proletarian both in its composition and in its tendency and that it is creating a proletarian art.

"Style is class." However, style is not born with a class at all. A class finds its style in extremely complex ways. It would be very simple if a writer, just because he was a proletarian, loyal to his class, could stand at the crossing of the roads and announce:

"I am the style of the proletariat!"

"Style is class"—not alone in art, but above all in politics. Politics is the only field in which the proletariat has really created its own style. But how? Not at all by means of a simple syllogism: each class has its own style; the proletariat is a class; it assigns to such and such a proletarian group the task of formulating its political style. No! The road is far more complex. The elaboration of proletarian politics went through economic strikes, through a struggle for the right to organize, through the Utopian schools of the English and the French, through the workers' participation in revolutionary struggles under the leadership of bourgeois democrats, through the *Communist Manifesto*, through the establishment of the Socialist Party, which, however, subordinated itself to the "style" of other classes, through the split among the socialists and the organization of the communists, through the struggle of the communists for a united front, and it will go through a whole series of other stages that are still ahead of us. All the energy of the proletariat that remains at its disposal after meeting the elementary demands of life has gone and is going toward the elaboration of this political "style" while, on the contrary, the historic rise of the bourgeoisie took place with a comparative evenness in all fields of social life. That is, the bourgeoisie grew rich, organized itself, shaped itself philosophically and aesthetically, and accumulated habits of government. On the other hand, the whole process of self-determination of the proletariat, a class unfortunate economically, assumes an intensely one-sided, revolutionary, and political character and reaches its highest expression in the Communist Party.

If we were to compare the rise in art with the rise in politics, we would have to say that here at the present time we find ourselves approximately in the same stage as when the first faint movements of the masses coincided with the efforts of the intelligentsia and of a few workers to construct Utopian systems. We heartily hope that the poets of "Kuznitsa" will contribute to the art of the future, if not to a proletarian, at least to a socialist art. But to recognize the monopoly of "Kuznitsa" to express "proletarian style" at the present super-primitive stage of the process would be an unpardonable error. The activity of "Kuznitsa" in relation to the proletariat is carried on the same plane as that of "Lef" and "Krug" and the other groups that try to find an artistic expression for the Revolution, and, in all honesty, we do not know which one of these contributions will prove to be the biggest.

For instance, many proletarian poets have an undoubted trace of Futurist influence. The talented Kazin has imbibed the elements of Futurist technique. Bezimensky is unthinkable without Mayakovsky, and Bezimensky is a hope.

"Kuznitsa's" manifesto pictures the present situation in art as extremely dark and makes the following indictment: "the NEP-stage of the Revolution found itself surrounded by an art that resembles the grimaces of a gorilla." "Money is assigned for everything....We have no Belinskys. Twilight hangs over the desert of art. We raise our voices and we lift the Red Flag..." etc., etc. They speak with great eloquence and even pompously of proletarian art sometimes as an art of the future and sometimes as an art of the present. "The monolith of class creates art in its own image only and in its own likeness. Its peculiar language, polyphonous, multicolored and multi-imaged...promotes the might of a great style by its simplicity, clarity, and precision." But if all this is true, why is there a desert of art and why the twilight over the desert? This evident contradiction can only be understood in the sense that the authors of this manifesto contrast the art that is protected by the Soviet Government and that is a desert covered by twilight with the proletarian art of big canvases and great style, which, however, is not getting the necessary recognition because there are no "Belinskys" and because the place of the Belinskys is taken by "a few comrades, publicists from our ranks, who were accustomed to draw cart-shafts." At the risk of being included among the cart-shaft order, I must say, however, that the manifesto of "Kuznitsa" is not penetrated with the spirit of class Messianism, but with the spirit of an arrogant small circle. "Kuznitsa" speaks of itself as the exclusive carrier of revolutionary art in the same terms as do the Futurists, Imagists, "Serapion Fraternity," and the others. Where is that "art of the big canvas, of the large style, that monumental art"? Where, oh, where is it? No matter how one may value the works of individual poets who are of proletarian origin—and they need careful and strictly individualized criticism—there is, nevertheless, no proletarian art. One must not play with big words. It is not true that a proletarian style exists and that it is a big and monumental one at that. Where is it? And in what? And why? The proletarian poets are going through an apprenticeship, and the influence of other schools, principally the Futurist, can be found without using, so to speak, the microscopic methods of the Formalist school. This is not said as a reproach, for it is no sin. But monumental proletarian styles cannot be created by means of manifestos.

Our authors complain that there are no "Belinskys." If we were in need of juridical proof that the work of "Kuznitsa" is imbued with the moods of the isolated little world of the intelligentsia or of a little circle or school, we should find the material evidence for this in this phrase in minor key: "There are no Belinskys." Of course Belinsky is referred to here not as a person, but as the representative of a dynasty of Russian social critics, the inspirers and directors of the old literature. But our friends of "Kuznitsa" do not seem to understand that this dynasty ceased to exist when the proletarian masses appeared on the political arena. In a way, and in a very essential way, Plekhanov was the Marxist Belinsky, the last representative of this noble dynasty of publicists. The historic role of the Belinskys was to open up a breathing hole into social life by means of literature. Literary criticism took the place of politics and was a preparation for it. But that which was merely a hint for Belinsky and for the later representatives of radical publicism has taken on in our day the flesh and blood of October and has become Soviet reality. If Belinsky, Tchernischevsky, Dobrolubov, Pisarev, Mikhailovsky, Plekhanov, were each in his own way the inspirers of social literature, or, what is more, the literary inspirers of an incipient social life, then does not our whole social life at the present time with its politics, its press, its meetings, its institutions, appear as the sufficient interpreter of its own ways? We have placed our entire social life under a projector, the light of Marxism illumines all the stages of our struggle and every institution is critically sounded from all sides. To sigh for the Belinskys under such a condition, is to reveal—alas!—the isolation of an intelligentsia group, entirely in the style (far from monumental) of the most pious populists of the Left—the Ivanov-Razumniks. "There are no Belinskys." But Belinsky was not a literary critic; he was a socially minded leader of his epoch. And if Vissarion Belinsky could be transported alive into our times, he probably would be—let us not conceal this from the Kuznitsa—a member of the Politburo. And, furious, he would most likely start drawing a cart-shaft. Did he not complain that he whose nature was to howl like a jackal, had to emit melodious notes?

⁓ ⁓ ⁓

It is not accidental that the poetry of small circles falls into the flat romanticism of "Cosmism" when it tries to overcome its isolation. The idea here approximately is that one should feel the entire world as a unity and oneself as an active part of that unity, with the prospect of commanding in the future not only the earth, but the entire cosmos. All this, of course, is very splendid, and terribly big. We came from Kursk and from Kaluga, we have conquered all Russia recently, and now we are going on toward world revolution. But are we to stop at the boundaries of "planetism"! Let us put the proletarian hoop on the barrel of the universe at once. What can be simpler? This is familiar business: we'll cover it all with our hat!

Cosmism seems, or may seem, extremely bold, vigorous, revolutionary, and proletarian. But in reality, Cosmism contains the suggestion of very nearly deserting the complex and difficult problems of art on earth so as to escape into the interstellar spheres. In this way Cosmism turns out quite suddenly to be akin to mysticism. It is a very difficult task to put the starry kingdom into one's own artistic world, and to do this in some sort of a conative way, not only in a contemplative, and to do this quite independently of how much one is acquainted with astronomy. Still, it is not an urgent task. And it seems that the poets are becoming Cosmists, not because the population of the Milky Way is knocking at their doors and demanding an answer, but because the problems of earth are lending themselves to artistic expression with so much difficulty that it makes them feel like jumping into another world. However, it takes more than calling oneself a Cosmist to catch stars from heaven, especially as there is so much more interstellar emptiness in the universe than there are stars. Let them beware lest this doubtful tendency to fill up the gaps in one's point of view and in one's artistic work with the thinness of interstellar spaces lead some of the Cosmists to the most subtle of matters, namely, to the Holy Ghost in which there are quite enough poetic dead bodies already at rest.

The nets and lassos thrown over the proletarian poets are the more dangerous because these poets are almost all young, some of them still hardly out of their teens. The majority of them were awakened to poetry by the victory of the Revolution. They did not enter it as people already formed, but were carried along on the wings of spontaneity and by the storm and the hurricane. But this primitive intoxication affected all the bourgeois writers as well, who afterwards paid for it by a reactionary, mystic, and every other kind of heavy head. The real difficulties and tests began when the rhythm of the Revolution slowed down, when the objective aims became more cloudy and when it was no longer possible simply to swim with the waves and to swallow and emit inspired bubbles, but one had to look around, dig oneself in, and sum up the situation. Then it was that the temptation came to jump straight off into the cosmos! But the earth? As in the case of the mystics, it may prove simply to be a springboard to the cosmos.

The revolutionary poets of our period are in need of being tempered—and a moral hardening is here more inseparable from an intellectual one than anywhere else. What is necessary here is a stable, flexible, activist point of view, saturated with facts and with an artistic feeling for the world. To understand and perceive truly, not in a journalistic way, but to feel to the very bottom the section of time in which we live, one has to know the past of mankind, its life, its work, its struggles, its hopes, its defeats, and its achievements. Astronomy and cosmogony are good things! But first of all, one has to know the history of mankind and the laws, the concrete facts, the picturesqueness, and the personalities of contemporary life.

■   ■   ■

It is curious that those who make abstract formulas of proletarian poetry usually pass the poet by who, more than anyone else, has the right to be called the poet of revolutionary Russia. No complex critical methods are needed to determine his tendencies or his social bases. Demyan Biedny is here in the whole, made out of one piece. He is not a poet who has approached the Revolution, who has come down to it, who has accepted it. He is a Bolshevik whose weapon is poetry. And in this lies Demyan Biedny's exclusive power. The Revolution is, for him, no material for creation, but the highest authority, which has placed him at his post. His work is a social service not only in the final analysis, as all art is, but subjectively, in the consciousness of the poet himself. And this has been true from the very first days of his historic service. He grew up in the Party, he lived through the various phases of its development, he learned to think and to feel with his class from day to day and to reproduce this world of thoughts and feelings in concentrated form in the language of verses that have the shrewdness of fables, the sadness of songs, the boldness of couplets, as well as indignation and appeal. There is nothing of the dilettante in his anger and in his hatred. He hates with the well-placed hatred of the most revolutionary Party in the world. Some of his things have the power of a great and finished art, but there is also much of the newspaper in him, of a daily and second-rate newspaper at that. Not only in those rare cases when Apollo calls him to the holy sacrifice does Demyan Biedny create, but day in and day out, as the events and the Central Committee of the Party demand. But taken in its entirety, his work represents the most unusual and unique phenomenon in its way. Let those little poets of various schools who like to sniff at Demyan Biedny and to call him a newspaper *feuilleton* writer (sic!) dig in their memory and find another poet who by his verses has influenced so directly and actively the masses, the working and peasant masses, the Red Army masses, the many-millioned masses, during the greatest of all epochs.

Demyan Biedny does not seek new forms. He even emphasizes the fact that he uses the sacred old forms. But they are resurrected and reborn in his work, as an invaluable mechanism for the transmission of Bolshevist ideas. Demyan Biedny did not and will not create a school; he himself was created by the school, called the Russian Communist Party, for the needs of a great epoch that will not come again. If one could free oneself from a metaphysical concept of proletarian culture and could regard the question from the point of view of what the proletariat reads, what it needs, what absorbs it, what impels it to action, what elevates its cultural level and so prepares the ground for a new art, then the work of Demyan Biedny would appear as proletarian and popular literature, that is, literature vitally needed by an awakened people. If this is not "true" poetry, it is something more than that.

The great historic figure, Ferdinand Lassalle, wrote at one time to Marx and Engels in London: "How willingly I would leave unwritten that which I know, in order to realize only part of that which I am "capable of." In the spirit of these words, Demyan Biedny could say about himself: "I willingly leave to others to write in new and more complicated form *about* the Revolution, that I myself may write in the old form *for* the Revolution."

CHAPTER SEVEN

Communist Policy Toward Art

There are Marxists in literature who have taken an arrogant attitude toward Futurists, the "Serapion Fraternity," Imagists, and all the "fellow travelers" in general, together or separately. That is why it has become quite the thing to run down Pilnyak and the Futurists have become quite adept at this. It is unquestionably true that Pilnyak is irritating because of some of his peculiarities. He is too light in great questions; he shows off too much and his mortar is too full of lyricism. But Pilnyak has shown the Revolution from the angle of the peasant in the provinces splendidly, and he has shown us the cattle car—thanks to Pilnyak all these stand before us immeasurably clearer and more tangible than ever before. And how about Vsevolod Ivanov? Have we not discovered Russia and felt its vastness, its ethnographic variety, its backwardness, and its sweep better after reading his "Guerilla-fighters," "The Armored Train," "The Blue Sands," in spite of all their sins in construction, their unevenness of style, and even their oleographics? Does anyone really think that this Imagist knowledge can be replaced with Futurist hyperboles or with the monotonous singing of syllables or with journalistic articles, which, day in day out, combine the same three hundred words in a different way? Throw out Pilnyak and Vsevolod Ivanov from our life and we shall be considerably the poorer. The organizers of the campaign against the fellow travelers—a campaign that shows an insufficient concern about perspectives and proportions—have selected Voronsky as one of their targets, the editor of the *Krasnaya Nov* and the leader of "Krug's" publishing house. We think that Voronsky is

177

carrying out a great literary and cultural work under the direction of the Party and, indeed, it is much easier to decree a communist art in a little article than to participate in the drudgery of its preparation!

In the question of form, our critics hewed to the line taken by the almanac *Raspad* some time ago (in 1908). But after all, one has to understand and sum up the differences in historic situations and the rearrangement of forces that has taken place since then. At that time we were a party driven underground. The revolution was retreating and the counterrevolution of Stolypin and of the anarchists and mystics was advancing along the entire line. In the Party itself, the intelligentsia played a disproportionately big part, and the groups of intelligentsia of various political shades exercised an influence upon one another. Under such conditions, for the self-protection of our ideology, a violent resistance to the literary moods of the reaction that began after 1905 was needed.

At the present time an entirely different process is taking place, a process that is fundamentally the reverse. The law of social attraction (toward the ruling class), which, in the last analysis, determines the creative work of the intelligentsia, is now operating to our advantage. One has to keep this fact in mind when shaping a political attitude toward art.

It is untrue that revolutionary art can be created only by workers. Just because the revolution is a working-class revolution, it releases—to repeat what was said before—very little working-class energy for art. During the French Revolution, the greatest works, which, directly or indirectly, reflected it were created not by French artists, but by German, English, and others. The French bourgeoisie, which was directly concerned with making the revolution, could not give up a sufficient quantity of its strength to recreate and to perpetuate its imprint. This is still more true of the proletariat, which, though it has culture in politics, has little culture in art. The intelligentsia, aside from the advantages of its qualifications in form, has also the odious privilege of holding a passive political position, which is marked by a greater or lesser degree of hostility or friendliness toward the October Revolution.

It is not surprising, then, that this contemplative intelligentsia is able to give, and does give, a better artistic reproduction of the revolution than the proletariat that has made the revolution, though the recreations of the intelligentsia are somewhat off line. We know very well the political limitations, the instability, and the unreliability of the "fellow travelers." But if we should eliminate Pilnyak, with his *The Bare Year,* the "Serapion Fraternity" with Vsevolod Ivanov, Tikhonov, and Polonskaya, if we should eliminate Mayakovsky and Yessenin, is there anything that will remain for us but a few unpaid promissory notes of a future proletarian literature? Especially as Demyan Biedny, who cannot be counted among the fellow travelers and who, we hope, cannot be eliminated from revolutionary literature, cannot be related to proletarian literature in the sense as defined by the manifesto of the *Kuznitsa.* What will remain then?

Does that mean that the Party, quite in opposition to its nature, occupies a purely eclectic position in the field of art? This argument, which seems so crushing, is, in reality, extremely childish. The Marxian method affords an opportunity to estimate the development of the new art, to trace all its sources, to help the most progressive tendencies by a critical illumination of the road, but it does not do more than that. Art must make its own way and by its own means. The Marxian methods are not the same as the artistic. The Party leads the proletariat but not the historic processes of history. There are domains in which the Party leads, directly and imperatively. There are domains in which it only cooperates. There are, finally, domains in which it only orients itself. The domain of art is not one in which the Party is called upon to command. It can and must protect and help it, but it can only lead it indirectly. It can and must give the additional credit of its confidence to various art groups, which are striving sincerely to approach the revolution and so help an artistic formulation of the revolution. And at any rate, the Party cannot and will not take the position of a literary circle that is struggling and merely competing with other literary circles.

The Party stands guard over the historic interests of the working class in its entirety. Because it prepares consciously and step by step the ground for a new culture and therefore for a new art, it regards the literary fellow travelers not as the competitors of the writers of the working class, but as the real or potential helpers of the working class in the big work of reconstruction. The Party understands the episodic character of the literary groups of a transition period and estimates them, not from the point of view of the class passports of the individual gentlemen literati, but from the point of view of the place that these groups occupy and can occupy in preparing a socialist culture. If it is not possible to determine the place of any given group today, then the Party as a party will wait patiently and gracefully. Individual critics or readers may sympathize with one group or another in advance. The Party, as a whole, protects the historic interests of the working class and must be more objective and wise. Its caution must be double-edged. If the party does not put its stamp of approval on the *Kuznitsa,* just because workers write for it, it does not, in advance, repel any given literary group, even from the intelligentsia, insofar as such a group tries to approach the revolution and tries to strengthen one of its links—a link is always a weak point—between the city and the village, or between the party member and the nonpartisan, or between the intelligentsia and the workers.

Does not such a policy mean, however, that the Party is going to have an unprotected flank on the side of art? This is a great exaggeration. The Party will repel the clearly poisonous, disintegrating tendencies of art and will guide itself by its political standards. It is true, however, that it is less protected on the flank of art than on the political front. But is this not true of science also? What are the metaphysicians of a purely proletarian science going to say about the theory of relativity? Can it be reconciled with materialism, or can it not? Has this question been decided? Where and when and by whom? It is clear to anyone, even to the uninitiated, that the work of our physiologist, Pavlov, is entirely along materialist lines. But what is one to say about the psychoanalytic theory of Freud? Can it be reconciled with materialism, as, for instance, Karl Radek thinks (and I also), or is it hostile to it? The same question can be put to all the new theories of atomic structure, etc., etc. It would be fine if a scientist would come along who could grasp all these new generalizations methodologically and introduce them into the dialectic materialist conception of the world. He could thus, at the same time, test the new theories and develop the dialectic method deeper. But I am very much afraid that this work—which is not like a newspaper or journalistic article, but a scientific and philosophic landmark, just as the *Origin of Species* and *Capital*—will not be created either today or tomorrow, or rather, if such an epoch-making book were created today, it would risk remaining uncut until the time when the proletariat will be able to lay aside its arms.

But does not the work of culture-bearing, that is, the work of acquiring the ABC of pre-proletarian culture, presuppose criticism, selection, and a class standard? Of course it does. But the standard is a political one and not an abstract cultural one. The political standard coincides with the cultural one only in the broad sense that the revolution creates conditions for a new culture. But this does not mean that such a coinciding is secured in every given case. If the revolution has the right to destroy bridges and art monuments whenever necessary, it will stop still less from laying its hand on any tendency in art, which, no matter how great its achievement in form, threatens to disintegrate the revolutionary environment or to arouse the internal forces of the revolution, that is, the proletariat, the peasantry, and the intelligentsia, to a hostile opposition to one another. Our standard is—clearly—political, imperative, and intolerant. But for this very reason, it must define the limits of its activity clearly. For a more precise expression of my meaning, I will say: we ought to have a watchful revolutionary censorship, and a broad and flexible policy in the field of art, free from petty partisan maliciousness....

It is quite evident that the Party cannot, not for one day, follow the liberal principle of laissez faire and laissez passer, even in the field of art. The question is only at what point should interference begin, and what should be its limits; in which case and between what should the Party choose. And this question is not at all as simple as the theorists of the "Lef," the heralds of proletarian literature, and the critics are pleased to think.

The aims, the problems, and the methods of the working class are incomparably more concrete, more definite, and theoretically better elaborated in economics than in art. Nevertheless, after a brief attempt to build an economy by means of centralization, the Party found itself compelled to admit the parallel existence of different and even of competing economic types. We have the State industries that are organized into trusts, we have enterprises of a local character, we have leased industries, concessional and privately owned enterprises, cooperatives, individual peasant economies, *kustar* or trade shops, collective enterprises, and so forth. The basic policy of the State is toward a centralized socialist economy. But this general tendency includes, for a given period, unlimited support for a peasant economy and for the kustar. Without this, the policy in the direction of a large-scale socialist industry becomes abstract and dead.

Our Republic is a union of workers, peasants, and petty-bourgeois intelligentsia, under the leadership of the Communist Party. Given the development of technology and culture, a communist society should develop in a series of stages out of this social combination. It is clear that the peasantry and the intelligentsia will not come to communism by the same road as did the workers. These roads cannot help but be reflected in art. The non-communist intelligentsia, which has not thrown in its lot unreservedly with the proletariat, and this comprises the overwhelming majority of the intelligentsia, seeks support in the peasantry because of the absence, or rather, the extreme weakness of bourgeois support. For the time being, this process has a purely preparatory and symbolic character, and expresses itself (with hindsight) in the idealization of the peasant elements of the Revolution. This peculiar neo-populism is characteristic of all the "fellow travelers." Later on, with the growth of the number of schools in the villages and of those who can read, the bond between this art and the peasantry may become more organic. At the same time, the peasantry will develop a creative intelligentsia of its own. The peasant point of view in economics, in politics, and in art, is more primitive, more limited, more egoistic than that of the proletariat. But this peasant point of view exists and will continue to exist for a long time and very earnestly. And if an artist, looking at life from the peasant, or more often from the intelligentsia and peasant point of view, is struck with the idea that a union of the peasants and the workers is necessary and vital, then his artistic work, given the necessary conditions, will be historically progressive. Through the influence of such art, the needed historical cooperation between the village and the city will be strengthened. The movement of the peasantry toward socialism will be profound, purposeful, many-sided, and many-colored, and there is every reason to believe that the creative work that will be done under its direct suggestion will add valuable chapters to the history of art. On the contrary, the point of view that opposes the organic, the age-old, the indivisible, the "national" village to the whirling city, is historically reactionary; the art resulting from such a point of view is inimical to the proletariat, incompatible with progress, and doomed to extinction. The conclusion can be drawn that such an art, even as far as form is concerned, can give nothing but rehashes and reminiscences.

Kliuev, the Imagists, the "Serapion Fraternity," Pilnyak, and such Futurists as Khlebnikov, Kruchenikh, and Kamensky, have a peasant underpinning. With some it is more or less conscious; with others it is organic; with still others, it is in fact a bourgeois underpinning, translated into peasant form. The Futurist attitude to the proletariat is the least dual of all. The "Serapion Fraternity," the Imagists, Pilnyak, deviate here and there into an opposition to the proletariat—at least, this was true until very recently. All these groups reflected, in an extremely uneven form, the state of mind of the village at the time of forced requisitions. It was then that the intelligentsia sought refuge from hunger in the villages and there accumulated its impressions. In its art, the intelligentsia summarized these years rather ambiguously. But this summary was made within the period that ended with the Kronstadt rebellion. At present, a considerable change has taken place in the peasant's point of view. This change has left its mark on the intelligentsia also and may, and in fact must, have an influence on the work of the peasant-singing "fellow travelers." This influence has already shown itself to a certain extent. These groups under the influence of social impulses will have internal struggles, splits, and reorganizations. All this must be followed very carefully and critically. A party that, not without some reason we hope, lays claim to ideological hegemony, has no right to answer such problems with cheap talk.

But cannot a purely proletarian art, broad enough in scope, illuminate and feed artistically the peasant movement toward socialism? Of course it *can*, just as a government electrical station *can* illuminate and feed its energy to a peasant hut or a barn or a flour mill. All that is necessary is to have such an electric station and the wires running from it to the village. By the way, under such conditions there will be no danger of antagonism between industry and agriculture. But we have no such wires yet. Even the electrical station is still nonexistent. There is no proletarian art. Proletarian art, which includes groups of working-class poets and communists-Futurists, is about as near to gratifying artistically the demands of the city and the village as, let us say, Soviet industry is near solving the problems of universal economics.

But even were we to leave aside the peasantry—and how can one leave it aside?—it will appear that, even with the proletariat, that basic class of Soviet society, matters are not as simple as they appear in the pages of the "Lef." When the Futurists propose to throw overboard the old literature of individualism, not only because it has become antiquated in form, but because it contradicts the collectivist nature of the proletariat, they reveal a very inadequate understanding of the dialectical nature of the contradiction between individualism and collectivism. There are no abstract truths. There are different kinds of individualism. Because of too much individualism, a section of the pre-revolutionary intelligentsia threw itself into mysticism, but another section moved along the chaotic lines of Futurism and, caught by the Revolution—to their honor be it said—came nearer to the proletariat. But when they who came nearer because their teeth were set on edge by individualism carry their feeling over to the proletariat, they show themselves guilty of egocentrism, that is, of extreme individualism. The trouble is that the average proletarian is lacking in this very quality. In the mass, proletarian individuality has not been sufficiently formed and differentiated. It is just such heightening of the objective quality and the subjective consciousness of individuality that is the most valuable contribution of the cultural advance at the threshold of which we stand today. It is childish to think that bourgeois belles lettres can make a breach in class solidarity. What the worker will take from Shakespeare, Goethe, Pushkin, or Dostoyevsky will be a more complex idea of human personality, of its passions and feelings, a deeper and profounder understanding of its psychic forces and of the role of the subconscious, etc. In the final analysis, the worker will become richer. At the beginning, Gorky was imbued with the romantic individualism of the tramp. Nevertheless, he fed the early spring revolutionism of the proletariat on the eve of 1905, because he helped to awaken individuality in that class in which individuality, once awakened, seeks contact with other awakened individualities. The proletariat is in need of artistic food and education, but that does not mean to say that the proletariat is mere clay that artists, those that have gone and those that are still to come, can fashion in their own image and in their own likeness.

Though the proletariat is spiritually, and therefore, artistically, very sensitive, it is uneducated aesthetically. It is hardly reasonable to think that it can simply begin at the point where the bourgeois intelligentsia left off on the eve of the catastrophe. Just as an individual passes biologically and psychologically through the history of the race and, to some extent, of the entire animal world in his development from the embryo, so, to a certain extent, must the overwhelming majority of a new class that has only recently come out of prehistoric life, pass through the entire history of artistic culture. This class cannot begin the construction of a new culture without absorbing and assimilating the elements of the old cultures. This does not mean in the least that it is necessary to go through step by step, slowly and systematically, the entire past history of art. Insofar as it concerns a social class and not a biological individual, the process of absorption and transformation has a freer and more conscious character. But a new class cannot move forward without regard to the most important landmarks of the past.

In its struggle for the preservation of continuity in artistic culture, the left wing of the old art, whose social basis has been destroyed by the Revolution more thoroughly than ever before in history, is compelled to seek support in the proletariat, or at least, in the new social environment that is being formed about the proletariat. In its turn, the proletariat takes advantage of its position as ruling class and tries and begins to make contacts with art in general, and thus to prepare the ground for an unprecedented influence of art. In this sense it is true that the factory news bulletins pasted on their walls represent a very necessary, though very remote, premise for the new literature of the future. No one, however, will say: Let us cross out everything else until the proletariat shall have risen from these walled bulletins to an independent craftsmanship of art. The proletariat also needs a continuity of creative tradition. At the present time the proletariat realizes this continuity not directly, but indirectly, through the creative bourgeois intelligentsia that gravitates toward the proletariat and which wants to keep warm under its wing. The proletariat tolerates a part of this intelligentsia, supports another part, half-adopts a third, and entirely assimilates a fourth. The policy of the Communist Party towards art is determined by the complexity of this process, by its internal many-sidedness. It is impossible to reduce this policy to one formula, to something short like a bird's bill. Nor is it necessary to do this.

CHAPTER EIGHT

Revolutionary and Socialist Art

When one speaks of revolutionary art, two kinds of artistic phenomena are meant: the works whose themes reflect the Revolution, and the works that are not connected with the Revolution in theme, but are thoroughly imbued with it, and are colored by the new consciousness arising out of the Revolution. These are phenomena that quite evidently belong, or could belong, in entirely different planes. Alexey Tolstoy, in his *The Road to Calvary*, describes the period of the War and the Revolution. He belongs to the peaceful Yasnaya-Polyana school, only his scale is infinitely smaller and his point of view narrower. And when he applies it to events of the greatest magnitude, it serves only as a cruel reminder that Yasnaya-Polyana has been and is no more. But when the young poet, Tikhonov, without writing about the Revolution, writes about a little grocery store (he seems to be shy about writing of the Revolution), he perceives and reproduces its inertia and immobility with such fresh and passionate power as only a poet created by the dynamics of a new epoch can do. Thus if works about the Revolution and works of revolutionary art are not one and the same thing, they still have a point in common. The artists that are created by the Revolution cannot but want to speak of the Revolution.

And, on the other hand, the art that will be filled with a great desire to speak of the Revolution, will inevitably reject the Yasnaya-Polyana point of view, whether it be the point of view of the Count or of the peasant.

There is no revolutionary art as yet. There are the elements of this art, there are hints and attempts at it, and, what is most important, there is the revolutionary man, who is forming the new generation in his own image and who is more and more in need of this art. How long will it take for such art to reveal itself clearly? It is difficult even to guess, because the process is intangible and incalculable, and we are limited to guesswork even when we try to time more tangible social processes. But why should not this art, at least its first big wave, come soon as the expression of the art of the young generation that was born in the Revolution and that carries it on?

Revolutionary art, which inevitably reflects all the contradictions of a revolutionary social system, should not be confused with socialist art for which no basis has as yet been made. On the other hand, one must not forget that socialist art will grow out of the art of this transition period.

In insisting on such a distinction, we are not at all guided by a pedantic consideration of an abstract program. Not for nothing did Engels speak of the socialist Revolution as a leap from the kingdom of necessity to the kingdom of freedom. The Revolution itself is not as yet the kingdom of freedom. On the contrary, it is developing the features of "necessity" to the greatest degree. Socialism will abolish class antagonisms, as well as classes, but the Revolution carries the class struggle to its highest tension. During the period of revolution, only that literature that promotes the consolidation of the workers in their struggle against the exploiters is necessary and progressive. Revolutionary literature cannot but be imbued with a spirit of social hatred, which is a creative historic factor in an epoch of proletarian dictatorship. Under socialism, solidarity will be the basis of society. Literature and art will be tuned to a different key. All the emotions that we revolutionists, at the present time, feel apprehensive of naming— so much have they been worn thin by hypocrites and vulgarians —such as disinterested friendship, love for one's neighbor, sympathy, will be the mighty ringing chords of socialist poetry.

However, does not an excess of solidarity, as the Nietzscheans fear, threaten to degenerate man into a sentimental, passive herd animal? Not at all. The powerful force of competition, which, in bourgeois society, has the character of market competition, will not disappear in a socialist society, but, to use the language of psychoanalysis, will be sublimated, that is, will assume a higher and more fertile form. There will be the struggle for one's opinion, for one's project, for one's taste. In the measure in which political struggles will be eliminated—and in a society where there will be no classes, there will be no such struggles—the liberated passions will be channeled into technique, into construction, which also includes art. Art then will become more general, will mature, will become tempered, and will become the most perfect method of the progressive building of life in every field. It will not be merely "pretty" without relation to anything else.

All forms of life, such as the cultivation of land, the planning of human habitations, the building of theaters, the methods of socially educating children, the solution of scientific problems, the creation of new styles, will vitally engross all and everybody. People will divide into "parties" over the question of a new gigantic canal, or the distribution of oases in the Sahara (such a question will exist too), over the regulation of the weather and the climate, over a new theater, over chemical hypotheses, over two competing tendencies in music, and over a best system of sports. Such parties will not be poisoned by the greed of class or caste. All will be equally interested in the success of the whole. The struggle will have a purely ideological character. It will have no running after profits, it will have nothing mean, no betrayals, no bribery, none of the things that form the soul of "competition" in a society divided into classes. But this will in no way hinder the struggle from being absorbing, dramatic, and passionate. And as all problems in a socialist society—the problems of life, which formerly were solved spontaneously and automatically, and the problems of art, which were in the custody of special priestly castes—will become the property of all people, one can say with certainty that collective interests and passions and individual competition will have the widest scope and the most unlimited opportunity. Art, therefore, will not suffer the lack of any such explosions of collective, nervous energy, and of such collective psychic impulses that make for the creation of new artistic tendencies and for changes in style. It will be the aesthetic schools around which "parties" will collect, that is, associations of temperaments, of tastes, and of moods. In a struggle so disinterested and tense, which will take place in a culture whose foundations are steadily rising, the human personality, with its invaluable basic trait of continual discontent, will grow and become polished at all its points. In truth, we have no reason to fear that there will be a decline of individuality or an impoverishment of art in a socialist society.

Can we christen revolutionary art with any of the names that we have? Osinsky somewhere called it realistic. The thought here is true and significant, but there ought to be an agreement on a definition of this concept to prevent falling into a misunderstanding.

The most perfect realism in art is coincident in our history with the "golden age" of literature, that is, with the classic literature of the noblemen.

The period of tendentious themes, when a work was judged primarily by the social ideals of the author, coincides with the period when the awakening intelligentsia sought an outlet to public activity, and tried to make a union with the "people" against the old regime.

The Decadent School and Symbolism, which appeared in opposition to the "realism" that ruled before them, correspond to the period when the intelligentsia tried to separate itself from the people and began to worship its own moods and experiences. Though, in fact, it submitted itself to the bourgeoisie, it tried not to dissolve itself into the bourgeoisie psychologically or scientifically. In this cause Symbolism invoked the aid of Heaven.

Pre-war Futurism was an attempt of the intelligentsia to rise out of the wreck of Symbolism, while still holding on to individualism, and to find a personal pivot in the impersonal conquests of material culture.

Such is the rough logic of the succession of the large periods in the development of Russian literature. Each one of these tendencies contained a definite social and group attitude toward the world that laid its impress upon the themes of the works, upon their content, upon the selection of environment, of the dramatic characters, etc. The idea of content does not refer to subject matter, in the ordinary sense of the term, but to social purpose. A lyric without a theme can express an epoch or a class or its point of view as well as a social novel.

Then there comes the question of form. Within certain limits, this develops in accord with its own laws, like any other technology. Each new literary school—if it is really a school and not an arbitrary grafting—is the result of a preceding development, of the craftsmanship of word and color already in existence, and only pulls away from the shores of what has been attained in order to conquer the elements anew.

Evolution is dialectic in this case, too. The new tendency in art negates the preceding one, and why? Evidently there are sentiments and thoughts that feel crowded within the framework of the old methods. But at the same time, the new moods find in the already old and fossilized art some elements, which when further developed can give them adequate expression. The banner of revolt is raised against the "old" as a whole, in the name of the elements that can be developed. Each literary school is contained potentially in the past and each one develops by pulling away hostilely from the past. The relation between form and content (the latter is to be understood not simply as a "theme" but as a living complex of moods and ideas that seek artistic expression) is determined by the fact that a new form is discovered, proclaimed, and developed under the pressure of an inner need, of a collective psychological demand, which, like all human psychology, has its roots in society.

This explains the dualism of every literary tendency; on the one hand, it adds something to the technique of art, heightening (or lowering) the general level of craftsmanship; on the other hand, in its concrete historic form, it expresses definite demands, which, in the final analysis, have a class character. We say class, but this also means individual, because a class speaks through an individual. It also means national, because the spirit of a nation is determined by the class that rules it and that subjects literature to itself.

Let us take up Symbolism. What is it understood to mean: is it the art of transforming reality symbolically, a method of artistic creation in form? Or is it that particular symbolic tendency that was represented by Blok, Sologub, and others? Russian Symbolism did not invent symbols. It only grafted them more closely to the organism of the modernized Russian language. In this sense, the future art, no matter what lines it will follow, will not wish to reject the Symbolist heritage in form. But the actual Russian Symbolism of certain definite years made use of the symbol for a precise social purpose. What was its purpose? The Decadent School, which preceded Symbolism, sought the solution of all artistic problems in the personal experiences of sex, death, and the rest, or rather of none but sex and death. It could not but exhaust itself in a very short time. From this—not from social impulses—followed the need to find a higher sanction for one's demands and feelings and moods, and so to enrich and elevate them. Symbolism, which made of the symbol not only a method of art, but a symbol of faith, seemed to the intelligentsia the artistic bridge to Mysticism. In this concretely sociologic sense, and not in any abstract formal sense, Symbolism was not merely a method of artistic technique, but the intelligentsia's escape from reality, its way of constructing another world, its artistic bringing up in self-sufficient daydreaming, contemplation, and passivity. In Blok we find Zhukovsky modernized! And the old Marxian symposiums and pamphlets (of 1908 and after) on the subject of the "literary decline," no matter how crude and one-sided some of their generalizations may have been, and no matter how they tended to mere scribbling, gave an incomparably more significant and correct social literary diagnosis and prognosis than Chuzhak did, for instance. He gave thought to the problem of form sooner and more attentively than many other Marxists, but because of the influence of the current schools of art, he saw in them the growing stages of a proletarian culture, and not the stages of the intelligentsia's growing estrangement from the masses.

What are we to understand under the term realism? At various periods, and by various methods, realism gave expression to the feelings and needs of different social groups. Each one of these realistic schools is subject to a separate and social literary definition, and a separate formal and literary estimation. What have they in common? A definite and important feeling for the world. It consists in a feeling for life as it is, in an artistic acceptance of reality, and not in a shrinking from it, in an active interest in the concrete stability and mobility of life. It is a striving either to picture life as it is or to idealize it, either to justify or to condemn it, either to photograph it or generalize and symbolize it. But it is always a preoccupation with our life of three dimensions as a sufficient and invaluable theme for art. In this large philosophic sense, and not in the narrow sense of a literary school, one

may say with certainty that the new art will be realistic. The Revolution cannot live together with mysticism. Nor can the Revolution live together with romanticism, if that which Pilnyak, the
Imagists, and others call romanticism is, as it may be feared, mysticism shyly trying to establish itself under a new name. This is
not being doctrinaire, this is an insuperable psychological fact.
Our age cannot have a shy and portable mysticism, something
like a pet dog that is carried along "with the rest." Our age
wields an axe. Our life, cruel, violent, and disturbed to its very
bottom, says: "I must have an artist of a single love. Whatever
way you take hold of me, whatever tools and instruments created
by the development of art you choose, I leave to you, to your
temperament and to your genius. But you must understand me as
I am, you must take me as I will become, and there must be no
one else besides me."

This means a realistic monism, in the sense of a philosophy
of life, and not a "realism" in the sense of the traditional arsenal
of literary schools. On the contrary, the new artist will need all
the methods and processes evolved in the past, as well as a few
supplementary ones, in order to grasp the new life. And this is
not going to be artistic eclecticism, because the unity of art is
created by an active world-attitude and active life-attitude.

■   ■   ■

In 1918 and 1919, it was not uncommon to meet at the
front a military division with cavalry at the head, and wagons
carrying actors, actresses, stage settings, and other stage properties in the rear. In general, the place of art is in the rear of the historic advance. Because of the rapid changes on our fronts, the
wagons with actors and stage properties found themselves frequently in a difficult position, and did not know where to go. At
times they fell into the hands of the Whites. No less difficult at
present is the position of all art, caught by the violent change on
the historic front.

The theater especially is in a difficult position for it absolutely does not know where to go and what to "show." And it
is most remarkable that the theater, which is perhaps the most
conservative form of art, should have the most radical theorists.
Everyone knows that the most revolutionary group in the Union

of Soviet Republics is the class of dramatic critics. At the first sign of a revolution in the West or in the East, it would be a good thing to organize them into a special military battalion of "Levtretsi" (left theatrical reviewers). When our theaters present *The Daughter of Madame Angot, The Death of Tarelkin, Turandot, The Cuckold,* then our venerable "Levtretsi" try to be patient. But when it comes to giving Martinet's play they nearly all rise on their hind legs (even before Meyerhold gave "The World on Its Hind Legs"). The play is patriotic. Martinet is a pacifist! And one of the critics even expressed himself in this wise: "This is all passé for us, and therefore of no interest." But all this "Leftism" is horrible philistinism, without an ounce of revolutionism behind it. If we are to begin, from the standpoint of politics, then Martinet was a revolutionist and an internationalist, when many of our present-day representatives of the extreme Left had not even begun to smell Leftist blessings. Moreover, what does it mean to say that Martinet's piece belongs to yesterday! Has the social revolution in France already taken place? Is it already victorious? Or shall we consider a French revolution not an independent historic drama, but only a boring repetition of what has happened to us? This Leftism covers, besides many other things, the commonest national narrowness. There is no question but Martinet's play is too long in spots, and that it is more literary than dramatic (the author himself hardly expected that the play would be put on the stage). But these defects would have remained in the background if the theater had taken this play in its national and historic simplicity, that is, as a drama of the French proletariat at a certain point in its great march, and not as a sketch of a world that is on its hind legs. To carry over the action of a definite historic milieu into an abstract constructivism is in this case a deviation from the revolution—from that real, true revolution that is developing obstinately and moving from country to country, and which appears, therefore, to some pseudo-revolutionists as a boring repetition.

I do not know whether the stage needs biomechanics at the present time, that is, whether there is a historic necessity for it. But I have no doubt at all—if I may speak my own point of view—that our theater is terribly in need of a new realistic revolutionary repertory, and above all, of a *Soviet comedy*. We ought to have our own *The Minors,* our own *Woes from Being Too Wise,* and our own *Inspector General.* Not a new staging of these three old comedies, not a retouching of them in a Soviet style, as for a carnival parody, though this would be more vital than 99 percent of our repertory—no; we need simply a Soviet comedy of manners, one of laughter and of indignation. I am using the terms out of the old literature textbooks on purpose, and I am not in the least afraid of being accused of going backwards. A new class, a new life, new vices, and new stupidity, demand that they shall be released from silence, and when this will happen we will have a new dramatic art, for it is impossible to reproduce the new stupidity without new methods. How many new minors are tremblingly waiting to be represented on the stage? How much woe is there from being too wise, or from pretending to be too wise, and how good it would be if a stage Inspector General would walk across our Soviet life. Please do not point to the dramatic censorship, because that is not true. Of course, if your comedy will try to say: "See what we have been brought to; let us go back to the nice old nobleman's nest"—then, of course, the censorship will sit on your comedy, and will do so with propriety. But if your comedy will say: "We are building a new life now, and yet how much piggishness, vulgarity, and knavery of the old and of the new are about us; let us make a clean sweep of them," then, of course, the censorship will not interfere, and if it will interfere somewhere it will do so foolishly, and all of us will fight such a censorship.

When, rare as it was, I had occasion to watch the stage, and politely hid my yawns so as not to offend anyone, I was strikingly impressed with the fact of how eagerly the audience caught every hint at present-day life, even the most insignificant. A very interesting manifestation of this can be seen in the operettas revived by the Art Theater, which are skittish with big and little thorns (there is no rose without thorns!). It occurred to me then that if we were not yet grown enough for comedy, we should, at least, stage a revue!

Of course, no doubt, and it goes without saying, in the future the theater will emerge out of its four walls and will merge in the life of the masses, which will obey absolutely the rhythm of biomechanics, and so forth, and so forth. But this, after all, is "futurism," that is, music of a very distant future. But between the past on which the theater feeds, and the very distant future, there is the present in which we live. Between *Passéism* and Futurism, it would be well to give "Presentism" a chance behind the foot-lights. Let us vote for such a tendency! One good Soviet comedy will awaken the theater for a few years to come, and then per-haps we will have tragedy, which is truly considered the highest form of literature.

▪   ▪   ▪

But can a great art be created out of our infidel epoch, ask certain mystics, who are willing to accept the Revolution if it can secure them immortality. Tragedy is a great and monumental form of literature. The tragedy of classic antiquity was deduced from its myths. All ancient tragedy is penetrated by a profound faith in fate, which gave a meaning to life. The Christian myth unified the monumental art of the Middle Ages and gave a sig-nificance not only to the temples and the mysteries, but to all human relationships. The union of the religious point of view on life with an active participation in it, made possible a great art in those times. If one were to remove religious faith, not the vague, mystic buzzing that goes on in the soul of our modern intelli-gentsia, but the real religion, with God and a heavenly law and a church hierarchy, then life is left bare, without any place in it for supreme collisions of hero and destiny, of sin and expiation. The well-known mystic Stepun approaches art from this point of view in his article on "Tragedy and the Contemporary Life." He starts from the needs of art itself, tempts us with a new and monumental art, shows us a revival of tragedy in the distance, and, in conclusion, demands, in the name of art, that we submit to and obey the powers of heaven. There is an insinuating logic in Stepun's scheme. In fact, the author does not care for tragedy, because the laws of tragedy are nothing to him as compared to the laws of heaven. He only wishes to catch hold of our epoch by the small finger of tragic aesthetics in order to take hold of its entire hand.

This is a purely Jesuitical approach. But from a dialectic point of view, Stepun's reasoning is formalistic and shallow. It ig-nores the materialistic and historical foundation from which the ancient drama and the Gothic art grew and from which a new art must grow.

The faith in an inevitable fate disclosed the narrow limits within which ancient man, clear in thought but poor in technique, was confined. He could not as yet undertake to conquer nature on the scale we do today, and nature hung over him like a fate. Fate is the limitation and the immobility of technical means, the voice of blood, of sickness, of death, of all that limits man, and that does not allow him to become "arrogant." Tragedy lay inherent in the contradiction between the awakened world of the mind, and the stagnant limitation of means. The myth did not create tragedy, it only expressed it in the language of man's childhood.

The bribe of spiritual expiation of the Middle Ages and, in general, the whole system of heavenly and earthly double book-keeping, which followed from the dualism of religion, and especially of historic, positive Christianity, did not make the contradictions of life, but only reflected them and solved them fictitiously. Medieval society overcame the growing contradictions by transferring the promissory note to the Son of God; the ruling classes signed this note, the Church hierarchy acted as endorser, and the oppressed masses prepared to discount it in the other world.

Bourgeois society broke up human relationships into atoms, and gave them unprecedented flexibility and mobility. Primitive unity of consciousness, which was the foundation of a monumental religious art disappeared, and with it went primitive economic relationships. As a result of the Reformation, religion became individualistic. The religious symbols of art having had their cord cut from the heavens, fell on their heads and sought support in the uncertain mysticism of individual consciousness.

In the tragedies of Shakespeare, which would be entirely unthinkable without the Reformation, the fate of the ancients and the passions of the medieval Christians are crowded out by individual human passions, such as love, jealousy, revengeful greediness, and spiritual dissension. But in every one of Shakespeare's dramas, the individual passion is carried to such a high degree of tension that it outgrows the individual, becomes super-personal, and is transformed into a fate of a certain kind. The jealousy of

Othello, the ambition of Macbeth, the greed of Shylock, the love of Romeo and Juliet, the arrogance of Coriolanus, the spiritual wavering of Hamlet, are all of this kind. Tragedy in Shakespeare is individualistic, and in this sense has not the general significance of *Oedipus Rex*, which expresses the consciousness of a whole people. Nonetheless, compared with Aeschylus, Shakespeare represents a great step forward and not backward. Shakespeare's art is more human. At any rate, we shall no longer accept a tragedy in which God gives orders and man submits. Moreover, there will be no one to write such a tragedy.

Having broken up human relations into atoms, bourgeois society, during the period of its rise, had a great aim for itself. Personal emancipation was its name. Out of it grew the dramas of Shakespeare and Goethe's *Faust*. Man placed himself in the center of the universe, and therefore in the center of art also. This theme sufficed for centuries. In reality, all modern literature has been nothing but an enlargement of this theme.

But to the degree in which the internal bankruptcy of bourgeois society was revealed as a result of its unbearable contradictions, the original purpose, the emancipation and qualification of the individual, faded away and was relegated more and more into the sphere of a new mythology, without soul or spirit.

However the conflict between what is personal and what is beyond the personal, can take place, not only in the sphere of religion, but in the sphere of a human passion that is larger than the individual. The super-personal element is, above all, the social element. So long as man will not have mastered his social organization, the latter will hang over him as his fate. Whether at the same time society casts a religious shadow or not, is a secondary matter and depends upon the degree of man's helplessness. Babeuf's struggle for communism in a society that was not yet ready for it, was a struggle of a classic hero with his fate. Babeuf's destiny had all the characteristics of true tragedy, just as the fate of the Gracchi had whose name Babeuf used.

Tragedy based on detached personal passions is too flat for our days. Why? Because we live in a period of social passions. The tragedy of our period lies in the conflict between the individual and the collectivity, or in the conflict between two hostile collectivities in the same individual.

Our age is an age of great aims. This is what stamps it. But the grandeur of these aims lies in man's effort to free himself from mystic and from every other intellectual vagueness and in his effort to reconstruct society and himself in accord with his own plan. This, of course, is much bigger than the child's play of the ancients, which was becoming to their childish age, or the medieval ravings of monks, or the arrogance of individualism that tears personality away from the collectivity, and then, draining it to the very bottom, pushes it off into the abyss of pessimism, or sets it on all fours before the remounted bull Apis.

Tragedy is a high expression of literature because it implies the heroic tenacity of strivings, of limitless aims, of conflicts and sufferings. In this sense, Stepun was right when he characterized our "on the eve" art, as he called it, that is, the art that preceded the War and the Revolution, as insignificant.

Bourgeois society, individualism, the Reformation, the Shakespearean dramas, the great Revolution, these have made impossible the tragic significance of aims that come from without; great aims must live in the consciousness of a people or of a class that leads a people, if they are to arouse heroism or create a basis for great sentiments that inspire tragedy. The Tsarist War, whose purpose did not penetrate consciousness, gave birth to cheap verse only, with personal poetry trickling by its side, unable to rise to an objectivity and unable to form a great art.

If one were to regard the Decadent and the Symbolist schools, with all their offshoots, from the point of view of the development of art as a social form, they would appear merely as scratches of the pen, as an exercise in craftsmanship, as a tuning up of instruments. The period in art when it was "on the eve" was without aims. Those who had aims had no time for art. At present, one has to carry out great aims by the means of art. One cannot tell whether revolutionary art will succeed in producing "high" revolutionary tragedy. But socialist art will revive tragedy. Without God, of course. The new art will be atheist. It will also revive comedy, because the new man of the future will want to laugh. It will give new life to the novel. It will grant all rights to lyrics, because the new man will love in a better and stronger way than did the old people, and he will think about the problems of birth and death. The new art will revive all the old forms, which arose in the course of the development of the creative spirit. The disintegration and decline of these forms are not absolute, that is, they do not mean that these forms are absolutely incompatible with the spirit of the new age. All that is necessary is for the poet of the new epoch to re-think in a new way the thoughts of mankind, and to re-feel its feelings.

■   ■   ■

In these latter years, architecture has suffered most of all, and this is true not only of our country alone; old buildings have been gradually destroyed, and new ones have not been built. Hence the housing crisis the world over. When work was resumed after the War, the people directed their energies, first of all, toward the most essential articles of consumption, and only secondarily toward the reconstruction of basic capital and houses. Ultimately, the destructiveness of wars and revolutions will give a powerful impetus to architecture, in the same way as the fire of 1812 helped to beautify Moscow. In Russia, the cultural material to be destroyed was less than in other countries, the destruction was greater than in other countries, while the rebuilding is immeasurably more difficult than in other countries. It is not surprising, then, that we have had no time for architecture, one of the most monumental of arts.

At present we are beginning to repair the pavements a little, to re-lay the sewage pipes, to finish the unfinished houses left to us as a heritage—but we are only beginning. We made the buildings of our Agricultural Exhibition out of wood. We must still put off all large-scale construction. The originators of gigantic projects, men like Tatlin, are given involuntarily a respite for more thought, for revision, and for radical reexamination. But one must not imagine that we are planning to repair old pavements and houses for decades to come. In this process, as in all other processes, there are periods of repair, of slow preparation and accumulation of forces, and periods of rapid development. As soon as a surplus will come after the most urgent and acute needs of life are covered, the Soviet state will take up the problem of gigantic constructions that will suitably express the monumental spirit of our epoch. Tatlin is undoubtedly right in discarding from his project national styles, allegorical sculpture, modeled monograms, flourishes and tails, and attempting to subordinate the entire design to a correct constructive use of material. This has been the way that machines, bridges, and covered markets have been built, for a long time. But Tatlin has still to prove that he is right in what seems to be his own personal invention, a rotating cube, a pyramid, and a cylinder all of glass. For good or bad, circumstances are going to give him plenty of time to find arguments for his side.

De Maupassant hated the Eiffel Tower, in which no one is forced to imitate him. But it is undoubtedly true that the Eiffel Tower makes a dual impression; one is attracted by the technical simplicity of its form, and, at the same time, repelled by its aimlessness. It is an extremely rational utilization of material for the purpose of making a high structure. But what is it for? It is not a building, but an exercise. At present, as everyone knows, the Eiffel Tower serves as a radio station. This gives it a meaning, and makes it aesthetically more unified. But if the tower had been built from the very beginning as a radio station, it probably would have attained a higher rationality of form, and so therefore a higher perfection of art.

From this point of view Tatlin's project for a monument appears much less satisfactory. The purpose of the main building is to make glass headquarters for the meetings of the World Council of People's Commissars, for the Communist International, etc. But the props and the piles that are to support the glass cylinder and the pyramid—and they are there for no other purpose—are so cumbersome and heavy that they look like unremoved scaffolding. One cannot think what they are for. They say: They are there to support the rotating cylinder in which the meetings will take place. But one answers: Meetings are not necessarily held in a cylinder and the cylinder does not necessarily have to rotate. I remember seeing once when a child a wooden temple built in a beer bottle. This fired my imagination, but I did not ask myself at that time what it was for. Tatlin proceeds by a reverse method; he wants to construct a beer bottle for the World Council of People's Commissars that would sit in a spiral concrete temple. But for the moment, I cannot refrain from the question: What is it for? To be more exact: we would probably accept the cylinder and its rotating, if it were combined with a simplicity and lightness of construction, that is, if the arrangements for its rotating did not depress the aim. Nor can we agree with the arguments that are given to interpret the artistic significance of the sculpture by Jacob Lipshitz. Sculpture must lose its fictitious independence, an independence that only means that it is relegated to the back-yards of life or lies vegetating in dead museums, and it must revive in some higher synthesis its connection with architecture. In this broad sense, sculpture has to assume a utilitarian purpose. Very good, then. But it is not at all clear how one is to approach the Lipshitz sculpture from such a point of view. I have a photograph of several intersecting planes, which are supposed to be the outlines of a man sitting with a stringed instrument in his hands. We are told that if today it is not utilitarian, it is "purposeful." In what way? To judge purposefulness, one has to know the purpose. But when one stops to think of the purposefulness and possible utility of those numerous intersecting planes and pointed forms and protrusions, one comes to the conclusion that, as a last resort, one could transform such a piece of sculpture into a hat rack. Still, if it had been the sculptor's plan to make a sculptured hat rack, he would have probably found a more purposeful form for it. At any rate, we cannot recommend that a plaster cast be made of it for hat racks.

We must therefore assume that the Lipshitz sculpture, like the word-forms of Kruchenikh, are merely exercises in technique, like the playing of scales and passages. They are exercises in the verbal and sculptural music of the future. But one should not hand exercises out as music. It is better not to let them out of the studio, nor to show them to a photographer.

           ▪   ▪   ▪

There is no doubt that, in the future—and the farther we go, the more true it will be—such monumental tasks as the planning of city gardens, of model houses, of railroads, and of ports, will interest vitally not only engineering architects, participators in competitions, but the large popular masses as well. The imperceptible, ant-like piling up of quarters and streets, brick by brick, from generation to generation, will give way to titanic constructions of city-villages, with map and compass in hand. Around this compass will be formed true peoples' parties, the parties of the future for special technology and construction, which will agitate passionately, hold meetings, and vote. In this struggle, architecture will again be filled with the spirit of mass feelings and moods, only on a much higher plane, and mankind will educate itself plastically, it will become accustomed to look at the world as submissive clay for sculpting the most perfect forms of life. The wall between art and industry will come down. The great style of the future will be formative, not ornamental. Here the Futurists are right. But it would be wrong to look at this as a liquidating of art, as a voluntary giving way to technique.

Take the penknife as an example. The combination of art and technique can proceed along two fundamental lines; either art embellishes the knife and pictures an elephant, a prize beauty, or the Eiffel Tower on its handle; or art helps technique to find an "ideal" form for the knife, that is, such a form that will correspond most adequately to the material of a knife and its purpose. To think that this task can be solved by purely technical means is incorrect, because purpose and material allow for an innumerable number of variations. To make an "ideal" knife, one must have, besides the knowledge of the properties of the material and the methods of its use, both imagination and taste. In accord with the entire tendency of industrial culture, we think that the artistic imagination in creating material objects will be directed toward working out the ideal form of a thing, as a thing, and not toward the embellishment of the thing as an aesthetic premium to itself. If this is true for penknives, it will be truer still for wearing apparel, furniture, theaters, and cities. This does not mean the doing away with "machine made" art, not even in the most distant future. But it seems that the direct cooperation between art and all branches of technique will become of paramount importance.

Does this mean that industry will absorb art, or that art will lift industry up to itself on Olympus? This question can be answered either way, depending on whether the problem is approached from the side of industry, or from the side of art. But in the object attained, there is no difference between either answer. Both answers signify a gigantic expansion of the scope and artistic quality of industry, and we understand here, under industry, the entire field without excepting the industrial activity of man; mechanical and electrified agriculture will also become part of industry.

The wall will fall not only between art and industry, but simultaneously between art and nature also. This is not meant in the sense of Jean Jacques Rousseau, that art will come nearer to a state of nature, but that nature will become more "artificial."

The present distribution of mountains and rivers, of fields, of meadows, of steppes, of forests, and of seashores, cannot be considered final. Man has already made changes in the map of nature that are not few nor insignificant. But they are mere pupils' practice in comparison with what is coming. Faith merely promises to move mountains; but technology, which takes nothing "on faith," is actually able to cut down mountains and move them. Up to now this was done for industrial purposes (mines) or for railways (tunnels); in the future this will be done on an immeasurably larger scale, according to a general industrial and artistic plan. Man will occupy himself with re-registering mountains and rivers, and will earnestly and repeatedly make improvements in nature. In the end, he will have rebuilt the earth, if not in his own image, at least according to his own taste. We have not the slightest fear that this taste will be bad.

The jealous, scowling Kliuev declares, in his quarrel with Mayakovsky, that "it does not behoove a maker of songs to bother about cranes," and that it is "only in the furnace of the heart, and in no other furnace, that the purple gold of life is melted." Ivanov-Razumnik, a populist, who was once a left Social-Revolutionist—and this tells the whole story—also took a hand in this quarrel. Ivanov-Razumnik declares that the poetry of the hammer and the machine, in whose name Mayakovsky speaks, is a transient episode, but that the poetry of "God-made Earth" is "the eternal poetry of the world." Earth and the machine are here contrasted as the eternal and temporary sources of poetry, and of course the eminent idealist, the tasteless and cautious semi-mystic Razumnik, prefers the eternal to the transient. But, in truth, this dualism of earth and machine is false; one can contrast a backward peasant field with a flour mill, either on a plantation, or in a socialist society. The poetry of the earth is not eternal, but changeable, and man began to sing articulate songs only after he had placed between himself and the earth implements and instruments that were the first simple machines. There would have been no Koltzov without a scythe, a plow, or a sickle. Does that mean that the earth with a scythe has the advantage of eternity over the earth with an electric plow? The new man, who is only now beginning to plan and to realize himself, will not contrast a barn floor for grouse and a dragnet for sturgeons with a crane and a steam hammer, as does Kliuev and Razumnik after him. Through the machine, man in socialist society will command nature in its entirety, with its grouse and its sturgeons. He will point out places for mountains and for passes. He will change the course of the rivers, and he will lay down rules for the oceans. The idealist simpletons may say that this will be a bore, but that is why they are simpletons. Of course this does not mean that the entire globe will be marked off into boxes, that the forests will be turned into parks and gardens. Most likely, thickets and forests and grouse and tigers will remain, but only where man commands them to remain. And man will do it so well that the tiger won't even notice the machine, or feel the change, but will live as he lived in primeval times. The machine is not in opposition to the earth. The machine is the instrument of modern man in every field of life. The present-day city is transient. But it will not be dissolved back again into the old village. On the contrary, the village will rise in fundamentals to the plane of the city. Here lies the principal task. The city is transient, but it points to the future, and indicates the road. The present village is entirely of the past. That is why its aesthetics seem archaic, as if they were taken from a museum of folk art.

Mankind will come out of the period of civil wars much poorer from terrific destructions, even without the earthquakes of the kind that occurred in Japan. The effort to conquer poverty, hunger, want in all its forms, that is, to conquer nature, will be the dominant tendency for decades to come. The passion for mechanical improvements, as in America, will accompany the first stage of every new socialist society. The passive enjoyment of nature will disappear from art. Technique will become a more powerful inspiration for artistic work, and later on the contradiction itself between technique and nature will be solved in a higher synthesis.

■   ■   ■

The personal dreams of a few enthusiasts today for making life more dramatic and for educating man himself rhythmically, find a proper and real place in this outlook. Having rationalized his economic system, that is, having saturated it with consciousness and planfulness, man will not leave a trace of the present stagnant and worm-eaten domestic life. The care for food and education, which lies like a millstone on the present-day family, will be removed, and will become the subject of social initiative and of an endless collective creativeness. Woman will at last free herself from her semi-servile condition. Side by side with technique, education, in the broad sense of the psychophysical molding of new generations, will take its place as the crown of social thinking. Powerful "parties" will form themselves around pedagogic systems. Experiments in social education and an emulation of different methods will take place to a degree that has not been dreamed of before. Communist life will not be formed blindly, like coral islands, but will be built consciously, will be tested by thought, will be directed and corrected. Life will cease to be elemental and for this reason stagnant. Man, who will learn how to move rivers and mountains, how to build peoples' palaces on the peaks of Mont Blanc and at the bottom of the Atlantic, will not only be able to add to his own life richness, brilliancy, and intensity, but also a dynamic quality of the highest degree. The shell of life will hardly have time to form before it will burst open again under the pressure of new technical and cultural inventions and achievements. Life in the future will not be monotonous.

More than that. Man at last will begin to harmonize himself in earnest. He will make it his business to achieve beauty by giving the movement of his own limbs the utmost precision, purposefulness, and economy in his work, his walk, and his play. He will try to master first the semiconscious and then the subconscious processes in his own organism, such as breathing, the circulation of the blood, digestion, reproduction, and, within necessary limits, he will try to subordinate them to the control of reason and will. Even purely physiologic life will become subject to collective experiments. The human species, the coagulated *Homo sapiens,* will once more enter into a state of radical transformation, and, in his own hands, will become an object of the most complicated methods of artificial selection and psychophysical training. This is entirely in accord with evolution. Man first drove the dark elements out of industry and ideology by displacing barbarian routine by scientific technique and religion by science. Afterwards he drove the unconscious out of politics, by overthrowing monarchy and class with democracy and rationalist parliamentarianism and then with the clear and open Soviet dictatorship. The blind elements have settled most heavily in economic relations, but man is driving them out from there also, by means of the socialist organization of economic life. This makes it possible to reconstruct fundamentally the traditional family life. Finally, the nature of man himself is hidden in the deepest and darkest corner of the unconscious, of the elemental, of the subsoil. Is it not self-evident that the greatest efforts of investigative thought and of creative initiative will be in that direction? The human race will not have ceased to crawl on all fours before God, kings, and capital, in order later to submit humbly before the dark laws of heredity and a blind sexual selection! Emancipated man will want to attain a greater equilibrium in the work of his organs and a more proportional developing and wearing out of his tissues, in order to reduce the fear of death to a rational reaction of the organism toward danger. There can be no doubt that man's extreme anatomical and physiological disharmony, that is, the extreme disproportion in the growth and wearing out of organs and tissues, give the life instinct the form of a pinched, morbid, and hysterical fear of death, which darkens reason, and which feeds the stupid and humiliating fantasies about life after death.

Man will make it his purpose to master his own feelings, to raise his instincts to the heights of consciousness, to make them transparent, to extend the wires of his will into hidden recesses, and thereby to raise himself to a new plane, to create a higher social biologic type, or, if you please, a superman.

It is difficult to predict the extent of self-government that the man of the future may reach or the heights to which he may carry his technique. Social construction and psychophysical self-education will become two aspects of one and the same process. All the arts—literature, drama, painting, music, and architecture will lend this process beautiful form. More correctly, the shell in which the cultural construction and self-education of communist man will be enclosed, will develop all the vital elements of contemporary art to the highest point. Man will become immeasurably stronger, wiser, and subtler; his body will become more harmonized, his movements more rhythmic, his voice more musical. The forms of life will become dynamically dramatic. The average human type will rise to the heights of an Aristotle, a Goethe, or a Marx. And above this ridge new peaks will rise.

Additional Resources

Trotsky, the Poets, and the Russian Revolution

The following selection of poems by writers active during the key decade of the Russian Revolution (1917–1927) is designed to offer readers of *Literature and Revolution* some sense of the writing that precipitated Trotsky's response. All of the writers sampled here are discussed by Trotsky except Osip Mandelstam, who is included because of the quality and reputation of his poetry and because of his relationship to Anna Akhmatova and other members of the Acméist group. For reasons of space, it is not possible to provide examples from writers of prose fiction, such as Boris Pilnyak, or playwrights, such as Vsevolod Meyerhold, who are important to Trotsky. The poets are arranged roughly in the order in which they appear in Trotsky's book.

Except in the cases of Akhmatova, Mayakovsky, and Biedny, all English translations come from two sources: *Twentieth Century Russian Poetry: Silver and Steel: An Anthology,* selected and with an introduction by Yevgeny Yevtushenko, edited by Albert C. Todd and Max Hayward, with Daniel Weissbort (New York: Doubleday, 1993), and *Modern Russian Poetry: An Anthology, With Verse Translations,* edited by Vladimir Markov and Merrill Sparks (Indianapolis: Bobbs-Merrill, 1966). The translations of Akhmatova are from *The Complete Poems,* translated by Judith Hemschemeyer, edited by Roberta Reeder (Boston: Zephyr Press and Edinburgh: Canongate Books Ltd., 1997). Mayakovsky's "To His Beloved Self" and "Order No. 2 to the Army of the Arts" are from *The Bedbug and Selected Poetry,* translated by Max Hayward and George Reavey, edited by Patricia Blake (Bloomington: Indiana University Press, 1960). Biedny's "Mil-

211

lion-footed" is from the RedWords edition of *Literature and Revolution,* foreword by Lindsey German (London, 1991), 44; no source for the English translation is given.

Andrey Biely
1880–1934

Born Andrey Nikolayevich Bugayev, Biely was a leading writer and theorist in the Russian Symbolist movement. He graduated from Moscow University in 1903 with a degree in mathematics; his interests also included German philosophy, literature, and music. He was attracted to the ideas of Friedrich Nietzsche and to the notion of a metaphysical opposition between the "mysterious East" and Western civilization. Biely is often celebrated for his experimentation with the Russian language. His collection of poems, *Symphonies,* appeared in four volumes between 1901 and 1908, and his remarkable and innovative novel, *Petersburg,* was published in 1912. He initially saw the Russian Revolution as retribution for the oppression of tsarism and as the beginning of spiritual and religious rebirth. But Trotsky is sharply critical of Biely's mysticism and "decadence" (54). He notes that Biely's very name (it means "white" in Russian) "testifies to his antithesis to the Revolution."

Despair
To Z.N. Grippius

Enough: do not wait, do not hope.
Disperse, my poor people, my race!
O torturous years without hope,
Break up, disappear into space!

Long centuries of serfdom and need.
O Motherland, allow me then
Tears for your expanses. I grieve
For your dark empty spaces again:—

Down in the humpbacked valley there,
Where a flock of green oak trees crowd

And stir as a raised thicket, bare
To the shaggy lead-colored clouds,

Where Stupor (a dry-armed bush) roams
Along field and pasture and crag
And piercingly whispers and moans
To winds with its rough, branchy rag,

Where, piercing my soul from the night
(Now risen hills like moons)
Are cruel yellow eyes leering bright—
The eyes of your crazy saloons.

O follow that hard rut from here,
Where sickness and death are ingrown...
Go off into space, disappear,
My Russia, O Russia, my own!

1908

Spirit

I was almost asleep...(Swift thoughts came rushing
In on some kind of spiraling express,
And on my realizing mind saw half-opened
Those heights not given to the consciousness):

I saw the Spirit...a spark in its beginning...
With an elusive face—like lightning fine—
And two wings—drilling gyres—which were tearing
The distances with a blood-colored shine.

This revealed: In the laws of precise numbers
And in the rebellious mental element
It was not I but good and kind hierarchies
Which had imprinted their Supreme intent.

The star...It has a shine that never changes...
But the star's flying beam runs on to bound
In diamonds on the mirror of the water
And dances shining arabesques around.

1914

To Vyacheslav Ivanov

What one had not expected happens...

You grow and take shape before me—
In ancient black frock-coat you stand
Among old armchairs and divans,
With a stamped volume in your hand:
'Transparence: Vyacheslav Ivanov.'

A green eye winks at me its blazes,
And then fly fireworks of phrases
In guttural tones of great lament.
Your absent-minded face is bent.
You toy with your tarnished ring—
A huge bright pentagram burning.

Now we are served rare Chinese tea...
Both of us eat the cookies.
And—we recall quite casually
The aphorisms of great men;
The sounds of ringing words are flying,
And they move me time and again
Like constant horn calls in a glen
And like a rooster's slender crying.

I've known you long—long, long ago,
Known you perhaps before my birth:
Your face with its pink-amber glow,
Your fingering your hair...like so,
And your long flapped coat (which I know
Must be booty for moths). And horrid
—Almost—how I know you who wore it,

How I know your large, browless forehead
Encircled by a gold halo.

1916

Nicolai Kliuev
1884–1937

Kliuev's work had its roots in Russian peasant culture—his mother was known as a reciter of folk epics. As a teenager he lived in a monastery and worked for the Flagellant sect of the Russian Orthodox Church. His correspondence with Alexander Blok in 1907 led to the publication of his first volume of poems, *Cry of the Pines,* which appeared with a foreword by Valery Bryusov. Kliuev at first welcomed the October Revolution but, along with other members of the literary group known as the Scythians, expected the peasantry to play the leading role in a Russian cultural revival. During the 1920s, his poetry was increasingly criticized as backward looking. Trotsky is more balanced in his assessment (65) than were many of his contemporaries, seeing Kliuev as "a poet of a closed-in world" but nevertheless "complex, exacting, ingenious." Kliuev was arrested in 1933 and exiled. Maxim Gorky secured his release for a time, but he was soon imprisoned again and held until his obscure death in 1937.

[Untitled: The autumns of the earth...]

The autumns of the earth are like a bishop's grave
Where incense and brocade—half-rotten, mix and set in
With the cadaver's mold. The aspen backwoods wave,
Browner than any brick. Like some crypt thieves can get in,
The sky is yawning wide. There—lees, the trash of cold
Graves, and the twangy talk, the sexton wind's endeavor:
'The omophorion and censer of pure gold
Are stolen; the most sacred grave profaned forever:
A miter—lump of dirt, the eagle-rug rags curled.'
The autumns of the earth are sad unendingly...
They are the living pledge the rich crypt of the world
Is stolen piece by piece—and without lock and key
Will be only received by the sacristan death.
Oh Lord, you pacify—with fire and wounds of war—
The spirit of the thief, the fats our bodies store;

But you soften the scabs with balms of Spring's fresh breath
And scare us with the fall—as with some dread landmark
At crossroads of the worlds where the graves' dusk is dark.

1917

[Untitled: This young girl will die in childbirth...]
To Annushka Kirillova

This young girl will die in childbirth soon...
And the sickly midwife doesn't know
That he pressed his shoulders hard to her
With fuzz on his boyish groin below,

That the fruit was heavy and like sap—
Windfall midst white blooming apple trees.
This girl in some interplanetary space,
Will birth radiant men of melodies.

In the grave—wormy as the windfalls are—
Her pubes will shine, like phosphorus.
And the girl's greedy eyes are like
White snowdrops, or lodges' lights for us.

In the grave are baptisms and births—
Blood to mold and heart to mineral.
Wet-nurse tales and ponds of feather beds
Foam up from the roaring lion squall.

In the whites of eyes sperm whales will splash.
In a walrus boat is death, eskimo iced...
And this girl, fragrant as honeycomb,
Will be cared for by the rainbow-Christ.

1917

Journey

"I am here"—replied the body
The thighs, the head, the palms, each hand,
And all the continents and islands
Which makes up my own orphaned land.

The promontory heart exalted
When suddenly one bright sail loomed:
"In my Madrid, Madrid so azure,
The almond trees and cypress bloomed!"

By the Aorta's reddened delta
The Sovereign Bark floats in the stream.
On barren mounds there in the darkness,
The mosses and the lichens gleam.

Here is the island, Liver. Over
It like sky does the Sacrum sweep.
In valleys with the green gall meadows
There are flocks of devoured sheep.

On their trees are grouse and chickens
And souls of millet—turnips too.
There is the navel-sun. The brown air
Is blind to each beam shining through.

The road leads past the polar circle
To Stomach and to Guts entire
Where such a fumy hell is blazing
From many milks that spit out fire.

Where the rendering plant and foundry,
Where tanneries and dump yard stand,
And where winged violent masses
Inhabit crests of the dry land.

O I am not your guest, pagans
Of flesh! Sail, sail, my boat (though crude)
To the continent of love and joy
Where the coast is incense and holy food.

The pubes is Morocco burning
Where neath fig trees a fountain can
Purr out its oriental singing
About Mohammed's caravan:

How through the star-flow of the desert
Came seven suns—the prophet's wives;

From Eve, the youngest—in the holy
Month—all the human race arrives.

Here Zoroaster, Christ, and Brahma
Plowed fields of fervid members. How
Two cannon balls, underground temples,
Keep watch over their diamond plow!

But also for the sun's own Magus
The altar hides the mystery...
And neath the pen's clairvoyant scratching
The paper sighs shudderingly.

Returning from the body's spaces,
The soul, a swallow homeward-bound,
Is bringing the first downy feather
Into the empty house of sound.

1917

From the cycle **Lenin**

I

Lenin has the spirit of an Old Believer,
Intones his decrees like a priest,
And looks to the Pomorian Responses
For the source of all our grief.

Now the land belongs to the peasants,
The Church is no longer a state serf.
Now a bright new world chimes forth,
And the people arise here on earth.

Shiny red as a flame or as leather,
That word opens up every soul.
It was long ago that the heel of Ivan
Forged the coin of his black iron rule.

Boris, Lord of the Golden Horde,
Rings proclamations on Ivan the Great.
But Lenin has raised the blizzard and storm
To the angel ranks of heaven.

It's pitch dark in Smolny, as dark as a thicket,
The air smells of pine and blueberries.
There, in a humble log-built grave,
The relics of Old Russia lie buried.

"Where are we going to bury the corpse?"
The band of the brave want to know.
They wind their way round the flask-shaped coast
From Konevets, raising dust like driven snow.

Ask instead of the clouds or the stars,
Or the dawns that turn the gorse bush red...
Ominous and bleak is that deserted graveyard
Where the robes of the Tsar lie interred.

The raven of fate will watch over them
In the faraway tombs of Hell.
So why must people mourn their loss
To the doom-laden Tartar death knell?

1918

Sergey Yessenin
1895–1925

The most popular Russian poet during the early years of the
Revolution, Yessenin came from a rural village in the Ryazan
province to study and work in Moscow in his teens. In 1914, he
began publishing his poems in journals. Their direct, lyrical evo-
cation of village life and landscape quickly won him admirers.
The success of this early poetry led him to move to Petersburg,
where he soon became a favorite in the literary salons. But Yessenin cultivated the identity of a wild, rebellious, uncompromising
outsider and was infamous for bouts of heavy drinking and un-
ruly behavior. At first, he welcomed the October Revolution but
insisted on keeping his poetry apart from political commitments
and loyalties. He joined Kliuev and other poets in founding a
movement they called "Imaginism," which prioritized imagery
and other formal features of verse. His personal admiration for
Mayakovsky did not prevent him from engaging in poetic dis-

putes with the older poet. In 1922, he published *Pugachev,* a verse tragedy about the peasant rebellion of 1773–1775. In the same year, he married the American dancer Isadora Duncan and toured the U.S. with her. They soon divorced, and he married the granddaughter of Leo Tolstoy. In the second chapter of *Literature and Revolution,* Trotsky positions "Yessenin (and the entire group of Imagists...) at the crossing of the road between Kliuev and Mayakovsky" (68). Trotsky is critical of *Pugachev* (the hero is "a sentimental romantic") but sees Yessenin in 1923 as a young writer still in the process of development. For his part, Yessenin became increasingly depressed and critical of the Bolsheviks. In 1925, he committed suicide by hanging himself in his room at the Hotel Angleterre in Leningrad, having first written his last poem in his own blood.

Trotsky's "To the Memory of Sergey Yessenin" appeared in *Pravda* on January 19, 1926. It is included in *Art and Revolution: Writings on Literature, Politics, and Culture,* edited by Paul N. Siegel (1992), 170–74.

[Untitled: I do not regret...]

I do not regret, complain, or weep,
All passes, like smoke off the white apple trees.
Autumn's gold has me in its withering grip.
I shall never be young again.

My heart has felt the chill,
It no longer beats as it once did.
The birch woods cotton print
No more tempts me to roam barefoot.

Spirit of wandering, less and less
Do you stir my lips' flame.
Oh, my lost freshness, storminess
Of eye, passion's flood time.

Oh life, do my desires
Grow tamer, or was it all a dream?
As though, in spring's echoing early hours,
I had galloped by on a pink steed.

We arc all mortal. Silently
The maples spill the copper of their leaves.
May you bc blessed for evermore
That you came—to flourish and to die.

1922

[Untitled: From the start…]

From the start, each living thing's
Got its own mark upon it.
I'd have been a thief and a cheat
If I'd not turned out a poet.

Scrawny and undersized,
Always the hero of the gang,
I'd often come back home
With my nose bashed in.

And when my scared mother saw me,
Through bleeding lips I'd murmur:
"It's nothing!—I tripped up.
I'll be all right tomorrow!"

Now that the seething cauldron
Of those days has cooled at last,
The restlessness and daring
Has spilt over into my verse—

A glittering heap of words,
And each line endlessly
Reflecting the bragging and bounce
Of an ex-daredevil and bully.

I'm still as bold and as proud.
Not for me the beaten track.
But now my soul's all bloodied,
Instead of my face getting bashed.

And it's no longer mother I'm telling,
But a mob of laughing strangers:

"It's nothing!—I tripped up.
I'll be all right tomorrow!"

1922

[Untitled: Now piece by piece...]

Now piece by piece we slip away
To that far land of peace and grace.
And perhaps must soon collect
My perishable chattels and set out.

Sweet birch groves, and you, earth,
And you, sands of the plain! I lack
The strength to hide the dread aroused
By this horde of party souls.

I have loved too much on earth
The things the soul owns in the flesh.
Peace to the aspens that spread their boughs
Admiring themselves in pink waters.

I have thought much in silence.
Sung many songs about myself.
And I rejoice that I have lived
And in this dark world drawn my breath.

I rejoice that I have kissed women,
Walked among flowers, and lounged on grass,
That I have never beaten about the head
Those dumb beasts that are our lower brothers.

I know the groves don't flourish there,
Nor does rye tinkle its swanlike neck.
Wherefore I always feel this dread
To see the horde of souls departing.

I know that in that land will be
No cornfields gleaming gold in haze.
Wherefore those men are dear to me
Who live with me on earth.

1924

The Son of My Bitch

Once again the years fly out from shadow,
And like meadows of daisies they bend.
Today I can clearly remember
The dog that was my childhood friend.

Like the maple that rots neath my window,
My youth rustled away. (How it ran!)
But I still see a girl in a white dress
For whom that dog was mailman.

Not everyone has such dear people,
But she was a song in my throat,
Because she never took from his collar
Any of the letters I wrote.

No, she never ever would read them.
She did not know my script. She was fond
Of dreaming for long times of something
By the snowball bush back of the pond.

I suffered. I wanted an answer…
It did not come. I left. And then
After years brought me fame as a poet,
I'm now back at my home gates again.

That dog has been dead for a long time,
But today I was met by her son—
With the wildest possible barking,
And her color—the same bluish one.

Holy Mary! They look like each other!
And the soul's pain flies out—as before.
And with this pain I seem to feel younger
And like writing letters once more.

I'm glad to hear the past singing.
But don't bark, you! Don't bark! Don't start!
Dog, you want me to kiss you
For the May you awoke in my heart?

I will kiss you, I'll press you close to me,
And take you home like a good friend would do...
Yes, I did like the girl dressed in white clothes,
But now I love one in blue.

1924

Anna Akhmatova
1889–1966

Akmatova was born near Odessa to aristocratic parents (her family name was Gorenko). In 1903, she met and began her relationship with Nicolai Gumilev; they married in 1910. The following year, with Mandelstam and several others, Akhmatova and Gumilev formed a circle of poets who called themselves "Acméists." Akhmatova published her first volume of poems in 1912, and her work continued to be published through the period of the Revolution. In 1918, she was divorced from Gumilev, who was executed in August 1921 for his involvement in a conspiracy against the Bolshevik government.

During the early 1920s, critical discussion of poetry in the Soviet Union was dominated by debate between the "Akhmatova faction" and the "Mayakovsky faction." In 1922, Mayakovsky himself attacked Akhmatova's "indoor intimacy" and characterized her poems as "pointless, pathetic and comic anachronisms." But in 1923, Alexandra Kollontai, a leading Bolshevik and the Soviet ambassador to Norway (she was the first woman ambassador in world history), defended Akhmatova by explaining why her poetry appealed to young women workers despite her distance from the Revolution and the Communist Party. Right through the period when Trotsky's *Literature and Revolution* was first being read and discussed, Akhmatova's poetry was also being read and discussed. In 1925, thirty-two of her poems were included in a major anthology entitled *Russian Poetry of the Twentieth Century.*

But these were the last of Akhmatova's poems to be published in the Soviet Union until 1940. Later in 1925, according to Akhmatova herself, an "unofficial" Communist Party resolution prohibited further publication of her work. In the same year, Trotsky was forced to resign his position as Commissar of War because of his increasingly outspoken opposition to the growing menace of Stalin's power within the state and party bureaucracy.

The editors of *Twentieth Century Russian Poetry* describe Akhmatova as "one of the two greatest women poets in the history of Russian poetry" (the other is Marina Tsvetaeva). They go on to say that her poetry is "distinguished...by its polished form, classical transparency, and thematic intimacy." Many of her lyrics, such as those included here, were published without titles. The first poem comes from the volume *White Flock* (1917), the second from *Plantain* (1921), and the last three from *Anno Domini MCMXXI* (1922). Akhmatova continued to live in the Soviet Union during the Stalinist era; her third husband, Nikolai Punin, died in prison, and her son was arrested and persecuted during the 1937–1938 purges. See *Against Forgetting: Twentieth-Century Poetry of Witness,* edited by Carolyn Forché (New York/London: Norton, 1993), 101–08, for selections from her poetic cycle *Requiem 1935–1940).*

[Untitled: We don't know how to say good-bye...]

We don't know how to say good-bye—
We keep wandering arm in arm.
Twilight has begun to fall,
You are pensive and I keep still.

Let's go into a church—we will watch
A funeral, christenings, a marriage service,
Without looking at each other, we will leave...
What's wrong with us?

Or let's sit on the trampled snow
Of the graveyard, sighing lightly,
And with your walking stick you'll outline palaces
Where we will be together always.

1917

[Untitled: I am listening to the orioles' ever mournful voice…]

I am listening to the orioles' ever mournful voice
And saluting the splendid summer's decline.
And through grain pressed tightly, ear to ear,
The sickle, with its snake's hiss, slices.

And the short skirts of the slender reapers
Fly in the wind, like flags on a holiday.
The jingling of bells would be jolly now,
And through dusty lashes, a long, slow gaze.

It's not caresses I await, nor lover's adulation,
The premonition of inevitable darkness,
But come with me to gaze at paradise, where together
We were innocent and blessed.

1917

[Untitled: I am not with those who abandoned their land…]

I am not with those who abandoned their land
To the lacerations of the enemy.
I am deaf to their coarse flattery,
I won't give them my songs.

But to me the exile is forever pitiful,
Like a prisoner, like someone ill.
Dark is your road, wanderer,
Like wormwood smells the bread of strangers.

But here, in the blinding smoke of the conflagration
Destroying what's left of youth,
We have not deflected from ourselves
One single stroke.

And we know that in the final accounting,
Each hour will be justified…
But there is no people on earth more tearless
More simple and more full of pride.

1922

[Untitled: Everything has been plundered...]
To Natalya Rykova

Everything has been plundered, betrayed, sold out,
The wing of black death has flashed,
Everything has been devoured by starving anguish,
Why, then, is it so bright?

The fantastic woods near the town
Wafts the scent of cherry blossoms by day,
At night new constellations shine
In the transparent depths of the skies of July—

And how near the miraculous draws
To the dirty, tumbledown huts…
No one, no one knows what it is,
But for centuries we have longed for it.

1921

[Untitled: Terror, fingering things in the dark...]

Terror, fingering things in the dark,
Leads the moonbeam to an ax.
Behind the wall there's an ominous knock—
What's there, a ghost, a thief, rats?

In the sweltering kitchen, water drips,
Counting the rickety floorboards.
Someone with a glossy black beard
Flashes by the attic window—

And becomes still. How cunning he is and evil,
He hid the matches and blew out the candle.
How much better would be the gleam of the barrels
Of rifles leveled at my breast.

Better, in the grassy square,
To be flattened on the raw wood scaffold
And, amid cries of joy and moans,
Pour out my life's blood there.

I press the smooth cross to my heart:
God, restore peace to my soul.
The odor of decay, sickeningly sweet,
Rises from the clammy sheets.

1921

Marina Tsvetaeva
1892–1941

A poet whose current reputation could hardly be higher: in *Twentieth Century Russian Poetry,* Todd and Hayward describe her as "[o]ne of the giants of Russian and world poetry." She was born in Moscow and traveled throughout Europe as a girl with her father (a professor) and mother (a pianist). Her first volume of poems, *Evening Album,* appeared in 1910. Her lyrics are often praised for their combination of intense passion and unconventional stylistic brilliance. In 1919, Tsvetaeva published a long verse narrative based on a folktale called *Maiden-Czar.* In 1922, she emigrated with her husband, Sergey Efron, to Paris. Trotsky mentions her only briefly in *Literature and Revolution,* all three times in connection with Akhmatova and "fellow travelers" whose poetry remains tied to Russian Orthodoxy and to pre-Revolutionary society. Tsvetaeva and her family returned to Russia in 1937, in the midst of the Stalinist Terror. Her husband was soon arrested and shot; her sister and daughter were both imprisoned. During World War II, Tsvetaeva was forced to evacuate to an area near Kazan where she committed suicide.

Return of the Leader

Horse—lame,
Sword—rusty.
Who—he?
Crowd's boss.

A step—an hour,
A sigh—an age,
Eyes—down.
People—there:

Foe.—Friend.
Thorn.—Laurel.
All—dreams…
He.—Horse.

Horse—lame.
Sword—rusty.
Cloak—old.
Back—straight.

1921

From **Two Songs**

2

Yesterday he could still look in my eyes, yet
Today—his looks are bent aside. Yesterday
He sat here until the birds began, but
Today—all those larks are ravens.

I am stupid, you are wise, alive,
While I am stunned and motionless: arise,
Lament of women in all times:
"My love, what was it I did to you?"

And tears are water, blood is
Water. A woman always washes in blood and tears.
Love is a stepmother, and no mother.
Then expect no justice and mercy from her.

Ships carry away the ones we love.
Along the white road they are taken away.
And one cry stretches across the earth:
"My love, what was it I did to you?"

Yesterday he lay at my feet. He even
Compared me to the Chinese Empire!
Suddenly he let his hands fall open,
And all my life fell out like a rusty kopeck.

A child-murderer, before some court
I stand—loathsome and timid I am.
And yet even in Hell I shall demand
"My love, what was it I did to you?"

I ask this chair, I asked the bed: Why?
Why do I suffer and live in penury?
His kisses stopped. He wanted to break you.
To kiss another girl, is their reply.

He taught me to live in fire, he threw me there,
And then abandoned me on the steppes of ice.
I know, my dear, what you have done with me.
"My love, what was it I did to you?"

I know everything, don't argue with me.
I can see now, I'm no longer a lover.
I understand wherever love has power
Death approaches soon, like a gardener.

The very thing—that shakes the tree!—
The apple will fall ripe when due…
For everything, for everything forgive me.
"My love, what was it 1 did to you?"

1920

Praise to the Rich

And so, making clear in advance
I know there are miles between us;
And I reckon myself with the tramps, which
Is a place of honor in this world:

Under the wheels of luxury, at
Table with cripples and hunchbacks…
From the top of the bell tower roof,
I proclaim it: I *love* the rich.

For their rotten, unsteady root
For the damage done in their cradle
For the absentminded way their hands
Go in and out of their pockets;

For the way their softest word is
Obeyed like a shouted order; because
They will not be let into heaven; and
Because they don't look in your eyes;

And because they send secrets by courier!
And their passions by errand boy!
In the nights that are thrust upon them they
Kiss and drink under compulsion.

And because in all their accountings
In boredom, in gilding, in wadding,
They can't buy me, I'm too brazen:
I confirm it, I *love* the rich!

And in spite of their shaven fatness,
Their fine drink (I wink—and spend),
Some sudden defeatedness,
And a look that is like a dog's

Doubting...
                    —not the core
Of their balance? But are the weights true?
I say that among all outcast
There are no such orphans on earth.

There is also a nasty fable
About camels getting through needles.
...For that look, surprised to death,
Apologizing for sickness, as

If they were suddenly bankrupt: "I would have been
Glad to lend, but" and their silence.
"I counted in carats once and then I was one of them."
For all these things, I swear it: I *love* the rich.

1922

The Poet

I

A poet's speech begins far away.
A poet is carried far away by speech,
By way of planets, signs, and the ruts
Of roundabouts parables, between *yes* and *no*,
In his hands even sweeping gestures from a bell tower
Become hooklike. For the way of comets

Is the poet's way. And the blown-apart
Links of causality are links. Look up
After him without hope. The eclipses of
Poets are not foretold in the calendar.

He is the one that mixes up the cards
And confuses arithmetic and weight.
He is the *questioner* from the desk,
The one who beats Kant on the head,

The one in the stone graves of the Bastille
Who remains like a tree in its loveliness.
And yet the one whose traces have always vanished,
The train everyone always arrives
Too late to catch…
                              —for the path of comets

Is the path of poets: they burn without warming,
Pick without cultivating. They are: an explosion, a breaking-in,
And the mane of their path on the curve of a
Graph cannot be foretold by the calendar.

1923

Nicolai Gumilev
1886–1921

The son of a physician serving in the navy, Gumilev studied philology in Moscow and in Paris, and traveled in Italy, Africa, and the Near East. He was married to Akhmatova from 1910 to 1918. He fought as a volunteer in the Russian army in World War I and eventually became a staff member of the Russian Expeditionary Force in Paris. Gumilev described himself to Victor Serge in these terms when they met in Paris in 1917: "I am a traditionalist, monarchist, imperialist, and pan-Slavist. Mine is the true Russian nature, just as it was formed by Orthodox Christianity" (see Serge's *Memoirs of a Revolutionary,* translated by Peter Sedgwick, London and New York: Writers and Readers Publishing, 1984, 59). Soon after the Revolution, Gumilev was elected the second president of the All-Russian Union of Poets, succeeding Alexander Blok. Trotsky mentions him once in *Literature and Revolution,* near the beginning of his chapter on Blok, saying that the latter "recognized Mayakovsky as a great talent, and yawned frankly over Gumilev." *The Pillar of Fire,* published in 1921, is usually regarded as Gumilev's best collection of poems. It was also in this year that he was executed for participating in a plot to undermine the Bolshevik government.

The Tram That Lost Its Way

The street was strange. Things made me wonder:
The sudden croaking of crows in the sky,
Then sounds of lutes, and distant thunder—
And then the tram was rushing by.

Somehow I jumped upon its platform
While the tram continued to rush and sway,
Leaving above a brilliant pathway
That remained undimmed in the light of day.

With a roar, like a tempest, dark and damned,
It was lost in the chasm of time…
Driver, you must stop the tram,
Driver, stop at once!

Too late. We rounded the city wall,
We cut through a grove of palms,
We crossed three bridges, three rivers in all—
The Neva, the Seine, and the Nile.

For an instant there flashed in the window frame
And threw us a searching stare
The bearded old beggar, of course the same
Who died in Beirut a year before.

Where am I? With languorous trepidation,
"Look over there"—my heartbeats reply:
"There are tickets at yonder railway station
To Spiritual India—for all to buy."

A signpost. Its blood-filled letters declare:
"Greengrocer's Shop." I know that instead
Of cabbages, carrots, and similar fare,
They sell human heads, cut off and dead.

Mine, too, was cut off. The butcher was dressed
In red shirt, and looked like an ox.
He put my head among the rest,
Here, on the floor of the slippery box.

And still, in that alley on a lawn of gray grass,
Stands the house with three windows, and a wooden fence...
Driver, you must stop the tram,
Driver, stop at once!

Masha, you lived here and sang for joy,
You wove me a carpet, my promised bride.
Where is your body now, where is your voice?
Can it be true that you have died?

Oh, how you suffered and moaned in your chamber,
While I, in the powdered wig and with chain,
Was being presented to the empress...
We never saw each other again.

Now I see: our freedom is only
Of light rushing in from beyond and far;

People and spirits wait at the entrance
To the zoo of planets and stars.

And now that sweet wind which I know and love
Brings to me, flying across the bridge,
The Horseman's hand in the iron glove
And two raised hooves of his steed.

The spire of St. Isaac's is cut into heaven
As a faithful stronghold of orthodox creed,
In there will be sung the thanksgiving service
For Masha's recovery, and a dirge for me.

And yet, the heart is forever tragic,
It is hard to breathe, and it hurts to live…
Masha, I never did imagine
That one can love and grieve like this.

1921

The Plague

A vessel with long red banners of the Prophet
Approaches Cairo.
By the sailor it's not hard to guess
They're from the East.

The captain shouting, bustling around,
Rough, guttural voices,
Swarthy faces in amongst the rigging,
And glimpses of the red of fezzes.

On the quay crowd children,
With their peculiar, delicate little bodies;
They've been gathered there since dawn
To see the strangers dock.

Storks sit perched on a roof
And stretch their necks.
Higher than everybody,
They see better.

Storks are aerial magicians.
Many secrets are revealed to them:
Like why a certain tramp
Has lilac blotches on his cheeks.

The storks screech out above the houses,
But no one hears their tale of how,
Together with the perfumes and the silks,
The plague insinuates itself into the town.

Words

In ancient days, when God cast down his gaze
Upon the newly created world,
Words could stop the sun,
Words could shatter cities.

Eagles didn't spread their wings,
And stars huddled, horror-stricken, round the moon,
Whenever word like pink flame,
Drifted through the heights.

But lower down in life came numbers,
Like domestic, subjugated cattle;
Clever numbers can convey
All shades of meaning.

The gray, old sage, who had transcended good and evil
And subdued them to his will,
Had not the nerve to risk a sound,
So, with his staff, he traced a number in the sand.

But we've forgotten that only words
Stay radiant among earthly troubles,
And in the Gospel of St. John
It does say that the word is God.

We have set their limits
At the meager boundaries of matter,
And, like bees in a vacated hive,
Dead words smell foul.

1921

The Worker

He stands before a red-hot furnace,
A short, old man.
The blinking of his reddish eyelids
Made his calm expression seem subservient.

All his comrades are asleep.
Only he still functions:
Still busy casting the bullet
That will sever me from the world.

Finished. His eyes brightened.
He leaves. The moon twinkles.
At home in a big bed
A sleepy, warm wife waits.

The bullet he cast will whistle
Over the gray, foaming Dvina,
The bullet he cast will seek out
My breast; I am its quarry.

I'll fall, in mortal melancholy,
I'll have a waking vision of the past,
Blood will push out onto the dry,
Dusty, crushed grass.

And the Lord will requite me in full measure
For my brief and bitter span.
This was done by a short, old man
In a light gray shirt.

1916

Osip Mandelstam
1881–1938

An important member of the Acméist group of poets, along with Akhmatova and Gumilev, Mandelstam came from a solid bourgeois family in St. Petersburg. On a visit to Paris in 1907, he became intensely interested in French Symbolism. His important collections of poems include *Stone* (1913) and *Tristia* (1922). The latter collection is based loosely on the Roman poet Ovid's sequence of elegies written during his years of exile in a remote area near the Black Sea; see the title poem from this volume below. Mandelstam's poems use plain language but are complicated in construction; they are often somber and at times fatalistic. Though he remained in Russia after the Revolution, Mandelstam wrote very little poetry after 1925. Because of a grotesque poetic portrait of Stalin, he was arrested in 1933 or 1934 and put in a prison camp, where he died.

Petersburg Strophes
To N. Gumilyov

Above the yellow Offices of State
A muzzy blizzard long swirled and fanned,
And mounting in a sleigh, an advocate
Closes his greatcoat with expansive hand.

The steamers at winter moorings. In the sun
The thickened glass of cabins has caught alight.
Monstrous, like a battleship in dock,
Heavy Russia lies at rest.

Above the river—the embassies of half the globe,
The sun and silence and the Admiralty;
The Empire's rigid porphyry robe
Is like the prickling shirt of poverty.

The northern snob has a lot to bear,
Onegin's old, outdated spleen:
A swollen snowdrift on Senate Square,
Bonfire smoke and bayonets' cold sheen.

The wherries have gathered water and the gulls
Are thick about the hemp shed
Where only peasants from some opera set
Wander, selling honey drinks or rolls of bread.

Through the mist a chain of motors streams
And modest, arrogant eccentric Eugene,
Forced to go on foot, is shamed by lack of means;
He curses fate and breathes in gasoline.

1913

An American Girl

American, twenty years old,
(Forgot what the *Titanic* told,
Sleeping below, dark as a crypt)
She's bound that she must reach Egypt.

America. The factory-whistles
Are singing. And the red skyscrapers
Watch their rising chimney tips
Give to the cold clouds their smudged lips.

The Louvre. Our daughter of the sea
Stands lovely as a poplar tree.
She climbs the Acropolis—a squirrel
That grinds away the sugared marble.

No meaning penetrates her brain,
But still she reads *Faust* on the train.
And she is sorry she must own
Louis is not now on the throne.

The hoofs of horses keep recalling
A time—rough, simple and remote…
So do the porters on their wooden
Benches, asleep in thick furcoats.

One, regal, lazy, hearing knocking
At an iron gate, got up. This man,
So animal-like in his yawning,
Brought back your image, Scythian,

When—full of aging love and mixing
Our snow and Rome in his song's parts—
Old Ovid sang of one ox-wagon
In campaigns with barbarian carts.

1914

Tristia

I've learned the science of farewells—at night
When those unloosened-hair laments are wept.
The oxen chew; the waiting lasts—till light
Ends those long vigil hours the city kept.
And I revere those night rites with cocks crowing,
When tear-red eyes, raising their load of long
Road sorrow, looked into the distance—flowing
A woman's weeping with the Muses' song.

Who knows what lies ahead with that "farewell,"
What kind of separation, and what this
First rooster's exclamation may foretell,
When the fire burns on the acropolis;
And at the dawn of some new life, new way,
While the ox chews lazily in his stall,
Why this same cock, herald of the new day,
Flaps loud his wings upon the city wall?

I love the regular routine of spinning:
The shuttle moves to, fro; the spindle hums…
Look, there is Delia—barefooted and grinning!
She flies toward you. And like swans down she comes!
O, how poor the language of joy and laughter,
That meager basic thread our lives invite!
All was before; all will repeat hereafter.
Only moments of knowing bring delight.

So be it: like a squirrel skin distending,
A small transparent figure lies
Upon a clean, clay platter. And there bending
Above the wax, a girl probes with her eyes.
We can't predict for the Greek Erebus;
Wax is for women what bronze is for men.

But where in battle our lot falls to us,
They die telling fortunes time and again.

1918

[Untitled: Last night I tell you…]

Last night I tell you, I do not lie,
Up to the waist in the melting snow,
I struggled from some strange railway halt.
I saw a hut and entered in:
Black monks were drinking tea and salt
While a gypsy girl made up to them.

At the bedhead all the while
She kept on beckoning with her eyes,
And foisting on them wretched talk:
There she sat until the dawn,
Repeating: Give me just a shawl,
Or anything, or half a shawl.

What once there was, you can't bring back.
An oaken table, in the salt a knife,
A fat hedgehog instead of bread:
They tried to sing but had no voice,
They tried to stand but merely arched
Through the window to the humpbacked yard.

And scarcely had a half-hour passed,
While their horses stomped and crunched
Their bowls of blackened cats,
When the gates screeched open in the dawn;
Their horses were harnessed in the yard
And they slowly, slowly warmed their hands.

The canvas gloom began to flush
As boredom will, for nothing, pour
Chalk that's settled out from water,
The milky day in the window peered
Through the transparent linen curtains
And a scrofulous jack flew flashing by.

1925

Alexander Blok
1880–1921

Regarded as the greatest of the Russian Symbolist poets, Blok is sometimes seen as the successor to Alexander Pushkin, who wrote the first Russian novel—in verse—*Eugene Onegin*. Born in Warsaw, where his father taught law at the university and his mother translated literary texts, he spent his teenage years with his grandfather in St. Petersburg where he studied jurisprudence and philology. *Verses on a Beautiful Lady,* Blok's first volume of collected poems, was published in 1904. His early poetry often emphasizes erotic desire and dark, forbidden passions. It also laments the corruption of Russian culture under tsarism. Blok welcomed the Bolshevik Revolution—most famously in "The Twelve," his long poem of 1918. He became the founding chairman of the Petrograd branch of the All-Russian Union of Poets, but the violence and suffering of the civil war led to his collapse into exhaustion and despair. Trotsky devotes the third chapter of *Literature and Revolution* to Blok, saying that he "belonged to pre-October literature, but he overcame this, and entered into the sphere of October when he wrote 'The Twelve.'" Blok "is not one of ours," he concludes, "but he reached towards us. And in doing so, he broke down. But the result of his impulse is the most significant work of our epoch. His poem, 'The Twelve,' will remain forever."

The Factory

The house next door has yellow windows.
Every night—every night
The wistful bolts begin to squeak,
Men walk slowly to the gate.

The heavy gates are double-locked,
And on the wall—on the wall
Someone silent, someone black
Sits motionless and counts them all.

His voice of brass calls to the men
Assembled down below

To bend their tortured backs again
To bend them low.

Inside they will disperse as ordered,
Each loaded with a heavy bag.
Behind the yellow windows laughter,
Because those beggars have been had.

1903

The Poets

Beyond the town a sterile quarter grew
On swampy and unsteady ground.
Here lived the poets—and each one met
The others with a supercilious smile.

In vain upon this dismal swamp
The bright-eyed day arose:
The inmates devoted their time
Only to wine and heavy work.

When drunk, they swore friendship, and talked
Cynical and salacious talk.
Toward dawn they puked. Then, locked up,
Labored dully and zealously.

Later from their kennels they crawled like dogs
And watched the sea burn,
And smitten by each passerby's
Gold hair, expertly raved.

Softening, they dreamed about the Golden Age,
Fondly cursed their publishers, and wept
Bitterly about a little flower,
And a little pearly storm cloud…

That's how the poets lived. O reader, friend!
You think, perhaps—it's worse
Than your own futile daily round,
Your own philistine mess?

But no, dear reader, blind critic!
The poet has at least the hair,
The cloud, the Age of Gold,
All inaccessible to you.

You rest content with self and wife,
With your bobtailed constitution.
While the poets' universal drinking,
Leaves them little constitution!

Should I die like a dog against a fence,
Should life stamp me into the earth—
Still I'll believe that God covered me with snow,
And that the blizzard kissed me!

1908

[Untitled: I want to live...]

I want to live, live to distraction:
To make the present live forever,
Make the impersonal human cover
With flesh whatever now has none!

What if life's torpor stifles me,
What if I suffocate and am dumb—
A happier young man maybe
Will say of me in the years to come:

Forgive his moods—was the momentum
Bitterness that made him write?
He was wholly on the side of freedom,
He was wholly on the side of light!

The Twelve

1

Darkness—and white
Snow hurled
By the wind. The wind!
You cannot stand upright

For the wind: the wind
Scouring God's world.

The wind ruffles
The white snow, pulls
That treacherous
Wool over the wicked ice.
Everyone out walking
Slips. Look—poor thing!

From building to building over
The street a rope skips nimble,
A banner on the rope:
ALL POWER TO THE CONSTITUENT ASSEMBLY.
This old weeping woman is worried to death,
She doesn't know what it's all about:
That banner—for God's sake—
So many yards of cloth!
How many children's leggings it would make—
And they without shirts—without boots…

The old girl like a puffed hen picks
Her way between drifts of snow.
"Mother of God, these Bolsheviks
Will be the death of us, I know!"

Will the frost never lose its grip
Or the wind lay its whips aside?
The bourgeois where the roads divide
Stands chin on chest, his collar up.

But who's this with the mane
Of hair, saying in a whisper:
"They've sold us down the river.
"Russia's down and out!"
A pen-pusher, no doubt,
A word-spinner…

There's someone in a long coat, sidling
Over there where the snow's less thick.
"What's happened to your joyful tidings,
Comrade cleric?"

Do you remember the old days:
Waddling belly-first to prayer,
When the cross on your belly would blaze
On the faithful there?...

A lady in a fur
Is turning to a friend:
"We cried our eyes out, dear..."
    She slips up—
Smack!—on her beam end.

    Heave ho
And up she rises—so!

The wind rejoices,
Mischievous and spry,
Ballooning dresses
And skittling passersby.
It buffets with a shower
Of snow the banner cloth:
ALL POWER TO THE CONSTITUENT ASSEMBLY,
And carries voices.

    ..."Us girls had a session...
    ...In there on the right...
      ...Had a discussion—
    Carried a motion:
Ten for a time, twenty-five for the night...
...And not a ruble less from anybody...
   ... Coming to bed...?"

Evening ebbs out.
The crowds decamp.
Only a tramp
Potters about.
And the wind screams...

Hey you! Hey
    Chum,
Give us a kiss...?

A crust!
What will become
Of us? Get lost!

Black sky grows blacker.

Anger, sorrowful anger
Seethes in the breast…
Black anger, holy anger…

Friend! Keep
Your eyes skinned!

2

The wind plays up: snow flutters down.
Twelve men are marching through the town.

Their rifle butts on black slings sway.
Lights left, right, left, wink all the way…

Cap tilted, fag drooping, every one
Looks like a jailbird on the run!

Freedom, freedom,
Down with the cross!

Rat-a-tat-tat!

It's cold, boys, and I'm numb!

"Johnny and Kate are living it up…"
"She's bank notes in her stocking top!"

"John's in the money, too, and how!"
"He was one of us; he's gone over now!"

"Well, Mister John, you son of a whore,
Just you kiss my girl once more!"

Freedom, freedom,
Down with the cross!

Rat-a-tat-tat!

It's cold, boys, and I'm numb

"Johnny and Kate are living it up..."
"She's bank notes in her stocking top!"

"John's in the money, too, and how!"
"He was one of us; he's gone over now!"

"Well, Mister John, you son of a whore,
Just you kiss my girl once more!"

    Freedom, freedom
  Down with the cross!
  Johnny right now is busy with Kate.
  What do you think they're busy at?

    Rat-a-tat-tat!

Lights left, right, left, lights all the way...
Rifles on their shoulders sway...

Keep a Revolutionary Step!
The Relentless Enemy Will Not Stop!

Grip your gun like a man, brother!
Let's have a crack at Holy Russia—

    Mother
    Russia
  with her big, fat arse!

Down with the cross!

3

The lads have all gone to the wars
To serve in the Red Guard—
To serve in the Red Guard—
And risk their hot heads for the cause!

    Hell and damnation,
    Life is such fun
    With a ragged greatcoat
    And a Jerry gun!

To smoke the nobs out of their holes
We'll light a fire through all the world,
A bloody fire through all the world—
   Lord, bless our souls!

4

The blizzard whirls; a cabby shouts;
Away fly Johnny and Kate with a 'lectric lamp
   Between the shafts...
   Hey there, look out!

He's in an army overcoat,
A silly grin upon his snout.
He's twirling a mustachio,
   Twirling it about,
   Joking as they go...

Young Johnny's a mighty lover
With a gift of the gab that charms!
   He takes silly Kate in his arms,
     He's talking her over...

She throws her head back as they hug
And her teeth are white as pearl...
   Ah, Kate, my Katey girl,
   With your little round mug...

5

Across your collarbone, my Kate,
A knife has scarred the flesh;
And there below your bosom, Kate,
That little scratch is fresh!

   Hey there, honey, honey, what
   A lovely pair of legs you've got!

You carried on in lace and furs—
Carry on, dear, while you can!
You frisked about with officers—
Frisk about, dear, while you can!

Honey, honey, swing your skirt!
My heart is knocking at my shirt!

Do you remember that officer—
The knife put an end to him…
Do you remember that, you whore,
Or does your memory dim?

Honey, honey, let him be!
You've got room in bed for me!

Once upon a time you wore gray spats,
Scoffed chocolates in gold foil,
Went out with officer-cadets—
Now it's the rank and file!

Honey, honey, don't be cruel!
Roll with me to ease your soul!

6

…Carriage again and cabby's shout
Come storming past: "Look out! Look out!…"

Stop, you, stop! Help, Andy—here!
Cut them off, Peter, from the rear!…

Crack—crack—reload—crack—crack!
The snow whirls skyward off the road!…

Young Johnny and the cabman run
Like the wind. Take aim. Give them one!…

For the road. Crack—crack! Now learn
To leave another man's girl alone!…

Running away, you bastard? Do.
Tomorrow I'll settle accounts with you!

But where is Kate? She's dead! She's dead!
A bullet hole clean through her head!

Kate, are you satisfied? Lost your tongue?
Lie in the snowdrift then, like dung!

Keep a Revolutionary Step!
The Relentless Enemy Will Not Stop!

7

Onward the twelve advance,
Their butts swinging together,
But the poor killer looks
At the end of his tether...

Fast, faster, he steps out.
Knotting a handkerchief
Clumsily round his throat
His hand shakes like a leaf...

"What's eating you, my friend?"
"Why so downhearted, mate?"
"Come, Pete, what's on your mind?
Still sorry for Kate?"

"Oh, brother, brother, brother,
I loved that girl...
Such nights we had together,
Me and that girl..."

"For the wicked come-hither
Her eyes would shoot at me,
And for the crimson mole
In the crook of her arm,
I shot her in my fury—
Like the fool I am..."

"Hey, Petey, shut your trap!
Are you a woman?"
"Are you a man, to pour
Your heart out like a tap?"
"Hold your head up!"
"And take a grip!"

"This isn't the time now
For me to be your nurse!
Brother, tomorrow
Will be ten times worse!"

And shortening his stride,
Petey slows his step...

Lifts his head
And brightens up...

What the hell!
It's not a sin to have some fun!

Put your shutters up, I say—
There'll be broken locks today!

Open your cellars: quick, run down...!
The scum of the earth are hitting the town!

8

God, what a life!
I've had enough!
I'm bored!

I'll scratch my head
And dream a dream...

I'll chew my cud
To pass the time...

I'll swig enough
To kill my drought...

I'll get my knife
And slit your throat!

Fly away, mister, like a sparrow,
Before I drink your blue veins dry
For the sake of my poor darling
With her dark and roving eye...

Blessed are the dead which die in the Lord...

I'm bored!

9

Out of the city spills no noise,
The prison tower reigns in peace.
"We've got no booze but cheer up, boys,
We've seen the last of the police!"

The bourgeois where the roads divide,
Stands chin on chest, his collar up:
Mangy and flea-bitten at his side
Shivers a coarse-haired mongrel pup.

The bourgeois with a hangdog air
Stands speechless, like a question mark,
And the old world behind him there
Stands with its tail down in the dark.

10

Still the storm rages gust upon gust.
    What weather! What a storm!
At arm's length you can only just
    Make out your neighbor's form.

Snow twists into a funnel,
A towering tunnel...

"Oh, what a blizzard!...Jesus Christ!"
"Watch it, Pete, cut out that rot!
You fool, what did Christ and his cross
Ever do for the likes of us?
Look at your hands. Aren't they hot
With the blood of the girl you shot?
Keep a Revolutionary Step?
The Enemy Is Near and Won't Let Up!"

    Forward, and forward again
      The working men!

11

...Abusing God's name as they go,
   All twelve march onward into snow.
      Prepared for anything,
      Regretting nothing...

Their rifles at the ready
For the unseen enemy...
In back streets, side roads
Where only snow explodes

Its shrapnel, and through quag—
Mire drifts where the boots drag...

      Before their eyes
      Throbs a red flag.

      Left, right,
      The echo replies.

      Keep your eyes skinned
      Lest the enemy strike!

Into their faces day and night
      Bellows the wind
      Without a break...

     Forward, and forward again
     The working men!

12

...They march far on with sovereign tread...
"Who else goes there? Come out! I said
Come out!" It is the wind and the red
Flag plunging gaily at their head.

The frozen snowdnft looms in front.
"Who's in the drift? Come out! Come here!"
There's only the homeless mongrel runt
Limping wretchedly in the rear...

"You mangy beast, out of the way
Before you taste my bayonet.
Old mongrel world, clear off I say!
I'll have your hide to sole my boot!"

…The shivering cur, the mongrel cur
bares his teeth like a hungry wolf,
droops his tail, but does not stir…
"Hey, answer, you there, show yourself."

"Who's that waving the red flag?"
"Try and see! It's as dark as the tomb!"
"Who's that moving at a jog
Trot, keeping to the back-street gloom?"

"Don't you worry—I'll catch you yet,
Better surrender to me alive!"
"Come out, comrade, or you'll regret
It—we'll fire when I've counted five!"

Crack—crack—crack! But only the echo
Answers from among the eaves…
The blizzard splits his seams, the snow
Laughs wildly up the whirlwind's sleeve…

    Crack—crack—crack!
    Crack—crack—crack!

    …So on they go with sovereign tread—
    Behind them limps the hungry mongrel,
And wrapped in wild snow at their head
    Carrying the flag blood-red—
    Soft-footed in the blizzard's swirl,
Invulnerable where bullets sliced—
Crowned with a crown of snowflake pearl,
    In a wreath of white rose,
    Ahead of them Christ Jesus goes.

1918

Vladimir Mayakovsky
1893–1930

Mayakovsky came from a rural background in Georgia and grew up speaking Russian with his family and Georgian with his friends at school. The family moved to Moscow in 1906, and in 1908, when he was fifteen, Mayakovsky joined the Bolshevik faction of the Social Democratic Labor Party. He was jailed for the first of several times the following year for engaging in subversive activity. In 1912, he moved to St. Petersburg and, with David Burlyuk, Velimir Khlebnikov, and Alexey Kruchenikh, published "A Slap in the Face of Public Taste," widely regarded as the manifesto of the Russian Futurist movement.

Mayakovsky began publishing his poems in the same year, and in 1913 gave dramatic readings of his poems on a tour of the provinces with his Futurist comrades. In 1915, he published his first major long poem, "The Cloud in Trousers," and became the lover of Lili Brick, wife of the critic Osip Brick. The couple contributed a flamboyant presence to literary and art circles. Trained as a draftsman and visual artist, Mayakovsky put these, as well as his writing skills, at the service of the Revolution between 1919 and 1921 by designing posters and writing short plays and other pieces for ROSTA, the Russian Telegraph Agency. In 1923, he co-founded the radical modernist journal *Lef* (short for *Left Front of the Arts*) with Osip Brick, and traveled widely in Europe, the United States, Mexico, and Cuba. With Stalin's rise to power in the late 1920s, Mayakovsky became increasingly alienated politically and depressed by developments in the Soviet Union. On April 14, 1930, he shot himself to death with a revolver. Tens of thousands of people attended his funeral.

Both before and after the October Revolution, Mayakovsky experimented boldly in his poetry with rhythm and metaphor as well as with the projection of poetic voice and persona. Trotsky devotes sustained critical attention to Mayakovsky, focusing especially on his revolutionary epic *The 150,000,000*. Unfortunately, this text has never been translated into English. The despair that led Mayakovsky to commit suicide in 1930 was both political and personal, and although Stalin celebrated his work, Mayakovsky's creative energy and daring are inimical to everything about Stalin's brutal dictatorship.

Trotsky's brief article on "The Suicide of Vladimir Maya-kovsky" appeared in the *Bulletin of the Opposition* for May 11, 1930. It is included in *Art and Revolution: Writings on Literature, Politics, and Culture,* edited by Paul N. Siegel (1992), 182–86.

To His Beloved Self, the Author Dedicates These Lines

Four words,
heavy as a blow:
"...unto Caesar...unto god..."
But where can a man
like me
bury his head?
Where is there shelter for me?

If I were
as small
as the Great Ocean,
I'd tiptoe on the waves
and woo the moon like the tide.
Where shall I find a beloved,
a beloved like me?
She would be too big for the tiny sky!

Oh, to be poor!
Like a multimillionaire!
What's money to the soul?
In it dwells an insatiable thief.
The gold of all the Californias
will never satisfy the rapacious horde of my lusts.

Oh, to be tongued-tied
like Dante
or Petrarch!
I'd kindle my soul for one love alone!
In verse I'd command her to burn to ash!
And if my words
and my love
were a triumphal arch,

then grandly
all the heroines of love through the ages
would pass through it, leaving no trace.

Oh, were I
as quiet
as thunder
then I would whine
and fold earth's aged hermitage in my shuddering embrace.
If,
to its full power,
I used my vast voice,
the comets would wring their burning hands
and plunge headlong in anguish.

With my eyes' rays I'd gnaw the night—
if I were, oh,
as dull
as the sun!
Why should I want
to feed with my radiance
the earth's lean lap!

I shall go by,
dragging my burden of love.
In what delirious
and ailing
night,
was I sired by Goliaths—
I, so large,
so unwanted?

1916

Can't Stand It

I couldn't stand sitting around reading
at home: Annensky, Tyutchev, Fet.
Wanting company and people again,
I go out
to the films, to some cafe or pub,
at the bar,

shining,
hope gleams in the idiot heart.
And if after a week
your Russian muzhik has changed,
I'll burn his cheeks, I'll fire his lips.
Carefully lifting my eyes
I stuff my fists in the heap of my coat.
"Get back!
Back! I say, back!
Get back!"
Fear screams from the pit of my heart,
races up and down my features with desperate sorrow.
I see I'm out of control.
A little to the left of me,
a most mysterious creature
unknown to the earth, to the depths of the seas,
is carefully working over
a carved leg of veal.
Looking at him you can't tell whether he's eating or not,
looking at him you can't tell whether
he's breathing or not.
Two yards of featureless rose-pink flesh;
I hope his number's sewn onto a corner,
and all that moves, rippling down to his shoulders,
are the gentle folds of his gleaming cheeks.
My heart in amazement
bursts up, pacing:
"Get back, I say!
What more do you want?"
I look to the left
My mouth agape.
I turn to the first and he's utterly changed;
after the second awful apparition
the first is something like
Leonardo da Vinci.
There are no people left.
Do you understand
the scream of a thousand and one tortured days?
Doesn't the spirit wish to steal away
silently
or to speak to someone?

I hurl myself to the ground,
with the peel of a stone,
I wipe off my face into blood,
washing the asphalt with my tears.
With lips exhausted from love from the thousandth embrace
I wash the tramcar's intelligent mouth.
I go back to my home.
I stick to the wallpaper:
Where is there a rose more tearlikc?
If you want
I'll read you,
scabby,
"Simple as a roar."

FOR HISTORY

When all are distributed through heaven and through hell,
conclusions will be drawn about this earth—
remember well:
In 1916 the beautiful people disappeared from Petrograd.

1916

Ode on the Revolution

Hissed offstage
mocked by the batteries.
To you,
to you,
ulcerated by querulous bayonets,
zestfully
I offer an ode's
solemn "O,"
suspended over the epithets!
O, beastlike!
Childlike!
O, pennylike!
Great one!
What else were you called?
How will you turn out, O two-faced one—
a graceful structure
or a pile of rubble?
You flatter,
flatter reverentially

the engine driver,
covered in coal dust,
the miner, who burrows deep amid ores,
the celebration of human labor's your task.
And tomorrow
Vasily the Blessed
will raise in vain
the cathedral rafters, begging for mercy,
the blunt-snouted hogs of your six-inch guns
will rake the Kremlin's millennia.
The *Glory*
wheezes on its death trip.
The sirens' thin scream is drowned.
You will send sailors
to the sinking ship,
where a forgotten kitten
meows.
And after?
After, you yelled like a whole drunken crowd.
Daredevil whiskers are twirled with a flourish.
Your rifle butts drive the gray admirals out,
heads down,
from the bridge in Helsingfors.
It licks and licks yesterday's wounds,
and again I see the opened veins.
As for you, my philistine
—o, may you be thrice cursed!—
and my
poetic
—o, four times famed, blessed one!—

1918

Order No. 2 to the Army of the Arts

This is for you—
the fleshy baritones
who, since the days
of Adam,
have shaken those dens called theaters
with the arias of Romeos and Juliets.

This is for you—
the *peintres,*
grown as robust as horses,
the ravening and neighing beauty of Russia,
skulking in ateliers
and, as of old, imposing Draconian laws on flowers
and bulking bodies.

This is for you—
who put on little fig leaves of mysticism,
whose brows are harrowed with wrinkles—
you, little futurists,
imaginists,
acmeists,
entangled in the cobweb of rhymes.
This is for you—
who have exchanged rumpled hair
for a slick hairdo,
bast shoes for lacquered pumps,
you, men of the Proletcult,
who keep patching
Pushkin's faded tailcoat.

This is for you—who dance and pipe on pipes,
sell yourselves openly,
sin in secret,
and picture your future as academicians
with outsized rations.
I admonish you,
I—
genius or not—
who have forsaken trifles
and work in Rosta,
I admonish you—
before they disperse you with rifle-butts:
Give it up!

Give it up!
Forget it.
Spit
on rhymes
and arias

and the rose bush
and other such mawkishness
from the arsenal of the arts.
Who's interested now
in—"Ah, wretched soul!
How he loved,
how he suffered…"?
Good workers—
these are the men we need
rather than long-haired preachers.
Listen!
The locomotives groan,
and a draft blows through crannies and floor:
"Give us coal from the Don!
Metal workers
and mechanics to the depot!"
At each river's outlet, steamers
with an aching hole in their side,
howl through the docks:
"Give us oil from Baku!"
While we dawdle and quarrel
in search of fundamental answers,
all things yell:
"give us new forms!"

There are no fools today
to crowd, open-mouthed, round a "maestro"
and await his pronouncement.
Comrades,
give us a new form of art—
an art
that will pull the republic out of the mud.

1921

Velemir Khlebnikov
1885–1922

Khlebnikov came from an academic professional family and himself studied science and mathematics at the University of Kazan.
He began publishing his poems in 1908 as a student at the University of St. Petersburg. Along with David Burlyuk and Alexey
Kruchenikh, he founded Russian Futurism. Contemporaries admired his demanding technical brilliance: Mayakovsky said of
him, "Khlebnikov is not a poet for the consumer, Khlebnikov is a
poet for the manufacturer." Khlebnikov worked to expand the
poetic resources of the Russian language and committed himself
to creating what he called a "trans-sense language" that could
become an adequate medium for the Futurists' new poetry.
Though he welcomed the October Revolution, he saw in it the
possibility of a kind of Slavic utopia rather than a democratic
workers' state. In 1921, Khlebnikov went with the Red Army to
Persia where he died of typhus. In Trotsky's chapter on "Futurism" in *Literature and Revolution,* he is generally skeptical of
Khlebnikov's linguistic experimentation and relates it to what he
sees as a "Utopian sectarianism" (118) in much Futurist work.

Manifesto of the Presidents of the Terrestrial Globe

> Only we, blasting your three years of war
> Through one swirl of the terrible trumpet,
> Sing and shout, sing and shout,
> Drunk with the charm of the truth
> That the Government of the Terrestrial Globe
> Has come into existence:
> It is We.
> Only we have fixed to our foreheads
> The wild laurels of the Rulers of the Terrestrial Globe.
> Implacable in our sunburned cruelty,
> Mounting the slab of the right of seizure,
> Raising high the standard of time,
> We fire the moist clays of mankind
> Into jugs and pitchers of time,
> We initiate the hunt for people's souls,

We howl through the gray sea horns,
We call home the human flocks—
Ego-e! Who's with us?
Who's our comrade and friend?
Ego-e! Who's behind us?
Thus we dance, the shepherds of people
And mankind, playing on the bagpipes.
Evo-e! Who else?
Evo-e! Who next?
Only we, mounting the slab
Of ourselves and our names,
Amid the sea of your malicious pupils
Intersected by the hunger of the gallows
And distorted by the horror of imminent death,
Intend by the surf of the human howl
To name and acclaim ourselves henceforth
The Presidents of the Terrestrial Globe.
What snots, some will say.
No, they're saints, others will object.
But we shall smile like gods
And point a finger at the Sun.
Drag it about on a string for dogs,
Hang it up on the words:
Equality, fraternity, freedom.
Judge it by your jury of jugglers
On the charge that once,
On the threshold of a very smileful spring,
It instilled in us these beautiful thoughts,
These words, and gave us
These angry stares.
It is the guilty one.
For we enact the solar whisper
When we crash through to you as
The plenipotentiaries-in-chief of its ordinances,
Its strict mandates.
Corpulent crowds of humanity
Will trail along the tracks
Which we have left behind.
London, Paris, and Chicago
In their appreciation
Will change their names to ours.

But we shall forgive them their folly.
This is the distant future,
But meanwhile, mothers,
Bear away your children
Should a state appear anywhere.
Youngsters, hustle away and hide in caves
And in the depths of the sea,
Should you see a state anywhere.
Girls and those who can't stand the smell of the dead
Fall in a swoon at the very word "borders":
They smell of corpses.
For every chopping block
Was once a good pine tree,
A curly pine.
The block is only bad because
It's used to chop off people's heads.
Such is the state and its government.
You are a very nice word from a dream—
There are ten sounds in it:
Much comfort and freshness.
You grew up in a forest of words:
Ashtray, match, cigarette butt.
An equal among equals:
But why do you, state, feed on people?
Why has the fatherland become a cannibal
And the motherland his wife?
Hey! Listen!
In the name of all mankind
We offer to negotiate
With the states of the past:
If you, O states, are splendid,
As you love to say of yourselves
And you force your servants
To say of you,
Then why this food of the gods?
Why do we people crunch in your maws
Between your incisors and molars?
Listen, states of space,
For three years already
You have pretended
That mankind is only a pastry,
A cookie melting in your mouth;

But what if the cookie jumps up like a razor and says:
Mommy!
What if we are sprinkled on it
Like poison?
Henceforth we order that the words "By the grace of God"
Be changed to "By the grace of Fiji."
Is it decent for the Lord Terrestrial Globe
(Long may his will be done)
To encourage communal cannibalism
Within the confines of himself?
And is it not the height of servility
On the part of the people, those who are eaten,
To defend their supreme Eater?
Listen! Even pismires
Squirt formic acid on the tongues of bears.
If there should be an objection
That the state of space is not subject to judgment,
As a communal person in law,
May we not object that man himself
Is also a bimanous state
Of blood corpuscles and also communal.
If the states be truly bad,
Then who among us will lift a finger
To cut short their dreaming
Under the blanket: forever.
You are dissatisfied,
O states and their governments,
You chatter your teeth in advance warning
And cut capers. But so what!
We are the higher power
And can always answer
The revolt of states,
With the revolt of slaves,
With a pointed letter.
Standing on the deck of the word "suprastate of the star"
And needing no cane in this hour of rolling,
We ask which is higher:
We, by virtue of the right to revolt,
And incontestable in our primacy,
Protected by the law of patents
In declaring ourselves the Presidents of the Terrestrial Globe,

Or you governments
Of the separate countries of the past,
These workday remnants by the slaughterhouses
Of the two-legged oxen, with whose
Cadaverous moisture you are smeared?
As regards us, the leaders of mankind,
Which we constructed according to the rules of rays
With the aid of the equations of fate,
We reject the lords
Who name themselves rulers,
States and other book publishers
And commercial houses of War & Co.,
Who have placed the mills of dear prosperity
Under the now three-year-old waterfall
Of your beer and our blood
With a defenselessly red wave.
We see the states falling on their sword
In despair that we have come.
With the motherland on your lips,
Fanning yourself with military regulations,
You have brazenly introduced war
Into the circle of the Brides of man.
But calm yourselves, you states of space,
And stop crying like girls.
As a private agreement between private persons,
Along with the societies for admirers of Dante,
The breeding of rabbits and the struggle against marmots,
You come under the umbrella of our published laws.
We shall not touch you.
Once a year you will assemble at an annual meeting
To make an inspection of the thinning forces
And observe the right of unions.
Remain a voluntary contract
Of private persons, needed by no one,
And important to no one.
As boring as the toothache
Of a seventeenth-century granny.
You compare to us
As a monkey's hairy hand and foot
Signed by an unknown fire god,
Compares to the hand of the thinker

Who calmly directs the universe,
This rider of saddled fate.
Besides, we are founding
A society for the defense of states
Against rude and cruel forms of address
On the part of the communes of time.
Like switchmen
At the cross ties of Past and Future,
We regard with as much composure
The replacement of your states
By a scientifically constructed mankind
As the replacement of a bast boot
By the gleaming glow of a train.
Comrade workers! Don't complain about us:
We, as architect workers,
Take a special path to the same goal.
We are a special weapon.
And so the battle gauntlet
Of three great words has been thrown down:
The Government of the Terrestrial Globe.
Intersected by a red flash of lightning,
The sky-blue banner of the firmament,
A banner of windy dawns, morning suns,
Is raised and flaps above the earth.
There you have it, my friends!
The Government of the Terrestrial Globe.

1917

From Good World

And so the castles of world trade,
Where gleam the chains of poverty,
With spite and rapture on your face
You will reduce to ash someday.
He who has tired of old disputes
And sees but torture in his stars,
Take in your hand the thunder dust,
And send the palace in the sky.
And if a cloud of deep blue smoke
Drowns in the flaming scarlet,

With bloodied hand, not bannered one,
Cast down to fate the gauntlet.
And if a bonfire hits the mark
And whips a sail of smoke about,
Step right into the blazing tent,
Your hidden firearm—take it out!
    And where grand profits spend the night,
    Encased in glass, at the tsar's castle,
    Explosive means are quite all right,
    As are the schemes of clever females.
When God himself seems like a chain,
You rich man's slave, where is your blade?
    O woman, smother with a curl
    Youth's murderer at meeting time,
    Because as a barefooted girl
    You once begged him for charity.
    Go softly, with a catlike gait,
    From tender midnight pure and clean.
    Consumptive one, give him a kiss
    Directly on his happy grin.
    And if your hand be without irons,
    Go up to a chained dog
    And kiss its foaming mug,
    Then kiss the foe until he disappears.
You rich man's slave, hey tallyho,
You were harassed by indigence.
You crawled like mendicant to king
And pressed a kiss upon his lips.
With a high wound afflicted,
Removing from red sky the latch,
Grab on the mustache of Aquarius
And slap the Canes on the back!
And may the space of Lobachevsky
Fly from the flags of nighttime Nevsky.

Now proceed creative men
In the place of gentlemen,
Congregation of the Goodworld
With the Workworld on a pole.
Now the uprising of Razin,
Flying to the sky of Nevsky,
Brings together the design

And the space of Lobachevsky.
May the curves of Lobachevsky
Adorn the city squares,
Arching round the straining neck
Of universal labor.
And the lightning will complain
That it must hurry like a serf,
And not a person will remain
To sell a bag of stolen wealth.

. . . .

Where the Volga will say "I,"
The Yangtze will add "love,"
And the Mississippi—"all of,"
Old Man Danube will add "the,"
And the Ganges's waters—"world."
Thus will the river idol
Outline the lands of green.
Forever, always, there and here!
For all, forever, everywhere—all!
Across the star will fly our call.
Above the world the language of love soars,
And into the sky the Song of Songs implores.
Draw not with chalk, but draw with love
The one that will be the design.
And as fate flies down to your pillow,
Wise spikes of rye it will incline.

1920

From **The Night Before the Soviets**

She came and spoke low:
"Milady, milady!"
"Now what's with you, I want to sleep!"
"They'll hang you soon, you know!
He-ee-he! Ee-he-he!
For your sins, your family tree!"
Just like a bag her face is gray
And a snicker crossed it quietly.
"Old hag, listen, it's time to sleep!
Go on home!

Now what nonsense is this,
I want to go to sleep!"
The big gray head shakes like a white lion.
"Must be a witch of some kind,
She would make a saint's mind go."
"Milady, milady!"
"What's with you?"
"They'll hang you soon, you know!"
Milord arrived. The clock grinds on:
White and streaked its ring.
"What's the matter. Again?"
"Milord, my darling one,
I keep looking at the clock,
Soon it will surely be ten!"
"There's just no rest, no end.
Now what nonsense is this?
She comes to me and says:
Tomorrow, they'll hang you then."

1920(?)

From **Washerwoman**

2

We don't live in castles,
Us no one caresses,
Us, the workingmen.
Grew up like whelps we did.
"Knife's mine!"
"Take it, swine!"
Nice knife.
Hey human hordes!
Knife's nice!
Know it, you,
In your brain
Make a notch.
But me, a sweet young girl,
But me, a black-haired girl,
Give love.
He, the pretty thing, long knife,

In the master's heart is right!
With a knife I regale you—
I, a simple girl:
Washerwoman-worker!
Aee it's nice, it's nice!
Knife.

7

Tsar! Send out a shot!
The head awaits, Your Majesty!
We've come out. Where are the bullets?
We're coming. And with us all Steaming Field's maidenry,
The criminal world's Smolny,
The stockade's high society.
But come on, cannons, thunder sternly:
Ding! Dong!
Or is someone there? Milyukov maybe?
Or Kerensky, could be?
Nope, no dopes today!
Today you know who goes
With the swarm of love
From the rotting city,
Whose flesh falls off today.
The hours for catching love
And trading eyes.
You march on.
—You march on!
Bullets
Sang ballads.
And burst in Steaming Field.

26

Writers of the knife are we!
Thinkers of the paunch are we!
Scientists of black bread,
Of sweatiness and sootiness,
High priests of ho-ho-ho.
We are tradeswomen of heavenly black eyes,
Profligates of gold in autumnal leaves,
Hoarders of yellow coins on the trees,

Violinists of the toothache are we,
We are in love with rheumatic cramp,
We are in love with the common cold,
Tradesmen of laughter,
Choirmasters of hunger,
Gluttons of yesteryear,
Drunkards of yesterday,
Lovers of the rainspout,
Savants of the crust of bread,
Artists of sootiness,
Accountants of jackdaws, crows,
Nabobs of the twilight glow—
All of us are tsars today!
Lovers of the belly,
Prophets of the dirty drawers,
Excavators of yesterday's dinners,
God's children are we.

1921

Demyan Biedny
1883–1945

Born Efim Alexeyevich Pridvorov, Biedny (his literary surname means "poor") came from a peasant family but managed to enroll as a student at the University of St. Petersburg from 1904 to 1908. A dedicated Bolshevik, he was admired for topical satiric poems rooted in folklore and for the direct, dramatic political engagement of his writing. Red Army soldiers are said to have carried cheap copies of his poems with them during the civil war of 1918 to 1921. Though he lived on into the Stalinist era and served on the presidium of the Writers Union in 1934, Biedny refused to temper his satiric honesty and directness to comply with official demands. He was expelled from the Communist Party in 1938, though he continued to publish antifascist poems in *Pravda* during World War II. Trotsky discusses Biedny near the end of Chapter 6 of *Literature and Revolution,* calling him "a Bolshevik whose weapon is poetry" and characterizing him as a poet who "does not seek new forms": "he uses the sacred old forms. But they are resurrected and reborn in his work" (175). Relatively little of Biedny's verse has been translated into English. In "Class and Art," Trotsky sees Biedny as "a product of the old, pre-October literature," and as "the revolutionary last-born child of our old literature" (*Art and Revolution: Writings on Literature, Politics, and Culture*, edited by Paul N. Siegel, 84).

Main Street
(A narrative poem)

Tra-ta-ta-tum!
Tra-ta-ta-tum!
Marching, marching, marching, marching,
Into chains of iron the links are forming,
In a thundering step they go grimly on,
go grimly on,
go on,
go on
To the last, the main redoubt.

Main Street is frantic,
Pale, trembling, as though out of its mind.
Bitten by mortal fear all of a sudden,
Bustling confusedly—businessman, in starched collar and shirt,
Crooked broker and wily banker,
Dealer in textiles and fashionable tailor,
Moneybags fur dealer, jeweler "by appointment,"
Each rushes, excited and worried
By the din and shouting heard from afar,
By buildings with luxury showcases,
Among their stocks and shares,
Russian and German, Frenchman and Jew,
Testing hinges, alarms, and bolts:
"Hey, there, lower the steel shutters!"
"Hurry!"
"Hurry!"
"Hurry!"
"They'll be taught a lesson, the cursed rabble,
and give up rioting for good!"
Down thunder the heavy lids
Of plate-glass windows, of oaken doors.

"Hurry!"
"Hurry!"
"But why do you drag your feet like cripples?
Does treachery lurk even here?
Are you in cahoots with all that scum?"
"D'you hear?"
"D'you hear?"
"D'you hear?"
"D'you hear?"
"Here they are...see them? Here they are, here!...
Here they come!
Here they come!"

Once again...
Once again.
The fatal wave beating...
The rotten base giving way...
The wall crashing heavily down.
"Heave ho!"
"Heave ho!"
"One-two-three,
Harder!"
"One-two-three,
Together!"
"One-two-three,
Forward!"
Nineteen hundred and seventeen comes like a thunder crash!
"Who goes there?
Who goes there
Sniveling in fear?" "Halt!"
"Who is shooting blanks
At the jaunty bloodsuckers?"
"Who holds back and minces his words?
Damn the lackeys of the bosses!"
"One-two-three,
Harder!"
"Once again
One!..."
"We need no bootlickers here!
The power is all the working people!"
"One-two-three,
Together!"

"One-two-three,
Forward!"
"Who can move us away from here?
No force in all the world!"
Main Street groans
Under the heel of the proletariat!

[Untitled: "Million-footed: a body..."]

Million-footed: a body. The pavement cracks.
A million mass: one heart, one will, one tread!
Keeping step! Keeping step!
On they march. On they march.
March, march...
Out of the factory quarters, smoke-wreathed,
Out of black dungeons, filthy rat holes,
He came—his finger bent like pincers,
Burst the thousand-year-old chains rattling about him—
Came now the new ruler of the street.
Like flecks of blood
Crimson flags waved above him. Steel-hard fists
Are raised aloft. The bones of the bourgeoisie whine.
But he speaks:
"All this is mine!
"Streets, palaces, canals, the Exchange, the Bank,
Arcades, granaries, gold, materials, food and drink,
Libraries, theaters, museums,
Pleasure grounds, boulevards, gardens and avenues,
Marble and splendor of bronze,
The poet's poem and the singer's song,
Towers, ships, cathedrals, space all round,
All this is mine!"
The houses thunder back. The highway clamors.
The giant stands fast.

1917

Chronology of Leon Trotsky's Life

1879
Trotsky is born Lev Davidovich Bronstein to Jewish parents in the Ukraine. His father, a prosperous farmer, sends him to school in Odessa.

1896
Becomes involved in revolutionary Marxist politics.

1898
Arrested for revolutionary activities and imprisoned in Siberia and other locations. One of his jailers is named "Trotsky."

1899
Marries Alexandra Sokolovskaya, who is also active in revolutionary politics.

1900
Trotsky's daughter, Zinaida, is born.

1902
A second daughter, Nina, is born. Trotsky manages to escape from detention and leaves Russia using a forged passport under the name "Trotsky."

1903
Attends the Second Congress of the Russian Social Democratic Labor Party in London, which ends in the split between Lenin's Bolsheviks and Martov's Mensheviks. Trotsky sides with the Mensheviks. Later that year, in Paris, Trotsky meets Natalya Sedova, who eventually becomes his second wife.

1905

"Bloody Sunday" (January 9) signals the start of the 1905 Revolution. In October, Nicholas II grants a constitution and a Duma with very limited representation. Trotsky becomes chairman of the Petrograd Soviet (workers' council) and is arrested and imprisoned at its last meeting.

1906

First son (with Natalya Sedova), Lev, is born. Trotsky stands trial with other members of the Petrograd Soviet and is again exiled to Siberia. While in prison he developed his theory of "permanent revolution," which eventually appears in *Results and Prospects*. Building on his analysis of Russia's uneven social and economic development, Trotsky argues that a socialist revolution is possible without an extended period of capitalist domination and bourgeois government.

1907

Escapes from Siberia to Vienna, where he lives and works as a journalist until 1914. A second son, Sergei, is born in 1908.

1914

With the outbreak of World War I, Trotsky moves to Switzerland, then to Paris again. Works on the internationalist newspaper *Our Word*.

1916

Expelled from France, goes to Spain.

1917

In January, moves to New York where he joins Nikolai Bukharin and Alexandra Kollontai in editing the paper *Novy Mir (New World)*. In March (February in the old Russia calendar), workers in Petrograd and Moscow lead an uprising that forces Nicholas II to abdicate. Provisional government under Prince Lvov is installed. In May, Trotsky returns to Russia and, in August, joins the Bolshevik Party. In September he becomes chairman of the new Petrograd Soviet. As head of the Soviet's Military Revolutionary Committee, he plans and carries out the insurrection in Petrograd that sparks the October Revolution and enables the Bolsheviks to seize power.

1918

Trotsky leads the negotiations with Germany that result in the Treaty of Brest-Litovsk. In March, with the beginning of the civil war, he is appointed People's Commissar for Military and Naval Affairs and organizes the Red Army.

1920–1921

Trotsky's suspicion of and conflict with Stalin sharpen.

1921

Directs the suppression of an anti-Bolshevik rebellion by naval forces at the port of Kronstadt (March).

1922

Lenin's health declines, weakening his ability to lead the Party and the government. Stalin becomes General Secretary of the Communist Party, and Trotsky's opposition to him intensifies. Stalin forms an alliance with Zinoviev and Kamenev to block Trotsky's influence.

1923

In October, Trotsky writes a letter to the Central Committee outlining his disagreements with Party policy.

1924

Lenin dies (January 21). The troika of Stalin, Kamenev, and Zinoviev assumes power. Trotsky becomes the most important leader of the Left Opposition.

1925

Despite Trotsky's enormous prestige among rank-and-file members of the Communist Party, Stalin uses his control over the bureaucracy and the Party machinery and forces Trotsky to resign as Commissar for Military and Naval Affairs.

1926

Stalin removes Trotsky from the Politburo. Kamenev and Zinoviev belatedly join Trotsky in an effort to check Stalin's power by launching the United Opposition.

1927
Trotsky is removed from the Central Committee in October and expelled from the Party in November.

1928
In January, Trotsky is exiled to Alma Ata in Kazakhstan. Trotsky's daughter, Nina, dies of tuberculosis in June. At the Sixth Congress of the Third Communist International (July–September), he fends off efforts to weaken and co-opt his opposition to Stalin's policies.

1929
Deported to Turkey, where he launches the *Bulletin of the Opposition*.

1930
Trotsky's autobiography, *My Life*, is published. The initial foundations of an international Left Opposition are organized in Paris.

1931
Trotsky's *History of the Russian Revolution* is published.

1933
Elder daughter Zinaida commits suicide. Trotsky leaves Turkey for France as Hitler and the Nazis seize power in Germany.

1935
Moves to Norway.

1936
Forced by Stalin's maneuvers to leave Norway, goes to Mexico. Completes *The Revolution Betrayed*. This is the year of Stalin's Moscow show trials; Zinoviev and Kamenev executed.

1937
Trotsky's son, Sergei, is convicted in the Moscow show trials and executed, as is his nephew, Boris.

1938
Elder son Lev dies following surgery. Trotsky and his political supporters found the Fourth International. Trotsky's elder brother, Alexander, executed in Moscow.

1940

In May, an unsuccessful attempt to kill Trotsky at his home is led by the prominent Mexican artist David Siquieros. In August, Trotsky is attacked by Rámon Mercader, a Spanish-born Stalinist, who had gained access to him months earlier by posing as a friend and supporter. Trotsky dies several days later, on August 21.

Glossary

Acméists: School of Russian poetry initiated in 1912 by Sergey Gorodetsky and Nicolai Gumilev as a reaction against the mysticism of the Symbolists. They were joined by Anna Akhmatova, Osip Mandelstam, and others. The Acméists emphasized clear, concrete, idiomatic expression. Trotsky sees them as practicing a version of neoclassicism.

Adamovich, Georgi Viktorovich (1884–1972): Influential émigré critic and minor poet who left Russia in 1922. Conventionally humanist in outlook, Adamovich was associated with Gumilev and influenced the Acméists. After leaving Russia, he became the leading critic for the review *Zveno* (1923–1928) and the daily newspaper *Postednie* (1928–1939).

Adler, Alfred (1870–1937): Austrian psychiatrist, early associate of Freud, and author of *The Practice and Theory of Individual Psychology* (1923).

Aeschylus (526–456 B.C.): Athenian writer of tragedies, including *The Persians, Seven Against Thebes, Prometheus Bound,* and the *Oresteia* trilogy.

Akhmatova, Anna: See Trotsky, the Poets and the Russian Revolution.

Aldanov, Mark (1886–1957): Pseudonym of Mark Alexandrovich Landau, a novelist who took part in the 1917 Revolution but soon emigrated to France. His tetralogy, *The Thinker* (1923–1927), deals with French history during the period 1793–1821. His later book *The Fifth Seal* (1939) is about the Spanish Civil War.

Amphiteatrov, Alexander Valentinovich (1862–1938): Russian journalist, critic, playwright, novelist, short story writer. In the 1890s, he became well known as a critic of the Romanov dynasty. In the 1910s, he helped found the important journal *Contemporary*. He left Russia at the time of the Revolution and wrote mainly anti-Bolshevik articles for newspapers in Paris, Warsaw, and Riga. His fiction includes *Viktoria Pavlovna* (1903, dealing with women's liberation), *Men of the Eighties* (1907–1908), and *Men of the Nineties* (1910).

Andreyev, Leonid Nikolayevich (1871–1919): Russian writer whose early stories of everyday life won the admiration of Maxim Gorky. He opposed the Bolsheviks in 1917, broke with Gorky, and went to Finland, where he died. His best works are the plays *The Red Laugh* (1905), *King Hunger* (1907), and *The Pretty Sabine Women* (1912).

Andreyevich: Pseudonym of Sergey Mikhailovich Soloviev (1885–1942). Russian poet, cousin of Alexander Blok, and intimate friend of Andrey Biely. He published in the Symbolist journals and issued numerous volumes of verse as well as some prose fiction and critical essays. Ordained as an Orthodox priest in 1916, he became a Catholic in 1923. After the 1917 Revolution, he taught Greek, Latin, and poetics and translated Virgil, Seneca, and other ancient Latin classics into Russian. He was arrested in 1931 and died in a psychiatric hospital.

Aristotle (384–322 B.C.): Greek philosopher who emphasized the metaphysical correspondence between the unchanging laws and categories of reason on the one hand, and the realms of physical existence and ethics on the other. Aristotle's *Poetics* is one of the most important ancient texts in the history of literary criticism and theory.

Arvatov, Boris Ignatievich (1896–1940): Literary and art critic and theorist. He joined the Communist Party in 1919 and was active in the *Proletkult*. His efforts to reconcile the claims of Marxism and Formalism were controversial but influential in the 1920s.

Avksentiev, Nikolai Dmitrievich (1878–1943): Socialist Revolutionary member of the Provisional Government, he opposed the October Revolution. He was a supporter of Russia's involvement in World War I. In 1918, he was an organizer of the counterrevolution in the Volga region and in Siberia. He left the Soviet Union in 1918.

Babeuf, François Noël (1760–1797): Militant French revolutionary who organized a radical uprising among artisans and soldiers against the "Directory." He led a secret revolutionary society called the Conspiracy of the Equals and advocated going beyond the goals of a bourgeois revolution and establishing a state based on the common ownership of property.

Balmont, Konstantin Dmitrievich (1867–1943): Russian poet and translator, who at first supported the Bolsheviks, then broke with them and emigrated to France. Influenced by the Symbolists, he translated Shelley, Ibsen, Poe, and Whitman (among other writers) into Russian.

Bebel, August (1840–1913): German socialist and Marxist closely associated with Wilhelm Liebknecht. He was instrumental in founding the German Social Democratic Party (SDP). Imprisoned by Bismarck in the 1870s, he later returned to active politics and represented the SDP for years in the Reichstag.

Beiliss, Mendel: A Jew accused in 1911 of murdering a Christian child and using the blood for ceremonial purposes. He was tried in Kiev and acquitted by a local jury. The acquittal was widely regarded as a defiant blow against the anti-Semitism of the tsarist regime.

Belinsky, Vissarion Grigoryevich (1811–1848): Russian writer and critic who advocated reliance on European literary forms and traditions. He was influential in arguing for the social basis and responsibilities of literary art and anticipated such priorities as emerged in the period of the Russian Revolution.

Bezimensky, Alexander Ilyich (1898–1973): Russian poet influenced by the *Proletkult* movement. He was active in both the Russian Association of Proletarian Writers (RAPP) and the All-Union Association (VAPP). He was a strong admirer of Mayakovsky. His verse drama of 1930, *The Shot*, won Stalin's approval for its conformity to the expectations of "socialist realism."

Biedny, Demyan: See Trotsky, the Poets and the Russian Revolution.

Biely, Andrey: See Trotsky, the Poets and the Russian Revolution.

Blok, Alexander: See Trotsky, the Poets and the Russian Revolution.

Bogdanov, Alexander Alexandrovich (1873–1928): Marxist literary theorist and writer. His early philosophical views are attacked by Lenin in *Materialism and Empiricocriticism* (1909). He became the main theoretician of the *Proletkult*. He wrote two science fiction novels, *Red Star* (1908) and *Engineer Manni* (1912), which reflect his training as a doctor and his belief that the future socialist society could be organized as an exact science. A founder for the Institute for Blood Transfusion in Moscow, he died as the result of an experiment he performed on himself.

Bohemian: Literally, someone from part of the old Austrian Empire known as Bohemia. The term was used from the seventeenth century on to mean "gypsy." In 1848, the Victorian novelist William Makepeace Thackeray first gave the word its extended modern sense: an artist or intellectual who lives in a free, unconventional way as a protest against dominant social norms.

Bolshevik: Name given to the branch of the Russian Social Democratic Labor Party which, in 1903, gained a majority in the debate over the future character and direction of the Party (the Russian word "Bolshevik" means "majority"). The Bolsheviks, following Lenin's leadership, stressed the importance of building a disciplined vanguard party within the working class in opposition to the "Mensheviks" (the "minority"), who favored a looser, more inclusive organization. In 1912 the Bolsheviks and Mensheviks became separate parties. Trotsky did not become a member of the Bolshevik Party until May of 1917.

Borgia, Cesare (1476–1507): Italian soldier and political figure; he is the prototype of the ruthless, realistic leader as analyzed in Machiavelli's *The Prince*.

Brick, Osip Maksimovich (1888–1945): Literary theorist and playwright. His wife Lili Brick had an extended affair with

Mayakovsky and inspired many of his poems. Following the 1917 Revolution, Brick worked in the Department of Fine Arts at the Commissariat for Education. He helped found the journals *Lef* (1923–1925) and *Novyi Lef* (1927–1928). He wrote important essays on the formal linguistic dimension of poetry, "Sound Repetitions" (1917) and "Rhythm and Syntax" (1927).

Briusov, Valery Yakovlevich (1873–1924): Poet, novelist, playwright, he became a proponent of Symbolism in the 1890s. In 1895, he published his first collection of poems, and in 1904 became editor of the Symbolist journal *Vesy*. He later broke with the Symbolists and devoted his energies to teaching and to translating such works as Virgil's *Aeneid* and Edgar Allen Poe's poetry and prose. After the 1917 Revolution, he headed the Department of Public Education's Division of Scientific Libraries. He joined the Communist Party in 1920 and organized LITO, the literary division of the Department of Public Education.

Budenny, Semyon Mikhailovich (1883–1973): Russian military officer in the tsarist cavalry, he joined the Communist Party in 1919 and served as a leader of the Soviet cavalry in the civil war of 1918–1921. He went on to serve as deputy commissar for defense under Stalin during World War II.

Bunin, Ivan Alexeyvich (1870–1953): Russian writer of prose fiction and poetry. From an aristocratic background, by 1900 he had come under the influence of Maxim Gorky. Yet much of his pre-Revolutionary writing laments the destruction of the Russian countryside and rural ways of life (*The Village*, 1909–1910, and *Dry Valley*, 1911). He scorned the 1917 Revolution and emigrated to Paris. In 1933, he won the Nobel Prize for literature.

Catherine the Great (1729–1796): Tsarina of Russia (1762–1796), she implemented legal reforms based on Enlightenment principles but responded to the peasant rising of 1773 with sharp repression and later extended serfdom and increased the power of the landed nobility. Her efforts to increase Russia's power at the expense of neighboring countries led to the Russo-Turkish Wars.

Changing Landmarks Group: Organized in 1921 by émigré nonrevolutionary writers hoping for reconciliation with the Bolshevik-led government. Alexey Tolstoy became a prominent member of the group when he returned to Russia in 1923.

Chekhov, Anton Pavlovich (1860–1904): Russian dramatist and short story writer noted for his emphasis on mood and internal emotional states. His work also reflects the social suffering and contradictions of tsarist Russia at the end of the nineteenth century. His best-known plays are *The Seagull* (1890), *Uncle Vanya* (1899), *The Three Sisters* (1901), and *The Cherry Orchard* (1904).

Chernov, Victor (1876–1952): A founder of the Socialist Revolutionary Party in Russia. He served as minister of agriculture under Kerensky in the Provisional Government of 1917 and was president of the January 1918 Constituent Assembly. An opponent of the Bolsheviks, he left Russia in 1921 and eventually died in New York.

Chirikov, Yevgeny Nikolayevich (1864–1932): Novelist and playwright, he became involved in revolutionary politics and was a member of Gorky's *Znanie* group. Early plays, such as *Jews* (1904) and *Peasants* (1906), were successful. His best-known novel, *The Life of Tarkhanov,* appeared in several installments between 1911 and 1925. A short story called "A Devastated Soul" (1921) focuses on the inner life of a Bolshevik activist. Chirikov later left the Soviet Union and died in Prague.

Chkheidze, Nikolai Semenovich (1864–1926): A Menshevik from Georgia who came to occupy important positions in the Russian labor movement and in the Petrograd Soviet in 1917. He worked with Tseretelli to strengthen ties between the Soviet and the Provisional Government. He aggressively opposed the Bolsheviks and argued against any cooperation with them. After the October Revolution, he returned to Georgia. In 1921, he emigrated to Paris, and in 1926 committed suicide.

Chukovsky, Kornei Ivanovich: Pen name of Nikolai Vasilyevich Korneichukov (1882–1969). Writer, critic, scholar, and translator, in 1903–1904 he worked in London as a correspondent for a Russian newspaper and studied English literature. He was associated for a time with Briusov and the Symbolist magazine *Vesy.* Throughout his early career, he also wrote extensively for children. He became well known for his Russian translations of Whitman, Twain, Wilde, and other American and British writers.

Chuzhak, Nikolai: Pseudonym of N.F. Nasimovich (1876–?). In 1921, he was involved with the Futurists and other avant-garde artists in the Institute for Artistic Culture (*Inkhuk*). He was also a leading member of the "Lef" group, along with Mayakovsky and Brick. He was purged and "disappeared" during the Stalinist era.

Constitutional Democrat: A member of the Constitutional Democratic or Cadet Party, a liberal reformist party first organized in 1905. The Cadets played a leading role in the Provisional Government following the February Revolution of 1917. After the October Revolution, many members supported the counter-revolution. The party split in 1921 and was no longer a significant political force.

Constituent Assembly: The representative body elected to govern Russia following the October Revolution of 1917. The Socialist Revolutionaries had the largest number of delegates (370), followed by the Bolsheviks (175), and a collection of "National groups" (86). But the Bolsheviks held the most powerful posts in the Council of People's Commissars, and on January 5, 1918, they dissolved the Constituent Assembly to prevent policies that would weaken and eventually destroy the new workers' state.

Constructivism: Artistic movement in Russia founded circa 1913 by Vladimir Tatlin (1885–1956). Naum Gabo and Antoine Pevsner joined Tatlin in emphasizing architectonic forms that represented the forces of modern technology. The Bolsheviks welcomed Constructivism at first, but the movement eventually came to be seen as esoteric and elitist.

Cubists, Cubism: Cubism originated in Paris circa 1907, primarily in painting, as a revolt against the sensuality and naturalistic conventions of much nineteenth-century painting. The Cubists developed an analytic system in which three-dimensional objects in space were taken apart and represented from multiple points of view simultaneously. Picasso and Braque were the most influential artists of early Cubism, which has sometimes been called "conceptual realism."

Dan: Pseudonym of Feodor Ilyich Gurevich (1871–1947). One of the most important leaders of the Mensheviks. He gave critical support to the Soviet government following the October Revolution. In 1922, he went into exile.

Dantchenko: Full name Vladimir Nemirovich-Dantchenko (1858–1943). Dramatist and stage director, a founder of the Moscow Art Theatre along with Konstantin Stanislavski.

Darwin, Charles (1809–1882): British naturalist who developed the theory of organic evolution, with its key principles of natural selection and survival of the best adapted species. His major books are *Origin of Species* (1859) and *The Descent of Man* (1871).

David, Jacques-Louis (1748–1825): The most influential artist in the era of the French Revolution and Napoleonic Empire. He made innovative, powerful use of themes and forms from ancient classical art in representing the ideals and tensions of a period of profound social conflict and change.

Decadent School: "Decadent" is a term loosely applied to artists and writers at the end of the nineteenth century who found aesthetic value in human experiences conventionally regarded as morbid, macabre, and immoral. The "decadents" are usually associated with the doctrine of "art for art's sake." In France, they include Rimbaud, Laforgue, Maeterlinck; in England Wilde, Pater, Beardsley.

Denikine, Anton Ivanovich (1872–1947): Russian general who joined General Kornilov in leading the counterrevolutionary White forces against the Bolshevik-led government. He gained control of large sections of southern Russia in 1918 but was defeated and forced to resign in 1920. He then moved to France and eventually to the United States.

Dobroluvov, Nikolai Alexandrovich (1836–1861): Literary critic who thought of himself as the successor to Vissarion Belinsky. Influenced by the German philosopher Feuerbach and the French utopian socialists, he became known especially for his interpretation of Goncharov's *Oblomov* and, near the end of his life, of Dostoyevsky's fiction.

Don: River in southwest Russia. It is linked by canal with the Volga River near Volgograd and flows into the Sea of Azov. Rostov-Na-Donu is the main city and port on the Don.

Don Aminado: Pseudonym of Aminad Petrovich Shpolyansky. A writer who emigrated from the Soviet Union soon after the 1917 Revolution.

Dostoyevsky, Feodor Mikhailovich (1821–1881): Russian novelist, author of *Crime and Punishment* (1866), *The Idiot* (1868), *The Brothers Karamazov* (1879–1880). Involved with a group of radical utopians in the 1840s, Dostoyevsky served four years at hard labor in a Siberian penal colony. Later in life he became disillusioned with radical politics. *The Possessed* (1871–1872) denounces the leftist revolutionaries he once admired.

Duma: The Russian word for representative assembly. The Revolution of 1905 led to the establishment of the Imperial Duma, whose representatives were elected by very limited suffrage. Tsar Nicholas II nevertheless eventually abolished this Duma and the reconstituted Dumas of 1907, 1907–1912, and 1912–1917. After the Revolution of February 1917, the Duma disintegrated and was replaced by the Constituent Assembly.

Ekaterinodar: City in southeast Russia founded in 1794 by Black Sea Cossacks on orders from Catherine the Great (hence its name) to serve as a military center protecting Russia's Caucasian frontier. In 1920, it was renamed Kransnodar.

Elbrus: The highest mountain in the Caucasus range, Georgia.

Engels, Friedrich (1820–1895): German revolutionary socialist, he was the son of a wealthy German manufacturer who sent him to England in 1842. In 1844, he met Karl Marx. In 1845, he published *The Condition of the Working Class in England,* and in 1848 he collaborated with Marx on the *Communist Manifesto*. Among his most important later works was the editing of volumes two and three of *Capital* after Marx's death and his own book *The Origin of the Family, Private Property, and the State* (1884).

Fedin, Konstantin Alexandrovich (1892–1970): Russian novelist whose early novels, *Cities and Years* (1924) and *The Brothers* (1928), address the role of the intellectual in Soviet society.

Fellow travelers: English translation of Russian *paputchiki,* a term invented by Trotsky in Chapter 2 of *Literature and Revolution* to refer to those writers who had accepted and were living with the Russian Revolution without having actively participated in or committed themselves to it.

Fet: Pen name of Afansay Afanasievich (1820–1892). Russian poet from an aristocratic family whose first volume of verse appeared in 1840. Politically conservative, his writing tended toward aestheticism and was attacked by leftist critics. He became famous for his love lyrics and eventually for a gloomy pessimism influenced by the German philosopher Arthur Schopenhauer.

Feuilleton: The section of a (French) newspaper devoted to books reviews and articles on literature and culture.

Fonvizin, Denis Ivanovich (1745–1792): Russian playwright. His first play, *The Brigadier* (1768–1769), a satire of eighteenth-century Russian imitation of French culture, was a great success. Later successes include *The Minor* (1785), considered his masterpiece.

Formalism: Any theoretical or analytical practice that emphasizes the formal features of the object of study rather than thematic, informational, or social content. In literary theory and criticism, Formalism focuses on textual patterns, structures, and relationships as determinations of meaning and aesthetic value.

Futurism: A movement in modernist painting, sculpture, and literature that flourished first in Italy and then elsewhere in Europe (particularly in Italy: Filippo Marinetti's first Futurist manifesto appeared in 1909). The Futurists sought to portray the dynamism of twentieth-century technology and urban experience. In Italy, their glorification of machines and technological warfare tended in a right-wing political direction that eventually led to alliances with Fascism. In France and Russia, Futurism took, instead, a left turn.

Gallifet, Gaston Alexandre August, marquis de (1830–1909): French general prominent in the Crimean War, the Franco-Prussian War, and various colonial campaigns. He led the brutal suppression of the Paris Commune in 1871. Later, he was minister of war during the Dreyfus Affair.

Goethe, Johann Wolfgang von (1749–1832): German poet, novelist, dramatist, critic—one of the towering literary figures of his age. His major works include *The Sorrow of Young Werther, Wilhelm Meister's Journeyman Years, Faust,* and many collections of lyric poetry.

Gogol, Nikolai Vsilyevich (1809–1852): Russian novelist, short story writer, playwright. Often considered the founder of Russian realism, his writing is nonetheless striking for its fantastical freedom and exuberance. His 1835 collection of stories, *Mirgorod,* contains "Taras Bulba." His best-known play is *The Inspector General* (1836); his best-known novel is *Dead Souls* (1842).

Goncharov, Ivan Alexandrovich (1812–1891): Russian novelist, author of *Oblomov* (1858), a realistic satirical representation of the indolence and corruption of the aristocracy. Less famous variations on this theme and perspective are *A Common Story* (1847) and *The Precipice* (1869).

Gorky, Maxim (1868–1936): Often regarded as the founding figure of Soviet literature and of "socialist realism," Gorky came from poor peasant origins and was self-educated. As a young journalist, his articles exposed the oppression and corruption of tsarism. *Sketches and Stories* (1898) was a sensation, and his 1907 novel *Mother* was enormously influential. He donated much of what he earned to the revolutionary movement. His best-known play is *The Lower Depths* (1902). Despite sharp differences with Lenin, he was an active, positive force during and after the 1917 Revolution.

Gorodetsky, Sergey (1884–1967): Traditionalist poet linked to the Acméist movement led by Gumilev, Akhmatova, and Mandelstam. He collaborated with Gumilev in founding the Poets' Guild in 1911, and contributed to the anti-Symbolist magazine *Apollon* in 1915. Gorodetsky subsequently broke with the Acméists and joined a group advocating the work of peasant poets. He eventually joined the Bolsheviks following the 1917 Revolution and, in 1921, published a collection of poems entitled *The Sickle.*

Gracchi: Two Roman statesmen and social reformers, Tiberius Sempronius Gracchus (died 133 B.C.) and Caius Sempronius

Gracchus (died 121 B.C.). Both worked for legal reforms that curbed the power and wealth of the nobility.

Gramsci, Antonio (1891–1937): Italian revolutionary socialist and writer. Originally trained in literary studies and philology, Gramsci was instrumental in founding the Italian Communist Party in 1921 and its newspaper, *L'Unità*. Mussolini outlawed the Party and imprisoned Gramsci in 1926. While in prison, Gramsci wrote his *Prison Notebooks,* which contain major contributions to Marxist political and cultural theory. They were not published until 1947, ten years after his death.

Griboyedov, Alexander Sergeyevich (1795–1829): Russian diplomat and playwright. His best-known play, *Wit Works Woe* (1825), is a satire on Moscow society. Griboyedov was killed while serving as Russian minister to Persia.

Gumilev, Nicolai: See Trotsky, the Poets and the Russian Revolution.

"Guzuv" (or "Gusev"): A story by Chekhov, one of the earliest (1890) reflecting his experiences on the island of Sakhalin. It tells of two men dying on a ship returning from the Far East.

Hegel, Georg Wilhelm Friedrich (1770–1831): German philosopher who exerted a profound influence on many areas of thinking in his own era and later. His system, sometimes called dialectical idealism, conceives of history as the conflicted process through which the mind, in its infinite potential, comes to be conscious of and to realize itself in the world. Hegel's method, developed in such works as *Phenomenology of Mind* (1807) and *Encyclopedia of the Philosophical Sciences* (1817) was an important influence on Marx, even though Marx's materialism has been said to "stand Hegel on his head."

Herzen, Alexander Ivanovich (1812–1870): Russian revolutionary leader and writer. After an early period of socialist activity in Russia, he went to Paris and supported the 1848 Revolution. He then went to England. His weekly journal, *Kolokol* (1857–1862), was widely read in Russia. *Who is to Blame?* (1847) is his most popular novel. Toward the end of his life, Herzen regarded Russian peasant communes as important forerunners of socialist society.

Hippius, Zinaida (1869–1945): Prolific poet, fiction writer, playwright, and essayist known for her expressions of transcendent spirituality. She was at the center of a significant literary and philosophical circle in St. Petersburg in the early years of the century. Though she welcomed the February Revolution of 1917 that forced the abdication of the tsar, she and her husband left Russia after the October Revolution, going first to Poland, then to Paris. She became one of the best known of the émigré writers.

Hoffmann, E.T. A. (1776–1822): German novelist and composer, famous for his fictional explorations of Gothic horror and the supernatural as resources for representing madness and grotesque fantasy. Among his important collections of stories are *The Serapion Brethren* (1819–1821) and *The Devil's Elixir* (1824–1826).

Hohenzollern: Family of German princes who ruled the state of Brandenburg from 1415 to 1918, the state of Prussia from 1525 to 1918, and the newly unified country of Germany from 1871 to 1918. Among the famous Hohenzollern rulers was Frederick II (Frederick the Great), who ruled Prussia from 1740 to 1786.

Iambics: A form of poetic meter in which the predominant rhythmic pattern is an unstressed followed by a stressed syllable —or, in some languages, a short followed by a long syllable.

Idealism, Idealist: In philosophy, "Idealism" is the term applied to those systems that give priority to ideas and other mental phenomena over material objects and phenomena, and that understand reality as either entirely or predominantly constituted by acts of mind. Plato is the most important Idealist philosopher of classical antiquity; Berkeley, Kant, and Hegel are influential modern Idealists.

Imaginism, Imaginist: Russian literary movement of the 1920s, founded by Vadim Shershenevich, that extended and intensified the Symbolists' concern with the renovation of form. The Imaginists were critical of the links between politics and art emphasized by openly pro-Revolutionary groups, including the Futurists. They advocated innovation and concreteness in poetic language.

Imagism, Imagist: "Imagism" usually refers to a movement in early twentieth-century poetry based on a repudiation of the intense sensuality and sentiment of much nineteenth-century poetry and an emphasis on the representation of ideas through a rendering in language of concrete objects and disciplined physical analogies. Ezra Pound was the most influential Imagist poet; he edited an anthology called *Des Imagistes* (1913).

Imaginism, Imaginist: Russian literary movement of the 1920s, founded by Vadim Shershenevich, that extended and intensified the Symbolists' concern with the renovation of form. The Imaginists were critical of the links between politics and art emphasized by openly pro-Revolutionary groups, including the Futurists. They advocated innovation and concreteness in poetic language.

"Isvostchik" or "Izvoychik": "The Cabby," a well-known poem by the nineteenth-century naturalist poet Nikolai Nekrasov (1821–1878).

Ivanov, Vsebolod Vyacheslavovich (1895–1963): Russian short story writer, novelist, and dramatist. Gorky admired the vivid detail and irony of his early work. His 1922 novel, *Armored Train 14–69,* deals with Soviet policy in Siberia, where Ivanov was born.

Ivanov-Razumniks: Pseudonym of Razumnik Vasilevich Ivanov (1878–1946). Critic and founder of the Scythian movement in Russian poetry, one of the "fellow traveler" groups discussed by Trotsky in Chapter 2. Politically, he was associated with the Socialist Revolutionaries.

Jakobson, Roman (1896–1982): Major literary and linguistic theorist and one of the founders of Russian Formalism. In 1915, he founded the Moscow Linguistic Circle. He moved to Prague in 1920, and in 1926 cofounded the Prague Linguistic Circle. When the Nazis invaded Czechoslovakia in 1938, he fled to Denmark and eventually settled in New York, where he taught at Columbia University. He later taught at Harvard and at MIT.

June Days: In French history, the name given to the workers' insurrection that played a key role in the Revolution of 1848. Between June 23 and June 26, thousands of workers took to the streets and fought violently against the government until they were savagely suppressed by the army under General Cavaignac.

Jung, Carl Gustav (1875–1961): Swiss psychiatrist. He met Freud in 1907 and collaborated with him until 1912, when his *Psychology of the Unconscious* signaled a break and a turn toward an emphasis on the archetypes of a "collective unconscious."

Kamensky, Vasily Vasilyevich (1884–1961): Poet and writer who came to be associated with Futurism. He was also one of the first Russian aviators. Immediately after the October Revolution, he became the main organizer of the Café of Poets in Moscow. His poetry is radically experimental in its language. His most popular work was "Stenka Razin" (see separate entry in this Glossary).

Kant, Immanuel (1724–1804): German philosopher, one of the dominant figures in the history of philosophy. Kant's "critical" philosophy attempts to overcome the conflict between rationalism and empiricism by showing that knowledge of reality depends upon categories and principles deriving from reason alone. *Kantianism* is still a major influence in epistemology, ethics, and aesthetics.

Kazin, Vasily Vasilievich (1898–?): Minor poet and journalist, a member of the "Kuznitsa" ("The Smithy") subgroup of the Proletarian Writers Organization. He became a loyal hack writer during the Stalin era.

Kerensky, Alexander Feodorovich (1881–1970): Russian political leader and a lawyer by training and profession. He was elected to the fourth Duma in 1912 as a representative of the reformist Labor Party. After the February Revolution of 1917, he joined the Socialist Revolutionary party and became war minister in the Provisional Government under Prince Lvov. In July 1917, he became premier. His determination to keep Russia in World War I and his failure to deal effectively with the economic crisis helped make possible the October Revolution. Kerensky fled to Paris after the Revolution and became a propagandist against the Bolshevik regime. In 1940, he moved to the United States.

Khlebnikov, Velemir: See Trotsky, the Poets and the Russian Revolution.

Khovin, Viktor: A minor figure in the Russian Futurist movement.

Kirillov, Vladimir Timofeevich (1890–1943): Poet and member of *Proletkult*. He became active in the revolutionary movement as a teenager, in 1905–1906. In 1918, he left the *Proletkult* and was a founding member of *Kuznitsa* ("The Smithy").

Kliuev, Nicolai: See Trotsky, the Poets and the Russian Revolution.

Koltzov, Alexey Vasilyevich (1809–1842): Russian poet from a peasant background, with little formal education. His direct, uncomplicated lyrics were admired for their representations of Russian peasant life.

Krashnaya Gazetta: A literary journal devoted to serious analysis and discussion, founded in 1921 with Lenin's support. It was edited by Alexander Voronsky and published work both by writers actively committed to the Revolution and by "fellow travelers."

Kronstadt: Russian port city on the small island of Kotlin, in the Gulf of Finland. In March 1921, sailors at a naval garrison revolted against the Bolshevik government at a moment of great vulnerability for the new workers' state. Trotsky organized the crushing of the revolt and later wrote a compelling account of the entire episode.

Kruchenikh, Alexey Eliseevich (1886–1969?): Poet and literary theorist prominent in the Futurist movement. He was, along with Mayakovsky, a signer of the manifesto "A Slap in the Face of Public Taste." After the Revolution, he was a member of Mayakovsky's "Lef" group. He became especially well known for his theory of "transrational language."

Krug Group: A literary group associated with the journal *Krug* (*Circle*), prominent in the mid-1920s.

Kühlmann, Richard von (1873–1948): German diplomat who led the delegation that negotiated the Treaty of Brest-Litovsk in March 1818, under the terms of which Russia withdrew from World War I.

Kuprin, Alexander Ivanovich (1870–1938): A prominent

member of the group (including Gorky) who published in the anthology *Znanie* (*Knowledge*). Before the Revolution, he was known for prose fiction depicting the brutalities of tsarist society. He emigrated to France after the 1917 Revolution.

Kusikov, Alexander B. (1886–?): One of the leading writers in the Imagist (or Imaginist) movement, which included Yessenin and Marienhof.

Kuzmin, Mikhail Alekseevich (1875–1936): A poet, prose writer, playwright, and critic who was at first associated with the Symbolists, then with the Acméists. Known for his often esoteric aestheticism, Kuzmin wrote openly of homosexual love. He remained in Russia after the 1917 Revolution.

Kuznitsa Group: *Kuznitsa* means "The Smithy" and was the name of a group formed by proletarian writers, especially lyric poets, who broke from the *Proletkult* in 1920. The founders included Gerasimov, Kirillov, Alexandrovsky, and Rodov. These writers proclaimed "complete freedom in the choice of literary method and style." At times romantic and idealistic in their approach to revolutionary art, many of the Kuznitsa Group left the Communist Party during the early 1920s.

Lassalle, Ferdinand (1825–1864): German socialist associated early in his life with the Left Hegelians. He met and read Marx and was influenced by him, though he moved away from Marx in emphasizing the role of the existing national state in providing socialist reforms. In 1863, he helped found the General German Workers' Association, which later developed into the Social Democratic Party.

Lef Group: "Lef" was the acronym for Left Front of Art, a literary group formed in 1922 mainly by former members of the Futurist movement. Mayakovsky and Brick were founding members. The main aim of the group was to confirm and carry forward an alliance between the Futurist avant-garde and the new workers' state. Mayakovsky described their journal, also called *Lef,* as "encompassing...the social theme by all the instruments of Futurism." *Lef* ceased publication in 1925.

Lenin, Vladimir Ilyich (1870–1924): Revolutionary socialist leader, founder of the Bolshevik Party, head of the Soviet government from the October Revolution until his death in 1924. Lenin was already active as a Marxist agitator in the late 1880s; he was exiled to Siberia in 1887, and in 1902 left Russia to continue his revolutionary activities abroad. In *What Is to Be Done?* (1902) he began to develop his theory that building a vanguard party within the working class was necessary if socialism was to be brought to a relatively backward country such as Russia. Lenin returned to Russia at the time of the 1905 Revolution but was forced to leave again in 1907. In Switzerland during most of World War I, Lenin urged Russian workers to oppose the war. Following the February Revolution of 1917 he was able to return to Russia. After an abortive mass uprising in Petrograd in July he was forced to escape to Finland, but after a few months he returned to Petrograd and joined Trotsky in organizing and leading the October Revolution. In 1919 Lenin led the establishment of the Third International or "Comintern" to advance the cause of socialism internationally. The stress of guiding the new workers' state through the period of civil war and foreign intervention took its toll: Lenin suffered serious strokes in 1922 and 1923. He died on January 21, 1924, but not before writing a testament criticizing Stalin and calling for his removal as general secretary of the Communist Party.

Lezhnev: Pseudonym of Abram Zakharovich Gorelik (1893–1938). Marxist critic and theorist, Lezhnev was a member of the so-called "Pereval Group." He wrote regularly for the journal *Krasnaya Nov'*. In the literary debates of the 1920s, he became a leading advocate of the "fellow travelers." Though increasingly marginalized during the rise of Stalin, he never left the Soviet Union. He was executed during the purges of the 1930s.

Lipschitz, Jacques (1881–1973): Important Lithuanian-born sculptor who worked mainly in France before moving to the United States during World War II.

Lunacharsky, Anatoli Vasilyevich (1875–1933): Russian dramatist and critic. An early member of the Bolshevik Party, he joined forces with Gorky and Bogdanov in internal opposition to Lenin. But in 1917, he joined Lenin and strongly supported the October overthrow of the Kerensky government. As Commissar of Education, Lunacharsky advocated a new "proletarian literature" and was a supporter of *Proletkult*. But he sided with Trotsky and Lenin on the question of Soviet culture's need to draw on bourgeois tradition and expertise.

Machiavelli, Niccolò (1469–1527): Italian writer and statesman, best known for his analysis of the real motives for gaining and holding onto political power in *The Prince* (published after his death in 1532). Machiavelli was defense secretary in the Florentine Republic of 1498–1512 and drew many of his ideas from the Republic's rise and fall.

Maecenas, Caius: Roman statesman and promoter of literary art. He was famous as the patron of the poets Horace, Virgil, and Propertius. Maecenas died in 8 B.C.; his name has come to be synonymous with the wealthy patron of the arts.

Makhno, Nestor (1889–1934): Anarchist leader of a large army of peasants who fought the White army during the civil war of 1918–1921. His conflict with Trotsky and the Red army eventually resulted in his being forced to leave the Soviet Union and settle in Paris.

Marat, Jean Paul (1743–1793): French revolutionary who founded the influential journal *L'Ami du peuple* (*Friend of the People*). Twice exiled during the early years of the Revolution, he was a major influence on the uprising of August 1792. Elected to the Convention in that year, he supported the Jacobins. Marat was stabbed to death by the Girondist Charlotte Corday.

Marienhof, Anatoly Borisovich (1879–1962): Poet, prose writer, and playwright who, from 1919 to 1927, was a leading member of the Imagist movement. A close friend of Yessenin, he also affected the latter's flamboyantly dissolute way of living. His best-known Imagist book is *Buyan-Island* (1920).

Marinetti, Filippo Tammaso (1876–1944): Poet, novelist, critic, and the founder of Italian Futurism. He was also an early member of the Fascist Party. Marinetti wrote in both Italian and French.

Martinet, Marcel: French dramatist whose 1922 play *La nuit* (*The Night*) was published in *Izvestia* with a preface by Trotsky ("A Drama of the French Working Class").

Marx, Karl (1818-1883): German political theorist and activist, the founding figure in modern revolutionary socialism. Marx studied law at the universities of Bonn and Berlin and eventually completed a doctorate in philosophy at Jena in 1841. He became editor of the *Rheinische Zeitung* in 1842, but when the paper was suppressed because of its calls for radical reform he went to Paris, where he began a lifelong friendship and collaboration with Friedrich Engels. Marx criticized the idealism and utopianism of early European socialism and developed instead a "scientific socialism" based on a method of "dialectical" and "historical" "materialism." In 1847 he joined the Communist League and in 1848 collaborated with Engels in writing the *Communist Manifesto*, in which the class struggle produced within capitalist society provides the basis for working-class revolution. The major project of Marx's intellectual career was *Capital*, a monumental analysis of modern capitalism as an economic and social system written while he was living in London (the first volume was published in 1867). Marx never abandoned his commitment to political organization and activism and was involved in many initiatives that he believed would eventually contribute to the creation of a mass working-class revolutionary party.

Materialism: In philosophy, positions that emphasize physical matter as determining reality, as opposed to idealism and its emphasis on the determining significance of thoughts and ideas. There are forms of materialism in ancient, Renaissance, and Enlightenment philosophy. Marx and Engels saw themselves as departing from the more static traditions of empiricist and mechanical materialism; they emphasize instead the role of dynamic conflict (dialectical materialism) and the history of socio-economic organization (historical materialism).

Mayakovsky, Vladimir: See Trotsky, the Poets and the Russian Revolution.

Maupassant, Guy de (1850–1893): French novelist and short story writer noted for the clarity and calm objectivity of his style and the psychological realism of his depictions of social life. His best-known stories include "The Necklace," "The House of Mme. Tellier," and "The Piece of String."

Menshevik: Originally one of the two main branches of the

Russian Social Democratic Labor Party. In 1903, the group led by Lenin gained a majority in the Party and were known as the "Bolsheviks" ("majority"). The Mensheviks, the "minority," opposed Lenin's emphasis on building a disciplined vanguard party and argued instead for a more loosely organized mass organization. The Mensheviks believed that socialism in Russia was possible only after an extended period of capitalist development and bourgeois democracy. They were thus directly opposed by Trotsky, with his theories of "combined and uneven development" and "permanent revolution." In 1912, the Bolsheviks and Mensheviks became separate parties. After the February Revolution, the Mensheviks joined the Provisional Government under Kerensky. They opposed the Bolshevik-led October Revolution, and they participated in the Constituent Assembly of January 1818 before it was dissolved. For the most part, however, the Mensheviks refused to side with the counterrevolution during the civil war of 1918–1921.

Mereykovsky, Dmitri Sergeyevich (1865–1941): Russian critic and novelist famous for his study *Tolstoy as Man and Artist* (1902). He wrote historical novels treating the lives of Julian the Apostate, Leonardo da Vinci, and Peter the Great. Mereykovsky and his wife, Zinaida Hippius (see separate entry in this Glossary), advocated a kind of religious humanism and opposed the 1917 Revolution.

Meyerhold, Vsevolod (1874–1940?): Russian theatrical director and producer whose experimental work with the Moscow Art Theatre was of lasting importance. A member of the Bolshevik Party, Meyerhold boldly refused to equate revolutionary culture with narrow concepts of naturalism and realism. He was an early practitioner of the "theater of the absurd," used spare constructivist sets, and urged his actors to minimize their own subjective self-involvement. He became an outspoken opponent of Stalinist "socialist realism" and was eventually a victim of Stalin's purges.

Mikhailovsky, Nikolai Konstantinovich (1842–1904): A leading figure in the Populist movement of the late nineteenth century. He was a theoretician of "agrarian socialism." Mikhailovsky was an important editor and worked to introduce western European writers—including Marx—to Russian readers.

Mont Blanc: Alpine mountain in France, near the Italian border, southeast of Geneva, Switzerland. It is the second highest peak in Europe (15,771 feet); huge glaciers cover its northwestern slopes.

Muratov, Pavel Pavlovich (1881–1950): Art historian and writer who edited the literary journal *Sofya* in 1914. He left Russia in 1922. His short stories and travelogues are the most widely read of his works. Muratov spent World War II in England and died in Ireland.

Nemirovich-Dantchenko, Vladimir: See entry under Dantchenko.

Nicholas I (1796–1855): Russian tsar from 1825 to 1855. He used the motto "autocracy, orthodoxy, and nationality" in his opposition to progressive thinking and reform. It was during his reign that the revolutionary movement in Russian first took serious form.

Nicholas II (1868–1918): The last tsar of Russia, son of Alexander III. Though he granted some concessions after the 1905 Revolution, he soon restricted the power of the elected Duma and led Russia into World War I. He was forced to abdicate in March 1917 following the February Revolution. Nicholas II and his family were executed on July 16, 1918, because they were an important focus for counterrevolutionary forces during the civil war.

Nikitin, Nikolai: A member of the Serapion Fraternity (see entry in this Glossary) and the author of a novel called *The Crime of Kirik Rudenko,* a fictional account of factory life in a Russian village.

Odoevtzeva, Irina (1901–?): Poet, novelist, wife of George Ivanov (1894–1958). Her poems were strongly influenced by Gumilev. Both Odoevtzeva and Ivanov were associated with the Acméists; they emigrated to Paris in 1922.

Opiskin: A despotic character in Dostoyevsky's comic tale, *The Village of Stepanchikovo.*

Orlov, Count (1734–1783): Russian nobleman and a lover of Catherine II, he led the conspiracy to depose Peter III and make

Catherine tsarina. He was later displaced by other court favorites, including Field Marshall Potemkin.

Orwell, George (1903–1950): Pseudonym of the British novelist and essayist Eric Arthur Blair. Best known for his political satires, *Animal Farm* (1946) and *Nineteen Eighty-Four* (1949), Orwell also wrote a brilliant autobiographical account of the Spanish Civil War, *Homage to Catalonia* (1938).

Ostrovsky, Nikolai Alexeyevich (1904–1936): Russian novelist, best known for *The Making of a Hero* (1936) and volume one of the unfinished *Born of the Storm* (1937).

Otsup, Nikolai A. (1894–1958): A poet associated with Gumilev and the Acméists who left Russia in 1922 and settled in Berlin, where he translated Russian poetry into German. During World War II he was arrested by the Nazis and sent to a concentration camp. He eventually escaped to Italy, where he joined the Resistance. Otsup eventually became a professor of Russian at the University of Paris.

Paris Commune: Insurrectionary government established in Paris in 1871 near the end of the Franco-Prussian War. Parisian workers opposed to the right-wing government of Adolphe Thiers seized power in March and elected a municipal council to govern the city. Troops loyal to the Thiers government laid siege to Paris and, at the end of May, finally defeated and brutally suppressed the *communards* (more than 17,000 were killed). In *The Civil War in France,* Marx recognizes the Paris Commune as the first great historical example of the working class seizing power and running society in its own interests.

Parnassians: A group of nineteenth-century French poets who founded a journal called *Parnasse contemporain* (Mount Parnassus in ancient Greece was sacred to Apollo and the Muses). The Parnassians were influenced by the ideas of Gautier; Verlaine is the only member of the group widely read today. In reaction against Romantic poetry, they emphasized stylistic discipline and a neoclassical control of emotion.

Pasternak, Boris Leonidovich (1890–1960): Russian poet, fiction writer, and translator. Son of a famous painter and a concert pianist, Pasternak was strongly influenced by Leo Tolstoy, who was a family friend. He established himself as a major poet in the years leading up to the 1917 Revolution. Pasternak at first embraced the Revolution but gradually became critical of the Bolsheviks. He came under severe pressure from Stalin during the 1930s and confined his literary activity mainly to translation. During this period he became a hero of many Russian intellectuals. After Stalin's death he began work on his famous epic novel, *Doctor Zhivago* (because of censorship in the Soviet Union, first published in Italy in 1957). In 1958 he was awarded the Nobel Prize in Literature.

Pavlov, Ivan Petrovich (1849–1936): Russian experimental psychologist and physiologist. In 1904, he won the Nobel Prize in Physiology and Medicine. He is best known as a founder of behaviorism, with its emphasis on conditioned reflexes. Trotsky's reference to Pavlov as "our psychologist" in Chapter 7 is significantly linked to his openness to Freud as also being a "materialist."

Peter the Great (1672–1725): Peter I, tsar of Russia and a major figure in the development of imperial Russia. His expansion of Russian territory through almost continuous war was combined with a campaign to "Europeanize" and modernize Russian society. Famous in conventional accounts for his "Western reforms," Peter sought throughout his reign to subordinate all classes to the needs of the state.

Pharisees: One of the two major religious parties within Judaism before and during the time of Jesus. Their opponents were the Sadducees. The Pharisees had their origins in the Maccabee campaign to free the Jewish people from Syrian domination. They came to stand for Jewish separatism and nationalism (in the ancient sense).

Philistines: An ancient non-Semitic people who came to Palestine from the Aegean area in the twelfth century B.C. According to ancient historians, they were the main rivals of the Jews for centuries, and Biblical myth turned them into the archetypal enemy of Judeo-Christian culture. The modern use of "Philistine" to mean an ignorant, uncultured person derives from the German equivalent *Philister,* a name applied by students in German universities to ordinary townspeople and nonstudents.

Pilnyak, Boris: Pseudonym of Boris Andreyvich Vogau (1894–1937?). Russian novelist and short story writer. His first widely read book was *The Naked Year* (1922), a novel based on the social conflicts that followed the 1917 Revolution. His novel, *Mahogany* (1927), was denied publication in Russia. *The Volga Falls to the Caspian Sea* (1930) was also criticized by the Stalinist regime. Pilnyak's responses to a visit to the United States are evident in *OK* (1932). He disappeared in 1937, presumably because he was arrested and executed.

Pilsudski, Joseph (1867–1935): Polish general and political leader who was imprisoned for activities against the Russian imperialist state. He joined the Polish Socialist Party in the 1890s. Later he led several anti-Russian militant organizations, including the Polish Legions during World War I. He was imprisoned in 1917 for refusing to follow Central Powers demands. Released in 1918, he returned to Warsaw and proclaimed an independent Polish republic. Forced to compromise with Paderewski and more conservative nationalists, he became chief of state in 1919. After expanding Poland's territory and influencing the terms of a peace treaty with Russia, he retired to private life. But in 1926, he led a coup that overthrew the existing government, and he thereafter ruled until his death in a quasi-fascist manner, both as premier and as war minister.

Pisarev, Dmitri Ivanovich (1840–1868): Russian journalist and critic, arrested in 1862 for authoring a revolutionary pamphlet. Much of his best writing was done while he was imprisoned in St. Petersburg. He became famous as a nihilist; his death by drowning may have been a suicide. An 1865 essay, "The Abolition of Aesthetics," is well known.

Plekhanov, Georgi Valentinovich (1857–1918): Russian revolutionary and Marxist theorist, sometimes called the "Father of Russian Marxism." A member of the Land and Freedom (Narodnik) organization as a young man, he left Russia in 1880 and spent a period in exile, mainly in Geneva. In 1883, he returned and helped found what would become the Russian Social Democratic Labor Party. He and Lenin founded *Iskra*, a revolutionary socialist newspaper, in 1900. Committed to the view that socialism would be possible in Russia only after an extended period of capitalist development, he joined the Mensheviks in their split from the Bolsheviks in 1903 and generally maintained a critical stance toward Lenin. He supported Russia's participation in World War I. After the February Revolution in 1917, he organized support for continued involvement in the war and opposition to Bolshevik policies. After the October Revolution he retired from public life.

Pletnov, Pyotr Alexandrovich (1792–1865): Russian poet, critic, and journalist, he became a tutor in Russian language and literature to the tsar's family. During the 1830s, he was close to Pushkin, who dedicated *Eugene Onegin* to him. Both his poetry and his criticism are cautious and conventional.

Pobedonostzev, Konstantin P. (1827–1907): Leader of the reactionary forces in Russia following the assassination of Tsar Alexander II in 1881. He was head of the Holy Synod of the Orthodox Church. Many readers have thought he was the model of Dostoyevsky's Grand Inquisitor in *The Brothers Karamazov*.

Polonskaya, Elizaveta Grigorieona (1890–1969): Russian poet, born in Warsaw, who began her career under the influence of Gumilev. Her first collection, *Banners*, was published in 1921. She later joined the Serapion Fraternity (see separate entry in this Glossary) and became a correspondent for *Leningradskaya Pravda*.

Populism: Originally, Russian "populism" (*narodnichestvo*) referred to the agrarian socialist movement of the late nineteenth century and the ideas of Alexander Herzen. Its influence extended to literature, music, and the other arts. The populist concept of *narodnost* continued to figure in literary and cultural debate during and after the 1917 Revolution.

Positivism: Philosophical approach or position that denies validity to anything except the describable properties of knowable physical phenomena. The term was first used by the French philosopher Auguste Comte (1798–1857), whose *Course of Positive Philosophy* appeared in 1830–1842 followed by *System of Positive Polity* in 1875–1877.

Proletkult: An organization and a journal founded by A.A. Bogdanov and A.V. Lunacharsky in early 1917 to promote proletarian literature and art. Trotsky's critical analysis of *Proletkult* and other institutions that assumed the existence of "proletarian literature" forms one of the major arguments of *Literature and Revolution.*

Protopopov, Alexander Dmitreyevich (1866–1918): Russian political leader connected to the Octobrist party and active in the Zemstvo, the assembly of local provincial government, from 1864 to 1917. He was vice president of the Duma from 1914. A friend of Rasputin, he was appointed minister of the interior in September 1916. Although insane in the later years of his career, Protopopov was protected by the tsarina. After the 1917 Revolution, he was arrested and executed.

Pugachev, Emelian Ivanovich (?–1775): Russian peasant leader who led the peasant rebellion of 1773–1774. He was a Don Cossack and virtually illiterate. Declaring the end of serfdom, his army overran substantial areas and threatened the control of Catherine II during Russia's war with Turkey. Eventually Pugachev was captured and beheaded. The rebellion provoked administrative "reforms" in 1775 that increased central government control and consolidated the institution of serfdom.

Pushkin, Alexander Sergeyevich (1799–1837): Russian poet, one of the greatest writers in Russian literature. He was born in Moscow into an aristocratic family; his mother's grandfather was Abram Hannibal, the Black African general who served under Peter the Great. Sent into exile in 1820 for his *Ode to Liberty* and his satires on the tsarist court, Pushkin returned and attained further literary success before being confined to his family estate (1824–1826) on order from the tsar. His masterpiece, *Eugene Onegin* (1825–1831), is a novel in verse. Pushkin died as the result of a duel with a French nobleman thought to have had an affair with Pushkin's wife.

Radek, Karl (1885–1939?): Communist leader and journalist, initially prominent in Warsaw in 1905 as a member of the Social Democratic Party of Poland and Lithuania. During World War I, he lived in Switzerland and strongly supported Lenin and the Bolsheviks. After the 1917 Revolution, he joined the Communist Party and had a role in negotiating the Treaty of Brest-Litovsk. In 1918, he was sent to Germany to forward the revolutionary cause there and was imprisoned. Upon his return to Russia in 1920, he became a leading official in the Comintern. He lost his position in 1924 and was expelled from the Party in 1927. Eventually, he recanted his opposition to Stalin and was reinstated in 1930. He went on to write for and edit *Izvestia*. But he was accused of treason during the purges of the later 1930s and is believed to have died in one of Stalin's prison camps.

Rakovsky, Christian Georgyevich (1873–?): The person to whom Trotsky dedicated *Literature and Revolution*. Born and initially active as a revolutionary socialist in Bulgaria, Rakovsky extended his work into Switzerland, Germany, France, and Romania. After the 1917 Revolution, he was briefly head of the Ukrainian government (1919). He went on to serve as a Soviet diplomat and became Russian chargé d'affaires in London (1924) and ambassador to France (1926–1927). Opposed to Stalin, he was expelled from the Communist Party in 1927 but later recanted (1934). In March 1938, he was convicted of treason during one of Stalin's show trials and probably died in prison.

Rasputin, Grigori Yefimovich (1872–1916): Self-styled "holy man" and the most notorious figure at the court of Tsar Nicholas II, Rasputin came from a peasant background and was semi-literate. He espoused a doctrine of salvation through religious fanaticism and sexual debauchery. He captured the fanatical loyalty of the tsarina and, through her, influenced Nicholas II. He was successful in promoting a host of corrupt, reactionary officials. His influence reached its height in 1915, during World War I, when the tsar left Moscow for the front. Rasputin's effect on the court and the government was so destructive that he was assassinated in December 1916 by a group of right-wing "patriots." His corpse was exhumed and burned during the February Revolution of 1917.

Razin, Stenka (?–1671): Cossack leader in the peasant revolt of 1670. His army of some 7,000 won the support of many serfs, peasants, and non-Russian minority people in its challenge to the power of the tsar. Finally defeated at Simbirsk, he was betrayed by landowning Cossacks and turned over to the government, which executed him. His exploits became the subject of popular legend and song.

Remizov, Alexey Mikhailovich (1877–1957): Russian novelist and short story writer, Remizov was an important influence on Isaac Babel and Boris Pilnyak. In early novels, such as *The Clock* and *The Pond* (both 1908), he emphasized the degrading living conditions of provincial Russian cities. He left Russia in 1921 and died in Paris.

Revolution of 1905: The so-called "dress rehearsal" for the 1917 Revolution, it was made possible in part by the disastrous Russo-Japanese War. It was during this uprising against the oppression of tsarism that the workers' councils called "Soviets" sprang up in the factories of St. Petersburg and other Russian cities for the first time, showing the Bolsheviks what kind of proletarian self-activity was possible. The 1905 Revolution forced Nicholas II to establish a constitution and a very limited representative assembly (Duma). But the reactionary government quickly curtailed these new freedoms.

Revolution of 1917: In February 1917, the massive suffering caused by Russian participation in World War I, along with the continuing oppression of Tsar Nicholas II's government, led to the outbreak of mass revolt. In March, Nicholas was forced to abdicate, and a provisional government under Prince Lvov was established. Weakened by contradictory class interests and unable to meet the demands of newly empowered workers organized in their Soviets, the provisional government was overthrown on October 25—with very little bloodshed—by the Bolsheviks and their supporters, who set about ending Russia's involvement in World War I and taking the initial steps toward creating the first workers' state in history.

Rodzianko, Mikhail (1859–1924): From a wealthy landowning family, he was elected to the third Duma in March 1911. He was a loyal supporter of the tsar and foresaw the possibility of revolution in Russia. He supported the Provisional Government of 1917 but disapproved of Kerensky. After the October Revolution, he emigrated to Yugoslavia.

Rozanov, Vasily Vasilevich (1856–1919): Critic, philosopher, and journalist who exerted considerable influence on the Russian Symbolists. His essay called "The Legend of the Grand Inquisitor by F.M. Dostoyevsky," though based on mistaken assumptions about Dostoyevsky's *The Brothers Karamazov,* became widely known. His last book, *The Apocalypse of Our Times* (1917–1918), offers a visionary tragic account of the 1917 Revolution.

Rousseau, Jean Jacques (1712–1778): Swiss-French writer of political theory, novels, and autobiography. Born in Geneva, Rousseau eventually moved to Paris and became part of the circle of Enlightenment intellects around Denis Diderot. He wrote articles on music for the famous *Encyclopédie.* His writings on the innate equality of human beings, which include the *Discourse on the Origins of Human Inequality* (1754) and *The Social Contract* (1762), were a major influence on the American Revolution and the French Revolution.

Russkiya Viedomosti: Widely read daily newspaper in Russia during the period of the Revolution.

Russo-Japanese War (1904–1905): An imperialist conflict grounded in the rivalry between Russia and Japan over control of Manchuria and Korea. The government of Tsar Nicholas II also believed that a victory over Japan would weaken the threat of political unrest and revolution inside Russia. But Japan won a series of surprising early victories. U.S. President Theodore Roosevelt oversaw the ending of the war through the Treaty of Portsmouth. Russia's disastrous miscalculation in this war was a key precipitating factor in the 1905 Revolution.

Sabaoth: A Hebrew word meaning "armies." It is also one of the names for "God" in Gnostic and cabalistic writing.

Saint John's Night: June 23, the night before the day in the Christian calendar on which the apostle John is celebrated. Saint John's Night is also traditionally regarded as a midsummer festival.

Saltikov-Shchedin, Mikhail Efgrafovich (1826–1889): Often considered the greatest Russian satirist of the nineteenth century. Though a tsarist government official, his radical political views resulted in his being exiled several times. In works such as *Provincial Sketches* (1856–1857), he satirizes the tsarist bureaucracy. In the 1860s, he engaged polemically with Dostoyevsky and others. His finest satire is *History of a Town* (1869),

a parodic account of Russian history cast as a chronicle of Glu-
pov ("Stupidville").

Schkapskaya, Maria (1891–1952): Russian poet, the daughter
of a tsarist official, educated in France. Her first two volumes of
poetry, *Mater Dolorosa* (1920) and *Drum of the Street Gentle-
man* (1922), are intensely religious. Trotsky associates her poetry
with that of Akhmatova and Tsvetaeva.

Serapion Fraternity (or Brotherhood): A literary group
founded in 1921 by Fedin, Polonskaya, and others who took
their name from a hermit who appears in the fiction of the German writer E.T.A. Hoffmann (see entry in this Glossary). They
affirmed the absolute freedom of the creative act and insisted on
diversity and pluralism in literary culture.

Shaginyan, Marietta Sergeevna (1888–1982): Russian poet
associated with the Symbolists. Her first important publication
was *Orientalia* (1912), stylized poems on exotic Caucasian
themes. After the Revolution, she worked as a journalist for
major newspapers and turned to prose fiction. Among her novels
are historical documentary narratives based on the life of Lenin.

Shakhmatov, Alexey Alexandrovich (1860–1920): Was the
leading authority on linguistics in pre-revolutionary Russia. As
professor of philology at St. Petersburg University, he devoted
himself to the history of the Russian language.

Shershenevich, Vadim Gabrielevich (1893–1942): Poet,
translator, playwright, screenwriter, he was first associated with
Futurism, then Imagism. In 1913, he founded a Futurist group
called Mezzanine of Poetry. His theoretical treatise of that year,
Futurism Without a Mask, was influential. With Yessenin and
Marienhof, he founded the Imagist Movement in 1919. A bold
stylistic experimentalist, he later worked with Mayakovsky
at ROSTA.

Shklovsky, Victor Borisovich (1893–1984): Russian theorist
and critic and a leading figure in the Formalist tradition, which
stressed a scientific approach to literary meaning through precise
analysis of formal structures. He was a prominent member of the
Society for the Study of Poetic Language (Opoyaz) in Petrograd,
founded in 1916.

Sinclair, Upton (1878–1968): American novelist and socialist. His 1906 novel, *The Jungle,* exposed the brutality of conditions in the Chicago stockyards and aroused great public anger that eventually led to legal reforms and inspection laws. Also in 1906, he established a short-lived socialist community in Englewood, New Jersey. His other important novels include *King Coal* (1917), *Oil!* (1927), *Boston* (1928, about the Sacco and Vanzetti case), and *Little Steel* (1938). In and out of the U.S. Socialist Party, Sinclair ran for governor of California as a Democrat in 1934. A late sequence of novels, beginning with *World's End* (1940), deals with international politics.

Sizov, A.: A writer associated with the Musaget publishing house in Moscow, established in 1909 by Biely and other Symbolist writers.

Socialist Revolutionary Party: An agrarian revolutionary party founded by various populist groups in Russia in 1901. In its 1906 program it called for the overthrow of tsarism, the establishment of a classless society, the redistribution of land to the peasantry on the basis of need, and self-determination for national minorities. The first leader of the Socialist Revolutionaries was Viktor Chernov. Although agrarian in ideological orientation, the party was initially made up mainly of students and intellectuals. It later gained some direct support from and involvement of the peasantry. Socialist Revolutionaries participated in the Petrograd Soviet in 1917 and in the provisional government established between the February and October revolutions. The party won a majority in the constituent assembly of January 1818. By looking to the peasantry instead of the working class the Socialist Revolutionaries threatened to undermine the very basis of the Revolution. The Bolsheviks realizing this disbanded the constituent assembly and extended their leading role in the Revolution by seizing control of the government.

Sologub, Feodor: Pseudonym of Feodor Kizmich Teternikov (1863–1927), Russian poet and writer of prose fiction, and one of the older members of the Symbolist movement. His best work of fiction is *The Little Demon* (1907), focused on the twisted behavior of an evil schoolmaster named Peredonov (the term *peredonovism* became common). His volumes of verse include *The*

Circle of Fire (1908) and *Pearly Stars* (1913). Politically, he was an opponent of the Bolsheviks.

Sophia, Saint or Hagia Sophia: The great architectural masterpiece of Byzantine culture in Istanbul. It was originally a Christian church, later became a mosque, and is now a museum of Byzantine art. The name means "holy wisdom."

Sophists: The term originally given to a group of itinerant teachers in ancient Greece, the best known of whom is Protagoras. Some associated with the group turned education into a matter of acquiring superficial skills, particularly those useful in advancing a political career. The Sophists were associated philosophically with skepticism. They came in for sustained criticism from both Plato and Aristotle. In modern usage "sophist" has come to designate someone who relies on a seemingly plausible but shallow and misleading argument.

Stammler, Rudolf (1856–1938): German jurist and legal philosopher; professor of law at Marburg, Giessen, and Berlin.

Steiner, Rudolf (1861–1925): German philosopher noted for his celebration of the occult. A founder of the German Theosophical Association, he eventually developed what he called "anthroposophy," which attempts to explain the world in ways independent of the senses. His books include *Investigations in Occultism* (1920) and *Philosophy of Spiritual Activity* (1922).

Stolypin, Piotr Arkadevich (1862–1911): Russian premier and minister of the interior for Tsar Nicholas II. He led the tsarist fight against the revolutionary movement—often with brutal repression, sometimes with reforms. Hundreds were executed under his direction in 1906–1907. Stolypin was especially eager to create a class of landowning peasants loyal to the tsar, and his land-reform efforts of 1906 were designed with this in mind. He was successful in manipulating the makeup of the Duma to obtain many of his objectives. He also encouraged anti-Semitic pogroms. Stolypin was assassinated in 1911.

Stepun, Fyodor: Russian philosopher, one of the émigré writers, associated with the "Club of Writers" in Berlin in the early 1920s. From 1910 to 1914, he edited the international philosophical journal *Logos.*

Suvorin, Alexey Sergeevich (1834–1912): Russian journalist and publisher. In the 1870s, he established an influential publishing empire in St. Petersburg. A strong proponent of Russian imperialism, he had a close relationship with Chekhov and other major writers critical of tsarism.

Symbolists: As a European literary movement, Symbolism originated in late nineteenth-century France as a reaction to realism and naturalism. The poetry of Verlaine, Rimbaud, and Mallarmé, influenced by the writing of Baudelaire, emphasized formal effects and experimentation and valued imaginative experience over historical and social reality. The impact of French Symbolism spread to England, Germany, and other countries, including Russia. The leading Russian Symbolists were Alexander Blok and Andrey Biely.

Tatlin, Vladimir (1885–1953): Russian sculptor and painter and a founder of the movement known as Constructivism, which featured suspended three-dimensional arrangements of nonrepresentational subjects.

Tchernischevsky, Nikolai Gavrielovich (1828–1889): Radical journalist, revolutionary, critic, and novelist. His journalistic opposition to the tsarist regime made him famous. Influenced philosophically by Hegel and Feuerbach, he developed his radical ideas independently of Marx. His 1855 essay, "The Aesthetic Relations of Art to Reality," proclaimed common people as the true arbiters of beauty. Critical of the limitations in Alexander II's emancipation of the serfs in 1861, his journal *Sovremennik* was shut down several times. His novel, *What Is to Be Done?* (1862), offers itself as a radical rival to Turgenev's *Fathers and Sons*. Tchernischevsky was sentenced to a labor camp in 1864; this was followed by twelve years of exile in the Arctic village of Irkutsk. He was a major inspiration for many twentieth-century socialists.

Terror: The term originated during the French Revolution and applied to political violence used both by the revolutionary forces and state (e.g., the "Reign of Terror," the "Jacobin Terror") and by the counterrevolutionary monarchists (the "White Terror"). During the Russian Revolution the "Red Terror" refers to the Bolshevik-led government's use of violence to defend the Revolution against the counterrevolutionary tsarists; the "White Terror" refers to the torture, executions, and genocide carried out by forces seeking to restore tsarism. Trotsky's most important analysis of terrorism is found in *Terrorism and Communism* (1920).

Three Sisters: One of Chekhov's best-known plays, first performed in 1901.

Tikhonov, Nikolai Semyonovich (1896–1979): Prolific Russian writer whose career began with a collection of poems called *The Horde* (1922), clearly influenced by Gumilev and the Acméists. Having been a hussar during World War I, he fought in the Red Army and produced a collection of poems about this experience called *Mead* (later in 1922). By this time he was associated with the Serapion Fraternity (see entry in this Glossary).

Tiutschev, Fyodor Ivanovich (1807–1873): Russian poet strongly influenced in his early career by German poetry. Later, in St. Petersburg, he wrote popular patriotic poems and deeply felt poems about nature shaped by German idealist philosophy.

Tolstoy, Alexey Nikolaevich (1883–1945): He began his career as a Symbolist poet in the early 1900s. A war correspondent in World War I, he emigrated to Berlin and Paris after the Revolution. But he returned in 1923, having published in 1921 the first of his novels on the Revolution, *The Sisters*. In the mid-1920s, he published two science fiction novels. His 1929 novel, *Peter the First,* established him as a major figure in the cultural scene that developed under Stalin's dictatorship.

Tolstoy, Count Leo (1828–1910): Russian novelist and philosopher, best known for *War and Peace* (1862–1869) and *Anna Karenina* (1873–1876), and for such masterful short stories as "The Death of Ivan Ilyich." From a noble family and a passionate if unconventional Christian, Tolstoy came to his own distinctive understanding of the crisis in Russian society. His late essay "What Is Art?" was certainly known to Trotsky, who wrote an essay entitled "Tolstoy: Poet and Rebel" in 1903 and an impressive obituary for *Pravda* when Tolstoy died in 1910.

Tseretelli, Iraklii Georgevich (1881–1959): A major figure in the Petrograd Soviet of 1917 and a proponent of "revolutionary

Defensism," the dominant Menshevik program of that moment advocating alliances between proletarian and bourgeois parties. In the opening session of the Constituent Assembly in January 1918, he delivered a famous attack on Lenin and the Bolsheviks. When the Bolsheviks dissolved the Assembly, Tseretelli fled to Georgia and became a diplomat for the Georgian republic. By 1929, isolated and disillusioned, he abandoned politics and emigrated first to Paris, then to New York, where he was living at the time of his death.

Tsvetaeva, Marina: See Trotsky, the Poets and the Russian Revolution.

Turgenev, Ivan Sergeyevich (1818–1883): Russian novelist, short story writer, dramatist. From a landowning family, Turgenev studied in Berlin and became an admirer of western European literary achievements. An early collection of stories, *A Sportman's Sketches* (1852), attacked serfdom and was thought to have influenced the tsar to emancipate the serfs in 1861. His great novels include *On the Eve* (1860), *Fathers and Sons* (1861), and *Smoke* (1867). His best play is *A Month in the Country* (1850).

Uncle Vanya: One of the most admired plays of Chekhov, first performed in 1899.

Vassili the Blessed: The name of the cathedral on Red Square, in Moscow.

Verkhovsky, A.I.: Minister of War under the "Directory" organized by Alexander Kerensky in September 1917 in an attempt to sustain the Provisional Government.

Versilove: A character in Dostoyevsky's novel *An Accidental Family*.

Vico, Giovanni Battista (1668–1744): Italian philosopher and historian, sometimes regarded as the first modern historian for his emphasis on history as the account of the emergence and development of human societies and institutions. His *Scienza Nuova* (*New Science,* 1725) has been much admired by critics and theorists of our own time, such as Edward Said. Trotsky probably regarded Vico's emphasis on the determining power of language and mythology and his belief that similar periods recur throughout history as mistakenly idealist.

Voltaire, François Marie Arouet de (1694–1778): French philosopher and writer, one of the great figures of the European Enlightenment. Famous for his satirical wit and skepticism, Voltaire was as controversial as he was influential. His "philosophical romance," *Candide* (1759), satirizes superficial optimism and idealism.

Voronsky, Alexander Konstantinovich (1884–1943): Editor, critic, and theorist who joined the Bolsheviks in his early twenties. After the Revolution he became editor of the newspaper *Workers Region*. In 1921, he moved to Moscow to edit the new literary journal *Krasnaya Nov'*. He was dismissed from this post in 1927 on suspicion of Trotskyism and lived a dangerous existence until 1939, when he was imprisoned until his death.

Weltanschauung: German, literally "worldview" or "world outlook."

Weltschmerz: German, literally "world pain"—that is, sorrow over present or future suffering in the world in general. The word is especially associated with the philosophical pessimism prominent in the writing of Arthur Schopenhauer.

Whites: Common term applied to the counterrevolutionary forces during the civil war of 1918–1921 who fought to restore tsarism to Russia.

Wilde, Oscar (1854–1900): Irish writer and flamboyant wit famous for his epigrammatic turns of phrase. Often associated with the aestheticist doctrine of "art for art's sake," Wilde actually used such positions to expose the hypocrisy of Victorian bourgeois society. His novel *The Picture of Dorian Gray* (1891) and his play *The Importance of Being Earnest* (1895) are his best-known works. Imprisoned for his homosexual relationship with a young aristocrat, he continued to write while in jail. In 1891, after hearing a speech by George Bernard Shaw, he wrote "The Soul of Man Under Socialism," advocating artistic freedom and individuality.

Wrangell, Baron Piotr Nikolayevich (1878–1928): Russian general who served in the Russo-Japanese War and World War I before becoming a leader of the White (counterrevolutionary) army in Southern Russia in 1917. After his defeat in the Crimea and retreat to Constantinople in November 1920, he fled into exile in Belgium.

Yasnaya-Potyana: Village in central Russia, the birthplace and residence of Tolstoy. Tolstoy's house was looted during the German occupation of the village in 1941 but has since been restored.

Yessenin, Sergey Alexandrovich: See Trotsky, the Poets and the Russian Revolution.

Yudenich, Nikolai Nikolayevich (1862–1933): Russian general who led the White army in the Baltic states after the 1917 Revolution. In October 1919, with British assistance, he attacked Petrograd but was defeated and forced to retreat. He died in exile in Paris.

Zaitzev, Varfolomei Alexandrovich (1842–1882): Literary critic and radical, closely associated with Pisarev. A mechanical materialist and "nihilist," Zaitzev attacked all forms of idealism and romanticism. His polemics against Saltykov and Tschernischevsky were notorious. Arrested in 1866, he fled to Italy in 1869 and founded the first Italian section of the International.

Zamyatin, Yevgeny Ivanovich (1884–1937): Fiction writer, dramatist, critic, he was an early member of the Bolshevik Party. A short novel, *A Provincial Tale* (1911), won widespread admiration. Trained as an engineer, he took on both careers during World War I. After the 1917 Revolution, he exerted major influence as a journal editor and translator. Known as an experimental modernist in his prose style, Zamyatin criticized the Bolsheviks under the pseudonym "M. Platanov." During the 1920s, he continued to produce fiction and plays. The Stalinists savagely attacked him in 1929. He left Russia in 1931 to live abroad. Zamyatin's anti-utopian novel of 1924, *We,* is thought to have anticipated Aldous Huxley's *Brave New World.*

Zhirmunsky, Viktor Maksimovich (1881–1971): Professor of philology at St. Petersburg University and contributor to the Formalist school of criticism and theory. His most influential work was *Introduction to Metrics* (1925). He also published careful analyses of the writings of Pushkin, Blok, Akhmatova, and others.

Zhukovsky, Vasily Andreyevich (1783–1852): Russian lyric poet and translator, best known for his translations into Russian of English, German, and French poems. He was a tutor to the future tsar, Alexander II.

Zoschenko, Mikhail Mikhailovich (1895–1958): Russian comic writer who spent most of his life in St. Petersburg. He published a very successful volume of short stories in 1922 and was popular during the 1920s and 1930s because of his willingness to make fun of a wide range of social phenomena. He also published novels in the 1930s and an autobiography, *Before Sunrise,* in 1943. During the literary purge of 1946, he was expelled from the Union of Soviet Writers. His writing was banned and not published again until 1956.

Suggestions for Further Reading

Volume two of Isaac Deutscher's three-volume biography of Trotsky, *The Prophet Unarmed: Trotsky, 1921–1929* (London, New York: Oxford University Press, 1959) and volume three of Tony Cliff's four-volume study, *Trotsky: Fighting the Rising Bureaucracy 1923–1927* (London: Bookmarks, 1991) are important both for their broader accounts of Trotsky's life, work, and ideas and for their specific discussions of *Literature and Revolution*. The best brief analysis of Trotsky's political ideas and their significance is Duncan Hallas's *Trotsky's Marxism and Other Essays* (Chicago: Haymarket Books, 2003; first published by Pluto Press, 1979).

For an overview of *Literature and Revolution*, Lindsey German's foreword to the 1991 RedWords edition is excellent. Also good are Alan Wald's essay, "Literature and Revolution: Leon Trotsky's Contributions to Marxist Cultural Theory and Literary Criticism," in *The Ideas of Leon Trotsky*, edited by Hillel Ticktin and Michael Cox (London: Porcupine Press, 1995), pages 219–32, and Paul N. Siegel's introduction to *Art and Revolution: Writing on Literature, Politics, and Culture* (New York: Pathfinder Press, 1992). The latter volume contains about thirty pages from *Literature and Revolution* and a valuable selection of Trotsky's other writings on literature and art.

More specialized critical engagement with Trotsky's ideas in *Literature and Revolution* may be found in Terry Eagleton's *Criticism and Ideology: A Study in Marxist Literary Theory* (London: Verso, 1978) and in Victor Erlich's *Russian Formalism: History-Doctrine* (The Hague, Paris, New York: Mouton, 1955).

See also Erlich's *Modernism and Revolution: Russian Literature in Transition* (Cambridge: Harvard University Press, 1994) for commentary on Trotsky and the writers of his era from a perspective mainly unsympathetic to the Bolsheviks.

Readers of French will also want to consult the recent edition of *Littérature et révolution,* translated by Pierre Frank, Claude Ligny, and Jean-Jacques Marie, preface by Maurice Nadeau (Paris: Les Éditions de la Passion, 2000).

Index

Soviet Union, 7, 8, 9, 10, 17, 224,
225, 256, 285, 288, 291, 300,
301, 306
Soviets, 39, 79, 271, 311
Spain, 279
Stalin, Joseph, 7–10, 15, 17, 225,
238, 256, 280, 281, 285, 287,
297, 300, 303, 306, 310, 317
Stammler, Rudolf, 152, 315
Steiner, Rudolph, 57, 85, 315
Stepun, Fyodor, 196, 199, 315
Stolypin, Piotr, 35, 178, 315
Strunsky, Elias, 22
Strunsky, Rose, 22, 23
subjectivists, 34
Surrealism, 10
Suvorin, Alexey, 32, 52, 316
Switzerland, 57, 59, 85, 279, 300,
304, 309, 310
Symbolic School, 30, 35, 105, 182,
191
Symbolism, 10, 18, 35, 36, 47, 54,
105, 120, 123, 190, 191, 192,
238, 287, 316
Symbolist(s), 37, 191, 199, 212,
242, 283–88, 293, 295, 296,
299, 311, 313, 314, 316, 317

T

Tatlin, Vladimir, 200, 201, 289, 316
Tchernischevsky, Nikolai, 172, 316
Terror, 52, 109, 228, 316, 317
"The Twelve", 37, 88, 89, 105–111,
242, 244, 251
Third International, 300
Tikhonov, Nikolai, 43, 61, 70, 179,
187, 317
Tiutschev, Fyodor, 115, 317
Tolstoy, Alexey, 38, 54, 55, 87, 100,
133, 187, 220, 288, 303, 305,
317, 320
Tsar Alexander II, 308, 316, 321
Tsar Alexander III, 304
Tsar Nicholas I, 304
Tsar Nicholas II, 52, 279, 291, 304,
310, 311, 312, 315
Tsar Nicholas the First, 90
Tsar Peter I (Peter the Great), 81,
303, 306, 309

Tsar Peter III, 304
Tsarina Catherine II, 304, 309
Tsarina Catherine the Great, 147,
287, 291
Tseretelli, Iraklii, 93, 288, 317, 318
Tsvetaeva, Marina, 50, 88, 144,
225, 228, 313, 318
Turgenev, Ivan, 55, 66, 316, 318

U

Uncle Vanya, 43, 120, 288, 318
United Opposition, 280
United States, 22, 256, 290, 297,
300, 307

V

Vassili the Blessed, 130, 318
Venus, 49
Verkhovsky, A.I., 101, 318
Versilov, 44, 45
Vetlugin, 39
Vetlugins, 41
Vico, Giovanni, 40, 318
Virgil, 284, 287, 301
Voltaire, 50, 319
von Kullmann, 94
Voronsky, Alexander, 177, 298, 319

W

Wald, Alan, 18, 322
Walling, William English, 22
Weimar, 57
White Army, 8, 301, 320
Whites, 37, 39, 193, 216, 319
Wilde, Oscar, 44, 289, 290, 319
Wilson, 131, 132
World War I, 8, 233, 279, 285, 297,
298, 300, 304, 307, 308, 309,
310, 311, 317, 319, 320
World War II, 228, 274, 287, 300,
304, 305
Wrangel, 90
Wrangell, Baron, 37, 319

Additional copyright information

About Leon Trotsky

Leon Trotsky was a leading figure in the 1917 Russian Revolution. After joining the Bolshevik Party in 1917, he held many positions in the new workers' state, including leading the Red Army in its defense of the Revolution. He wrote extensively, including the definitive *History of the Russian Revolution*. After V.I. Lenin's death in 1924, he fought against Stalin's destruction of the newly formed workers' government, forming the Left Opposition. He was killed by Stalinist agents while in exile in Mexico in 1940.

About William Keach

William Keach taught at Rutgers University before coming to Brown University in 1986 and was supported by a Guggenheim Fellowship in 1988–89. In 1983, he was given a Lindback Award for Excellence in Teaching at Rutgers, and in 1998 a Distinguished Scholar Award by the Keats-Shelley Association of America. He is the author of *Elizabethan Erotic Narratives* (Rutgers, 1976), *Shelley's Style* (Routledge, 1984), and *Arbitrary Power: Romanticism, Language, Politics* (Princeton, 2004), and he edited *Coleridge: The Complete Poems* for the Penguin English Poets series (1997). His articles have appeared in *Studies in Romanticism*, *European Romantic Review*, the *Keats-Shelley Journal*, *Left History*, and other scholarly journals, and he contributed the section on "Poetry, after 1740" in volume four of *The Cambridge History of Literary Criticism* (1997).

Keach is a member of the Campaign to End the Death Penalty and the International Socialist Organization. He lives in Boston.

ALSO FROM HAYMARKET BOOKS

WHAT'S MY NAME, FOOL? SPORTS AND RESISTANCE IN THE UNITED STATES

Dave Zirin   1 931859 20 5   July 2005

Edgeofsports.com sportswriter Dave Zirin provdes a no-holds-barred commentary on the personalities and politics of American sports. "Zirin is America's best sportswriter."—Lee Ballinger, *Rock and Rap Confidential*

WOMEN AND SOCIALISM

Sharon Smith   1 931859 11 6   May 2005

The fight for women's liberation is urgent—and must be linked to winning broader social change.

A PEOPLE'S HISTORY OF IRAQ: THE IRAQI COMMUNIST PARTY, WORKERS' MOVEMENTS, AND THE LEFT 1924–2004

Ilario Salucci   1 931859 14 0   April 2005

Iraqis have a long tradition of fighting against foreign and domestic tyranny. Here is their story.

THE WORLD SOCIAL FORUM: STRATEGIES OF RESISTANCE

José Corrêa Leite   1 931859 15 9   April 2005

The inside story of how the worldwide movement against corporate globalization has become such a force.

YOUR MONEY OR YOUR LIFE (3rd edition)

Eric Toussaint   1 931859 18 3   June 2005

Globalization brings growth? Think again. Debt—engineered by the IMF and World Bank—sucks countries dry.

THE DISPOSSESSED: CHRONICLES OF THE DESTERRADOS OF COLOMBIA

Alfredo Molano   1 931859 17 5   April 2005

Here in their own words are the stories of the Desterrados, or "dispossessed"— the thousands of Colombians displaced by years of war and state-backed terrorism, funded in part through U.S. aid to the Colombian government. With a preface by Aviva Chomsky.

THE THEORY OF REVOLUTION IN THE YOUNG MARX

Michael Löwy   1 931859 19 1   June 2005

The ideas of Marx's early writings come alive in this important examination of their lasting relevance.

THE STRUGGLE FOR PALESTINE

Lance Selfa, editor   1 931859 00 0   2002

In this important collection of essays, leading international solidarity activists offer insight into the ongoing struggle for Palestinian freedom and for justice in the Middle East.

THE FORGING OF THE AMERICAN EMPIRE

Sidney Lens   0 745321 00 3   2002

This is the story of a nation—the United States—that has conducted more than 160 wars and other military ventures while insisting that it loves peace. In the process, the U.S. has forged a world empire while maintaining its innocence of imperialistic designs. Includes a new introduction by Howard Zinn.

AMERICAN SOCIALIST MOVEMENT: 1897-1912

Ira Kipnis   1 931859 12 4   2004

The American Socialist Party, at the height of its power, had more than 150,000 members and won almost a million votes for its presidential candidate. Few books have more to offer to the student of the movement than this one.

THE CASE FOR SOCIALISM

Alan Maass   1 931859 09 4   2004

"[Maass'] book charts a game plan for realistic radicals, who haven't given up hope for making revolutionary changes in a society that finds itself in the grip of a remorseless political entropy. Take cheer: History isn't over. In fact, it's hardly even begun for us. Read Maass. Then go out and make some."
                                        —Jeffrey St. Clair, coeditor of CounterPunch

Order these titles and more online at www.haymarketbooks.org
or call 773-583-7884.

Haymarket Books is distributed to bookstores by Consortium Book Sales
and Distribution, www.cbsd.com.

ABOUT HAYMARKET BOOKS

Haymarket Books is a non-profit, progressive book distributor and publisher, a project of the Center for Economic Research and Social Change.

We believe that activists need to take ideas, history and politics into the many struggles for social justice today. Learning the lessons of past victories, as well as defeats, can arm a new generation of fighters for a better world. As Karl Marx said, "The philosophers have merely interpreted the world; the point however is to change it."

We take inspiration and courage from our namesakes, the Haymarket Martyrs, who gave their lives fighting for a better world. Their struggle for the eight-hour day in 1886, which gave us May Day, the international workers' holiday, reminds workers around the world that ordinary people can organize and struggle for their own liberation. These struggles continue today in every corner of the globe—struggles against oppression, exploitation, hunger and poverty.

It was August Spies, one of the Martyrs who was targeted for being an immigrant and an anarchist, who predicted the battles being fought to this day. "If you think that by hanging us you can stamp out the labor movement," Spies told the judge, "then hang us. Here you will tread upon a spark, but here, and there, and behind you, and in front of you, and everywhere, the flames will blaze up. It is a subterranean fire. You cannot put it out. The ground is on fire upon which you stand."

Visit our online bookstore at www.haymarketbooks.org.

We could not succeed in our publishing efforts without the generous financial support of our readers. Many people contribute to our project through the Haymarket Sustainers program, where donors receive free books in return for their monetary support. If you would like to be a part of this program, please contact us at info@haymarketbooks.org.

Printed in the USA
CPSIA information can be obtained
at www.ICGtesting.com
JSHW012048140824
68134JS00035B/3318